M000031725

Escaping the Shadows

Travis Verge

Palmetto Publishing Group
Charleston, SC

Escaping the Shadows
Copyright © 2019 by Travis Verge

All rights reserved
No portion of this book may be reproduced, stored in a retrieval system, or
transmitted in any form by any means–electronic, mechanical, photocopy,
recording, or other–except for brief quotations in printed reviews, without
prior permission of the author.

First Edition

Printed in the United States

ISBN-13: 978-1-64111-285-7
ISBN-10: 1-64111-285-9

Table of Contents

Preface

But the Spirit explicitly says that in later times some will fall away from the faith, paying attention to deceitful spirits and doctrines of demons, by means of the hypocrisy of liars seared in their own conscience as with a branding iron, men who forbid marriage and advocate abstaining from foods, which God has created to be gratefully shared in by those who believe and know the truth.
   —1 Timothy 4: 1-4

Now is the time for a book that will challenge your thinking and, at times, leave you breathless and begging for more. You will ask questions and you will get a lot of answers. I do not profess to have all the answers, but, by sharing my knowledge and experiences, I truly believe I can shed some light through the use of Scripture, so we are no longer walking in the shadows. This book will stretch your view of the world we live in while strengthening your understanding of God. I am convinced that the more we learn of the dark world, the more we will believe that God truly exists and He holds all the power. Through my experiences with people involved in the satanic occult and with professed Devil worshippers, God has revealed Himself to me in ways that are unfathomable. I struggle with painting a clear picture for you of the one implanted in my mind that illustrates the experiences I have had, but the canvas is set.

My faith in God has grown so much because of what I have seen. I hope this book will give you a glimpse of the enormity of God's power and goodness. I feel like Paul when he was called up to the third heaven in 2 Corinthians 12 and heard things which were inexpressible. In this book, I have included Scripture in every section, so that you will not just see my own words and interpretations. Enjoy the illustrations in this book, but allow God's Holy Spirit to move you by the untainted truth of God's Word. As you read this book, the one thing I ask is do not look to me as special or heroic because of the experiences I have gone through, but rather, view me as a simple minister who has a deep love and passion for God and is trying to make a difference in today's predominantly corrupt world.

Satan is extremely powerful and he is the prince of this world, according to John 16:11 NASV when it says, "the prince of this world now stands condemned." In this book, we will take a deep look into a dark world that is corrupted by the influence of Satan, his angels, and evil spirits. We will not only look at darkness, but because of the darkness, we will appreciate the light even more. Many may believe Satan's influence is not widespread, but is this belief because of ignorance? That was the way it was for me. What I did not see, hear, or know of in the evil world did not really exist for me. The reality is that many of us are ignorant of Satan's schemes and he deceives us without us even knowing. This can change and we can answer God's calling to be the church.

Many of us live our lives in the shadows. The shadows represent living among the world's deception and lies due to our own ignorance. This ignorance is simply because we have always believed what we have heard without examining the Scriptures to see if what we have heard is true. The shadows I am referring to in this book are false beliefs based on the inaccurate teachings that we have heard. God did not intend for us to live in the shadows, so he gave us the light of the world and His Spirit so we could behold truth. God did not give us the Bible and said, while laughing, "Ha, ha, figure this out."

The Bible is not for the ordained priests and ministers of the world to dictate its interpretation. First Peter 2:9 says: "But you are a chosen people, a royal priesthood, a holy nation, a people belonging to God, that you may declare the praises of Him who called you out of darkness into His wonderful light." Does that seem peculiar? We are not even out of the first chapter and we are already challenging the traditions of churches. According to 1 Peter 2:9 in which Peter is talking to Christians, he refers to them all as priests. Do not fall into the deception that the Word of God is hard to understand. Most of the Scriptures are simple enough for even a child to understand.

I have heard an inspirational quote that fits perfectly into this book: "You don't need to fear shadows because it means there is a light shining nearby." Although, it was C.S. Lewis who said, "I believe in Christianity as I believe that the sun is risen: not only because I see it, but because by it I see everything else." This is not a book intended to instill fear of evil with knowledge, but rather the objective is to prove that shadows do exist and that we may be walking in them without even realizing it. In this world, when we are standing in a shadow outdoors, we are unable to see the sun. Likewise, when we are in the shadow of deception, we are also unable to see the Son.

May this book help us see Christ, the source of true light, so that the shadows can dissipate in our lives and we can be in direct contact with the true light of Christ. Remember, if we are in the shadows, the true shining light is close by. Together, let us see the true light of Christ and allow the ever-present God to expose the shadows.

We can choose to live in the light instead of the shadow, but we will have to be open-minded while searching the Word of God diligently. Our comfort is that the shadows can only be seen when light is present. In 1 John 1, John says, "God is light and in him is no darkness." It is time for us to allow God to shed some light on the truth of Satan and his followers. In 1 Timothy 4:1-4, it says, "But the Spirit explicitly says that in later times some will fall away from the faith, paying attention to deceitful spirits and doctrines of demons, by means of the hypocrisy of liars seared in their own conscience as with a branding iron, men who forbid marriage and advocate abstaining from foods, which God has created to be gratefully shared in by those who believe and know the truth." This Scripture clearly says there are deceitful spirits and even doctrines of demons that will mislead people. These deceitful spirits are in the world today, proving that not all the people who claim to know God are following truth. With Satan being the deceiver, it would seem that he has distorted truth far more than we previously believed.

Could we not expect one of Satan's main tactics to be perverting the Scriptures so many of us can be misled? Is that not what he tried to do with Jesus in the wilderness in Matthew 4, but Jesus was not ignorant of his schemes. It did not work on Jesus, but could it work on us? Satan's job on earth would be a lot easier if he could get people to feel as if they are walking with God when, in fact, they are actually walking in the shadows.

Also, should we expect that distorting salvation through Christ would be one of the first things Satan would pervert? Jesus clearly says in Matthew 7:13-14: "Enter through the narrow gate. For wide is the gate and broad is the road that leads to destruction, and many enter through it. But small is the gate and narrow the road that leads to life and only a few find it." What does it mean when Jesus says that few will find it? We never want to believe in the simplicity of this statement. Why will only few find it? Is it because God has hidden it or made it too complex? Of course not! It is because Satan has provided so many other ways to "be saved" through traditions and man-made ideas that are found nowhere in the Scriptures. If anything, they clearly divert from the truth found only in God's Word.

I have committed myself to the Word of God, so I do not fall prey to the one who hates God and hates His Word. In the end, I do not know how God is going to sort it out, and I will not get caught up trying to play God. The one thing I do know is God is not a liar and He will be as merciful as His very words allow Him to be, but do not expect Him to compromise His own words.

Our responsibility is not to be like the Pharisees, who thought they had it figured out when it came to God's desires for mankind. Instead, our responsibility is to live faithfully based on what we know while humbly continuing to learn and grow in the understanding we gain from His unaltered Word. We will all stand before God and it will be His Word that judges us. Let us not act as judges, but let us live obedient and faithful to our King, allowing Him to be the Judge.

At times when we read the Scriptures, we make assumptions about what we believe the writer is trying to say and get across to us. There are times in the Bible where we can make assumptions, but the problem is that people make assumptions when the facts are there and obvious. An example of this is in 1st John. We can read chapter 1 and try to figure out why this book was written. We can make all kinds of different assumptions, but we do not need to assume when the fact is, the true purpose of the book is written clearly in 1 John 5:13: "I write these things to you who believe in the name of the Son of God so that you may know that you have eternal life." Many people believe so many different things about Christian religion based on incorrect assumptions instead of on the clearly stated truth. As you read through this book, I challenge you to make as few assumptions as possible from the Scriptures so the truth can be clearly seen.

At times, you will be challenged to view a Scripture differently than you have always heard it, but that is what reading Scripture open-mindedly is all about. For example, I was taught to read and see 1 Timothy 2:8 a particular way. 1 Timothy 2:8 says, "I want men everywhere to lift up holy hands in prayer, without anger of disputing." I was taught to read this as saying that only men are authorized by God to pray everywhere," which would exclude women from praying anywhere that Christian men are present. What if I read this differently? Could it be that Paul was writing about a specific issue—that men were praying when they had anger and divisive issues that would cause their hands to not be clean or holy as they raised them in prayer? The following verse on women cannot be interpreted just for women to adorn themselves properly. Wouldn't that be absurd if women were to be modest and men were not? Similarly, it would be absurd for men only to pray without anger and for women to pray as they please. Read 1 Timothy and see what Paul was dealing with.

For those of us who have been brought up with religion, our minds have been conditioned to see the Scriptures the way the people whom we love and respect taught us to understand them. Through years of prayer and my goal of reaching humility, I realized it was all right not to be perfect and right in my understanding of everything in the Bible, as long as I was open and obedient while I continued to grow and learn. With this attitude, it is now God starting to teach me the truth through His Word. I believe that, for many years, I had been blinded by my own pride because I felt I had to be perfect in my understanding of the Scriptures or my life with God would be discredited.

I finally realized I was not converting people to Christ but to my way of thinking, and, by doing that, I had fallen prey to the shadows and lies of our enemy. Now I see Christian life as a journey where I learn new things and then become obedient to what I have learned. This is because my life is motivated by love for God, not by a sense of pride where I think I have all the right answers.

I did not realize that believing things a little differently to what I was taught and what my past teachers taught would cause judgments and, at times, resentment. Being a follower of Christ instead of a follower of traditions and names can result in persecution from family, friends, and, sadly, other churches. I would rather follow Christ and endure with Christ then to live my life in the shadows because of people. I want to enjoy the abundant life God gives, not allow my enemy to rob me of what God wants to give me because of legalism and deception.

May this book bless your life as you humble yourself before the Almighty God and see clearly the truth God has set before you, letting Him expose the shadows of deception, so we can escape for our lives.

CHAPTER 1

Walking Away From the Shadow

Those who oppose him he must gently instruct, in the hope that God will grant them repentance leading them to a knowledge of the truth, and that they will come to their senses and escape from the trap of the Devil, who has taken them captive to do his will.
   —2 Timothy 2:25-26

It was January 2006 when I received a call from a girl in our youth group who worked at a Christian book store. She called about a twenty-six-year-old mother named D. J. who repeatedly came into the store in central Florida claiming she was involved in a Devil worshipping cult right there in town. She started to talk to the Christian store teenage employees about her life. When they asked her why she continued to come into the store, she stated that she was curious. A few of the teenage workers called me because I was their youth minister, and I told them, not knowing what I was getting into, that I had past experience in dealing with people involved in the occult.

At the Christian bookstore, these teenagers became very frightened because the things they heard shocked them and kept them awake at night. At that time, they did not know if D. J. wanted attention or if her story was even true. From the way she was acting, they assumed that the claims were true. She continued to come into the Christian bookstore and sometimes stayed for hours at a time, talking with the manager and the teenage girls.

One day I received a call from a member of my youth group who worked in the store, who told me she was there. I jumped in my car and hurried down there to meet her. I did not know what I was going to say or how I was going to say it. I just knew I wanted to have a chance to talk to her.

As I walked into this Christian bookstore, D. J. was in the back of the store watching a Jesus video so she could learn about the man she was told to hate. As I got to where she was sitting, all I saw was the back of her head with her fists clutching her long, jet black hair. Her head was down and she was fighting with herself to look at the movie. The girls who worked there told her I had arrived, but she would not even look back to greet me. When the movie ended, she leapt up and, not caring who was in her path, took off outside to pace and smoke a cigarette. As I caught a glimpse of her face, she appeared as a witch with her dark complexion, black hair, and long fingernails. The girls told me to leave her alone, but I took off outside to talk to her. I introduced myself and told her I was there to help her. I began asking her questions about the occult group. After fifteen minutes of talking, she said she needed to catch the bus on the corner and I respectfully let her go.

As I went to my car, I felt uneasy about the conversation. She was crying out for help and God had sent me. I got in my car and went to the corner where she was waiting to get the bus. I gave her my phone number and said, "Can I pray for you?" She said, "If you want." So I put my hand on her shoulder and said the quickest prayer ever, but she pulled away and yelled, "Stop that!" I did not realize she meant for me to pray for her later instead of right there with her. But I'd wanted a chance that night to pray for her deliverance from this evil.

To my surprise, she called me the next day to talk. She told me she was amazed that I was not afraid but that I was bold and confident. I said, "There is no reason for me to be afraid because God is stronger than Satan. In fact, God defeated Satan." She then asked, "How do you know that is true?" I told her, "We need to meet so I can show you." And we began meeting that very day, unaware that both our lives would never be the same again.

The first time we got together she told me some things about herself and the only life she had ever known. I learned D. J. was a twenty-six-year-old woman who claimed her family members were in the satanic occult. But no one knew if she could be trusted. She said that at the age of six, she had been dedicated to Satan and, from that point on, she had invited the evil spirits to possess her. D. J. remembered at least twenty different occasions where she had invited evil spirits into her. No one knew how involved in the occult she really was, but the fact remained, this woman had evil controlling her.

The community, as she called it, had different practices, such as infant sacrifice, incest, and so many other horrific things that would make you cringe and bring tears to your eyes. D. J. explained how Devil worship was different than Satanism. Satanism was more about gratifying any desire you have, while Devil worship was more about honoring and praying to Satan.

She told me that inside these cults there are different sectors, which could be compared to church denominations. There are different opinions on the way things should be done, as well as various roles for men and women. In some of the sectors, women are not even allowed to go outside. It was undeniable that D.J. knew more than most people about occult practices.

In my first actual meeting with her, she mentioned some of the levels in the Devil worshipping cult, such as Servant, Soldier, Lord Master, and High Priest. The Servant is the lowest, of course, because that is the opposite of what Jesus said. Each level did not know what the level greater than them knew until they were promoted. As a person moved up in rank, the responsibilities would be greater and the crimes would be worse. D. J. claimed she was a Soldier because of her years of service to the group.

She told me things that no one else could have believed or understood. One thing D. J. said that frightened people was that she saw coverings on people. She could see whether or not people were wearing a strong covering, meaning they were strong with Christ. She would shy away from people coming in the store who had this strong covering. There were times when the covering was so strong she could not look at them. It was encouraging to me when she said I was one of those she could not look at when she first met me. She mentioned how many in the world do not have strong coverings, and many came into the Christian bookstore with no covering at all.

Doesn't that make you think about what she would see if she looked at you? She knew "so-called" Christians who had no coverings at all. For the sake of readers who come from diverse backgrounds, I will not mention the different religious groups who appear as no threats to these cults because of their lack of coverings. What I will say is that the groups follow various religious traditions and, at times, other Scriptures besides the true inspired Word of God.

She also told me cult members could not say Jesus Christ so she referred to Jesus as "J. C." She never referred to the Bible as the Bible, but always as "your Bible." Anytime she would hear biblical Scripture, she would cover her ears and, at times, pull out her hair.

I read her Scriptures about how Satan was a liar from John 8:42-44. "Jesus said to them, If God were your Father, you would love me, for I came from God and now am here. I have not come on my own; but he sent me. Why is my language not clear to you? Because you are unable to hear what I say. You belong to your father, the Devil, and you want to carry out your father's desire. He was a murderer from the beginning, not holding to the truth, for there is no truth in him. When he lies, he speaks his native language, for he is a liar and the father of lies."

She started swinging her head back and forth uncontrollably while squealing, "No, no, no." She described the Word of God as jumbled and heard only through loud screaming in her mind. I knew, at this point, it was going to be a long haul to teach her about the truth of Jesus. There was no doubt that my mind had been opened to much about this evil empire.

For weeks, we kept in touch to meet and discuss the truth about Jesus Christ, and, even on one occasion, she had the strength to sneak out of what she called "the cult house" on a Sunday morning and go to church.

Oh, boy, was that an experience! It was obvious to everyone there was something wrong with this young lady. She said how it hurt her from within when she listened to God's Word. Actually, the first time she came to church, she spent fifteen to twenty minutes vomiting outside the church and in the church bathroom because of sitting through service. At that point, I realized this was no joke.

Her five-year old son went to Bible class and actually enjoyed it. He asked his mother after class, "Do we follow Jesus or Satan?" D. J. answered with the question, "Who do you want to follow?" The innocence of her son answered, "I want to follow Jesus." It reminded me of the innocence and purity on the day in Matthew 18 where Jesus called the children to Him and, once again, made a profound statement:

> At that time the disciples came to Jesus and asked, "Who is the greatest in the kingdom of heaven?" He called a little child and had him stand among them. And he said, "I tell you the truth, unless you change and become like little children, you will never enter the kingdom of heaven. Therefore, whoever humbles himself like this child is the greatest in the kingdom of heaven. And whoever

welcomes a little child like this in my name welcomes me. But if anyone causes one of these little ones who believe in me to sin, it would be better for him to have a large millstone hung around his neck and to be drowned in the depths of the sea" (Matthew 18:1-6).

Her child was learning the truth, but would she ever come to see it?

After a few months of studying with her, she decided on March 12, 2006, that she would no longer follow Satan, after a tough Saturday night when she said the leaders of her cult found out that she had been going to a Christian bookstore, searching and asking questions about Jesus. The punishment she said she received that night in the woods where the cult met was so bad that I cannot write about it. It was worse than anything I had ever heard in my entire life of anyone doing to someone else outside of murder. Actually, murder would have even seemed better.

She said, "It was obvious. Satan made it extremely clear to the High Priest about my curiosity and pursuit of Christianity." It also didn't help things when her five-year old son came home from church the Sunday she visited and innocently told the family members, "I went to church today!"

My wife and I prayed intently that she would be able to get up on Sunday morning and leave, and that no one in the cult community house where she was living would wake up, even though it was nine o'clock in the morning. She had actually tried to wake up her dad because she was confused about leaving, but he would not wake up, so she was able to gather most of her things.

She showed up to our church on Sunday morning in tears with her two children and as many of her things as she had been able to gather. She was so scared because they did not know she had left. When she told me the story that day, I was reminded of Acts 12:6-10 where the angel came and released Peter from jail, and how God caused a deep sleep to fall on the people and guards:

> And behold, an angel of the Lord suddenly appeared, and a light shone in the cell; and he struck Peter's side and roused him, saying, "Get up quickly." And his chains fell off his hands. And the angel said to him, "Gird yourself and put on your sandals. " And he did so. And he said to him, "Wrap your cloak around you and follow me. " And he went out and continued to follow, and he did not know that what was being done by the angel was real, but thought he was seeing a vision. And when they had passed the first and second guard, they came to the iron gate that leads into the city, which opened for them by itself; and they went out and went along one street; and immediately the angel departed from him.

When I showed her this passage, D. J. was amazed because now it all made sense.

On that Sunday, we searched for a shelter opening for her and I realized how hard it was to find help for people. Our church leaders decided to put her in a weekly hotel until she could find permanent housing. At this point, I was unsure as to the validity of all the statements she had made, but it was clear that she was afraid and fighting the evil within her.

It was tough for me because on that very same day my wife, Teresa, and I were to lead a youth group spring break trip from March 12th though March 14th for our older high school youth. As church service ended that morning, we were ready to leave. What could I do? D.J. could possibly be in danger, and I was one of only a few who knew her in the church.

I am proud to say that people in our church stepped up to the plate. It started with a family who took her to find housing that afternoon, despite the safety issues. I was so pleased when our leaders helped financially, as well, even though there were so many con artists out there preying on churches for their money. I see this as being the hands and feet of Jesus.

While we were away on the trip, our youth prayed intently for D.J. all three days because we knew of the temptation she would feel to go back to the cult's community house. She was not a Christian and was still very much under the direction of Satan.

I had received calls from her the first two days. She told me, "I am going crazy with my two boys. I am so scared they will come after me and kill me. Will you come see me when you get home?" Because she had witnessed so many criminal acts, I told her, "God is watching over you and I trust He will protect you. Write down the things the people in the cult did that were illegal, and seal up the envelope. I will give it to someone in the church. Once you do that, call your cult and let them know you do not want that life anymore. The ball is in your court because you could put them all in jail for many years with what you know. Tell them if they threaten anyone related to this situation, or try in any way to find you, the envelope filled with descriptions of their crimes will be turned over to the authorities immediately."

As soon as she got off the phone, she did what I had asked.

March 14, 2006, was a day I will never forget. That was the day God opened my eyes to see things which I have a hard time putting into words. But let me try.

We had just returned from the three-day youth trip. She called me, and it seemed as if she had plans and no longer cared if I came by to study with her. This was unlike the first two days when she could not wait until I got back so these evil spirits would be gone. I knew something was up and I knew I wanted her to be saved.

She said, "I can't meet tonight because I have a birthday party to go to for my son." I knew we had to go straight from this youth event to her hotel, even before going home. There was no time to spare. The spiritual battle was getting fierce.

My wife and I arrived at the hotel where she had been staying for the last few nights, and somehow I knew this was the day she would be released from Satan and his evil spirits. To be honest, my confidence was in the fact that God was there, and I knew He wanted her saved. There is a lot of controversy around the subject of demon possession and exorcism, but all I knew was, I had no power within myself to do save her. That would only happen through the power of the Almighty God. As I walked into the hotel room, she would not even look at me. Later on, she would write in her journal, "The spirits told me to just act normal and he would go away."

She wrote, "As Travis came in that day, he was more assertive and stronger than ever."

I knew it was through the Holy Spirit because of how much prayer I had been a part of during the past three days. I opened the Bible and began to show her more passages. She started with jerks and uncontrollable slaps to her face, but I kept talking. My wife took our twin two-year-old boys out of the hotel room along with D. J.'s one-year-old and five-year-old sons. This was no place for children. We continued to study about how God could release her from all her past sins and the evil spirits, but she lost more control of her body as each minute went by.

My wife came back in the room to get something for one of her boys and D. J. got up and ran to the bathroom and locked the door. After Teresa left, I went to the bathroom door where I heard banging on the wall and bathtub. I could not believe what was going on. I just knew, at that very hour, a major battle was going on for her soul.

I shouted through the door, "Do not let the spirits rule you! Open the door!" After five minutes of pleading, she finally unlocked the door. D. J.

was sitting on the floor in the bathroom hitting her head on the porcelain bathtub. She began to bleed, and I knew I needed to pray. I grabbed her hand and she began kicking and hitting me, so I grabbed her arms and just prayed. I prayed, "Father release her from this and give her the strength to choose for herself who she will serve."

As the prayer went on, she began to calm down. After the prayer, I pleaded with her, "Take God's strength! He is giving it to you! He is stronger than the evil within you!" As she calmed down and took hold of God's strength, I knew it was time to confess Jesus as Lord and baptize her into His name. There was no time to change or find my wife. We were in the midst of a spiritual battle and the heat was on. It was time to go to the hotel swimming pool.

I grabbed my video camera and we ran to the pool. On the way, she took off. I did not run after her, but shouted, "D. J., take God's strength, it is there." She stopped and I later found out that the evil spirits were trying to kill her by making her run into the busy street in front of moving cars. This happened two times on the way to the pool.

Finally, we got to the pool area and I said, "I am going to videotape your confession so you will always have it and know you did it."

As we sat on the lounge chairs next to the pool, I finally heard the evil spirits. The sound of those voices will never leave my mind. I asked her to confess Jesus as Lord, but the spirits would not let her. The evil spirits controlled everything by throwing her into fits of rage and screaming in her head, "Kill him! Just Kill Him!"

The amazing thing was, there were no people around the pool area. I challenged her by saying, "If the spirits do not leave, I will give you a hundred dollars and send you on your way. You will never have to see me again." I had to trust that God would be faithful to His Word.

Finally, after approximately ten minutes of videotaping, I asked God, "Shut the mouths of these spirits and let her confess." With the sound of a painful squeal, she did it. She confessed, "Jesus is Lord!"

At that point, all hell broke loose. The evil spirits began to speak to me as she was uncontrollably hurting herself by pulling out clumps of her hair, slinging her head back and forth, and slapping her face. The spirits were speaking through her in a voice I had never heard saying, "You cannot have her. Kill him. I hate you! Leave! Run! Last chance!"

I somehow boldly responded by saying, "I am glad you hate me because you hate God," and "It is too late because she has already confessed Jesus as Lord. It is time for you to leave her." I shut off the camera, and we struggled as I was getting her into the water. I told her I did not want to force her to be baptized. I asked her to tell me, and for the spirits to keep quiet. I asked, "Do you want to be a Christian?"

She said, "Yes." We got in the shallow end of the pool, and I said, "Based on your confession, I baptize you in the name of the Father, Son, and Holy Spirit for the forgiveness of your sins." Then, she fell backward into the water as I was grabbing her arm. Her hair spread out over the water like something out of a horror movie and she let out the most excruciating scream. I told her once again, "Take God's strength and go under!" I then helped her under the water to be changed forever.

She came out of the water with a jolt and began weeping. As I hugged her, I said, "It is now all over. The spirits are gone." I said it not because I had ever witnessed anything like this before, but it was due to pure faith in God that her sin was gone and God's Spirit was there instead. For the first time in twenty years she was free.

We got out of the water and I turned on the camera again and she said with no problem, "Jesus is Lord! Jesus is Lord! I can say it so clear and easy." She began humming and touching her ears and I asked her, "Is everything ok?" She responded, "You are talking so loud now and, for the first time that I can remember, there are not any voices or screaming in my head." Walking back to the hotel room, she acted like a deaf women who had just heard sound for the first time. The twitching, slapping, and fighting were gone. With a smile on her face, she was set free.

This was such a relief for me because I'd had to just trust that God would take the spirits away.

As a side note, the evil spirits did not leave when she confessed Christ, but they took flight when she became obedient to her faith and was baptized. We will look at this further in the chapter entitled, "The Shadow of Salvation."

We got back to her hotel room and she was singing and humming in complete amazement. I opened up the Bible to James 4:7 where is says, "Submit to God. Resist the Devil and he will flee from you." Before I got this verse out of my mouth she began crying again, saying, "This is the first time I have clearly heard the Word of God. Every time you would read the Bible to me before, it would be mixed with screaming and voices telling me that it was all lies."

The day was not over. My next thought after all of this was, where were my wife and the children? I acted as if I was not concerned, but as we began to walk around the hotel, I noticed that Teresa was not by the lake or at the front, and was nowhere to be found. Now I was getting concerned. I could not imagine she would leave the area. The thought jumped into my head, "This is how Satan gets me." I was so scared, there was a pit in my stomach and my adrenaline raced.

We began to walk around the hotel again and I asked the people in the front office if they had seen a woman with four children, and they said they had, but thirty minutes ago. Our car was parked by the room and I prayed, trying to not show the fear I was feeling. I knew I needed to have faith, but fear overwhelmed me with the thought that this victory might cost me my family. Then a young man we had asked earlier said, pointing across the road, "Is that them?" We learned that the bathroom was broken in the lobby so they had gone to the restaurant next door. I thanked God.

I was so glad to see them. From the images I had just seen of evil, I knew that Satan wanted to destroy them and could, if God allowed it. My eyes had been opened to the real evil that is in the world. I was so glad that I followed the all-powerful God because I knew, from the voices of the evil spirits, that Satan hated me.

We left to go home, and I felt like Paul in 2 Corinthians 12 when he said, "I had heard inexpressible things that I was permitted to speak." I could not wait to get home so I could play the DVD of what I could never explain. As we were going home, I was trying to explain the story to my wife, but ended up telling her just to wait and see the DVD. We got home a few minutes later and I went right to work, putting the video onto a DVD to play it.

I told my wife, "It would be just like Satan to not allow this to play." No sooner had I gotten the words out of my mouth and put the DVD in the player did I see that the disc was unreadable. I worked on it for a few hours to try to get it to work, but it never did. The images were gone. I prayed because I knew this video would change the world, but it simply would not play. To this day, I wonder if God allowed Satan to ruin the DVD so people would have to believe the Bible instead of gaining their faith from a DVD. Even so, I was sorry. Satan might have stopped the images of that unbelievable day from being seen, but do not let him stop you from reading this book.

Now, do these things line up with the Scriptures? Can they give us more insight on the power of God as well as the spiritual world that exists? The remainder of this book will work through some questions about Satan and evil spirits from the Bible, so we do not remain ignorant of Satan's schemes.

Some of you may ask why we do not hear or see examples of Devil worship if it is so widespread. I have to say that many, just like me, are so ignorant to the grip that Satan has on so many people—even so-called Christians. The people in these satanic cults do not want to draw any attention to themselves. They want to fly under the radar. I believe also, at times, people want to just cover their eyes and pretend it does not exist.

Even now that D. J. is a Christian, people have a hard time accepting the fact that occult activity happens regularly in the woods less than a mile from where some of them live. We have people in the church who question this activity and D.J's involvement. There were some lies we found out about her past after her conversion, but after I heard the voices, saw the terror, and witnessed her complete change after her baptism, I was a believer that she had been very much controlled by Satan.

I learned that cult members live in the very same neighborhoods where Christians live and their children attend the same schools where our Christian children are going. Some cult members are law enforcement officers, Little League coaches, and even politicians in the areas where we live. Many of them have clean records on paper because they have yet to be caught. It was eye-opening for me to find out where this cult community house was in the city where I live. As my wife and I drove by, I noticed a church van across the street from the cult house. Apparently, a church minister lives across the street. I wonder if he has met his neighbors yet. There is said to be at least ten other houses like it in the surrounding area, near Orlando. Satanism and Devil worship are not as rare as we have been led to believe. The deception of Satan is not as miniscule as we were once taught.

God is at work in this world, but we are deceived if we think Satan's power is not. It starts with those who choose to surrender to Satan and it ends with those who surrender to him unknowingly because they have not surrendered to Christ. Even though we are around so much evil, God is greater, and it is important to walk faithfully and confidently with Him.

CHAPTER 1 WORKSHEET

What were some new things you learned about evil from this breathtaking story?

_____

_____

_____

What are some things you noticed about God from this chapter?

_____

_____

_____

What fears do you have which keep you from helping those who are distraught?

_____

_____

_____

How can God remove those fears?

_____

_____

_____

Do you know anyone right now who is battling with their demons? What can you do to help them?

_____

_____

_____

The Shadow of Satan

And no wonder, for Satan himself masquerades as an angel of light.
2 Corinthians 11:14-15

What you will read in this chapter about Satan may surprise—if not shock—you. You will read about many of the traditions that have been passed down through the years, but that may not be biblically accurate. Satan has been the talk of many centuries, starting at the beginning of time as he took the form of a serpent. Many who worship in the occult believe that Satan was Jesus's brother, and that God chose Jesus over Satan. This would be the reason why the Devil rebelled initially. Many have referred to him as the great archangel, Lucifer, and so on, but are those descriptions even accurate? The point of this chapter is to educate you in Scripture and help you see the importance of studying God's Word. Your first thought in hearing some of these biblical truths of who Satan is may be that you want to go and check to see if what I am writing is correct. May the heavens rejoice if we begin to search God's Word instead of listening to mere men! So, what are the shadows or lies? You should determine your thoughts from the Scriptures, as I have.

The Shadow of Satan as God

There is a belief out there that Satan and Jesus are brothers. It is taken from the pattern of Abraham and Isaac. The Bible teaches that Isaac was the only begotten son of Abraham, even though Abraham had a son named Ishmael. Abraham is an antitype of God and Isaac is an antitype of Jesus. I do not believe that argument validates this theory. Jesus is God, and Satan is not.

What defines the person of God are four major characteristics that neither Satan nor anyone created has ever had or ever can have. These characteristics are eternal (no beginning or end), omnipotent (all powerful, holds all power), omniscient (all knowing, holds all knowledge), and omnipresent (can be everywhere at once). It seems clear from the Scriptures that Satan does not hold any of these characteristics that define God. It is also clear from the Scriptures that Jesus holds all of these characteristics, thereby proving conclusively that Jesus is, in fact, God.

One of the Scriptures that proves Jesus is God is John 1:1, 14:

> In the beginning was the Word, and the Word was with God, and the Word was God. ... The Word became flesh and made his dwelling among us. We have seen his glory, the glory of the One and only, who came from the Father, full of grace and truth.

This is the verse that goes farther back than any other verse in the Scriptures. If you copied the Bible in chronological order, this would be the very first verse before anything. This verse clearly says that Jesus was there in the beginning and that He was God.

Other verses related to the topic of Jesus being God are Hebrews 1:5-8: "For to which of the angels did God ever say, "You are my Son; today I have become your Father?" Or again, "I will be his Father, and he will be my Son?" And again, when God brings his firstborn into the world, he says, "Let all God's angels worship him." In speaking of the angels he says, "He makes his angels winds, his servant's flames of fire." But about the Son he says, "Your throne, O God, will last forever and ever, and righteousness will be the scepter of your kingdom."

This verse is intriguing because the Father is talking about the Son, and the Father clearly calls the Son, Jesus, God. This book is not about proving the deity of Christ, so let me give you a few more verses for your own study if you need some convincing from the Scriptures that Jesus is God. These passages are found in Isaiah 9:6; John 8:58; John 10:30; John 14:9; John 20:28; Romans 9:5; Colossians 2:9; Hebrews 1:3; and Revelation 5:13-14.

Now to prove Satan is not God, we must prove that Satan does not have any of God's characteristics.

First, Satan is not eternal. He was created by God for a purpose. Therefore, he has a beginning and cannot be the brother of Jesus, who did not have a beginning. This idea of eternity is hard even to imagine because all we have ever experienced is a definitive time period. Take time as a book. God is the one looking at the book, and He can choose to see the beginning of the book or end of the book whenever He pleases. He is not bound inside of the book like us. One day, we also will dwell out of the "book of time."

Everything we have ever seen has had a start and finish or a beginning and end. God says in Revelation 1:8: "'I am the Alpha and the Omega,' says the Lord God, 'who is, and who was, and who is to come, the Almighty.'" The angels, and everything ever created, whether on earth or in heaven, are not eternal because all of it had a beginning. What God did before He created the world baffles scholars. My thought is, why think about it? It will just give you a headache. Until we are outside of time, we will never understand how everything works. We only have five entrances into our mind and, outside of that, we cannot comprehend anything.

Second, Satan is not omnipotent. He cannot hold all power as God does because he is limited in his power. In Job, he asked to tempt Job and hurt him and his family. God limited his power even in that situation. If Satan had all power, he could do what he wanted, even with Job, without permission from God. Many do not understand Satan's power. I believe Satan is extremely powerful because that is the way God created him. Satan is so powerful he convinced a third of the angels that he could defeat the Father. That is a lot of power. I am reminded of the Scripture in 1 John 4:4 that says, "Greater is he who is in you than he who is in the world."

To illustrate this second point, I'd like to tell you a story.

I mentioned earlier that I have had a few experiences with the occult. One of those was in January, 1996, in Lubbock, Texas. Within the Bible Belt of America, Lubbock was a city of approximately 200,000 people at the time, with churches on every corner. It is a city with so many godly people that you would never think the occult would be so strong. Surprisingly, the occult still existed there and was quite prevalent. Would Satan have positioned himself strategically in this location because of all the believers?

On January 28, 1996, my wife, who was my girlfriend at that time, and I went to lead Bible study with a girl named Carolyn, whom we had met months before and were teaching about the Bible. She was living by herself in a new apartment away from the projects. Back then, I had been praying for God to reveal a glimpse of the spiritual world to me because I'd been reading books such as *This Present Darkness, Seeing the Unseen,* and *Piercing the Darkness.* It was a Saturday night, and I was excited because I knew Carolyn was ready to give her life to Christ. We had already been through months of study, and she was evaluating the possibility of complete surrender in her life. That evening we were studying with Carolyn, her sister, Patti, and her cousin, Deanne. A knock came at her door, and a young man in his twenties walked in. His name was Lafayette, and his face will forever be imprinted in my mind. Because that night would challenge my faith far more than anything I had ever experienced thus far in my life.

Lafayette came in and we explained we were studying the Bible, and he was more than welcome to join us. As our study continued, I realized he was going to confuse Carolyn and the other girls because he had a warped view of God. He said he had been in a Satanic cult, but that he'd gotten out of it not long ago. The girls continued to study with me in their room while Teresa sat at the dining room table and studied with Lafayette. I was not going to let Satan use this opportunity to confuse Carolyn. If I could do that night over again, I would have stayed with Lafayette and let Teresa continue studying with Carolyn.

After my study was over with Carolyn that night, she decided to be baptized. I went out to tell Teresa the good news. She said she wanted Lafayette to explain a few things he had told her previously. He talked about some experiences he'd had while practicing the occult. He said he'd been sent on missions to kill people for financial reasons or because that person mistreated one of their own. Lafayette said, "The only time cult members would hurt Christians was if Christians were trying to convert someone or were interfering with someone they were also try-ing to convert." I did not realize at the time, that this included us. He discussed in detail how they would actually gut people's stomachs, as well as other methods of brutality which I cannot describe in this book. He described the many people he had murdered.

Teresa asked him, "If you were still in the cult, could you kill us if you wanted to?"

He replied in a serious tone, "I could not tonight because you are cur-rently being guarded."

Do we have guardian angels? Or was it because we were in a very threatening situation? It was amazing to see the insight he had on the spiritual world. He told us, "Not every time I was sent on a mission to kill did I succeed. Sometimes, the spiritual force was so strong that I could not even enter through that person's front gate at night."

This is really eye-opening and encouraging. Satan cannot touch you without God's permission. He is in submission to God and His power. Lafayette told us that he knew what people said and discussed when he was not around because evil would tell him. He described the ranking system within the occult practice, with the High Priest being the highest in the community. These people definitely had powers, but like Satan, they were limited by God's power.

Teresa and I had to go and get a different car to take Carolyn for her baptism in our pool at the apartment complex where we were living at that time in a program called AIM Adventures in Missions. As we left and got in my Nissan two-seater, I told Teresa, "I know for sure Lafayette is lying. I believe the Spirit told me he is still in the cult." The Holy Spirit spoke so clearly that I was warned.

As we went and picked up our friend's four-door sedan, it was very clear that we needed to get Carolyn, Patti, and Deanne and leave immediately. We were not going to act as if we knew anything, but would tell Lafayette there were not enough seats for him to come along. Wisdom told us that there was no way we were going to show him where we lived. Not after all he had just told us.

We got back to Carolyn's apartment and walked in the door. There was Lafayette, rubbing his nose violently. I asked in humor, "Does your nose itch?"

He said, "You know they say if your nose itches, it means someone has been talking about you." I had heard the phrase about a person's ears burning, but this statement got my attention. Especially when he related with complete accuracy and direct quotes all that Teresa and I had said on our trip to pick up the car.

Then he gave me the most evil look, so I knew he knew. I believe, to this day, that Satan and/or his followers had heard Teresa's and my entire conversation, and told Lafayette everything. It was obvious he knew the exact things we had said. I knew we had to get out of there. We immediately went to the car, and he called Carolyn back. As Lafayette talked to her, she began to cry. After a few minutes of waiting and watching, she got in the car and continued to cry. I asked her, "Do you still want to be baptized?"

In tears, she just nodded her head yes.

I asked her, "What did he say to you before we left?"

She replied, "He is still in the cult and if I do this, he will kill me, my family, and you two later tonight."

It was amazing, but I did not fear my life. Lafayette had made it clear we were protected, and I knew God would continue to protect us. We got to our apartment around eleven p.m. that night, and I baptized her into Christ in fifty-degree water in the pool.

For the sake of Teresa's safety, I took Carolyn, Patti, and Deanne back home after the baptism and praying with them. I told them to call the police if he was there or if he came back. Lafayette was not joking. After I dropped them off and told them to go in and lock their doors, I heard he came back later, armed and ready to keep his promise.

After I got home again, Teresa came over to my apartment and we just sat on the couch talking and praying. Then it happened! At approximately three a.m. that Sunday morning, I got a call. Lafayette had just been outside pounding on their window, threatening to kill Carolyn and her family if they did not open up. He said he was going down the street, and he would be back to kill them. I asked if they had called 911, and they said no, they'd called me first. I told them to hang up and we would both call 911.

It was silent for the rest of the night. I could not call them to see if the police got there in time because they had called from a pay phone outside their room. As you might suspect, I did not get much sleep that night. I had to just trust that God would protect them and us. We had to go off to the respective churches we had been assigned in AIM the Adventures in Missions program for that entire Sunday, not knowing what had happened. All I knew was that Carolyn would be saved if something terrible had happened.

That Sunday evening we got a call from Carolyn, saying, "He came right back after Patti hung up with you. It was scary. He was busting out our front window with his knife. The police arrived just as he was reaching in to unlock the door. I was so relieved when they arrested him and hauled him off to jail." That night, they'd arrested him with a foot-long knife in his hand. He also had a large amount of crack cocaine, all of which would put him away for a good while. We later saw this attempted break in on the news and we were so thankful the police got there in time.

This understanding about Satan and evil spirits should not frighten us, because as Christians, we have the all-powerful God on our side. It should be the most encouraging thing for Christians, but it should frighten the socks off those who are not saved.

So, getting back to the proof that Satan is not God, we move on to the next characteristic he lacks.

Third, Satan is not omniscient. He does not have all knowledge pertaining to the future because he truly believed Job would curse God in Job 1. Also, he would never have killed the Son of God if he knew the cross was part of the plan to save mankind. In 1 Peter 1:12, the Scripture says that angels long to look into these things. Even the mystery of God in saving the Gentiles was hidden from his own angels. Many believe psychics must be from Satan, but people cannot figure it all out. Can psychics really tell the future? Satan might be able to know your past and guess the future, but he cannot know the future definitively. We know from the Scriptures that Satan is not all-knowing.

Fourth, Satan is not omnipresent. Satan cannot be in all places at once. In 1 Peter 3:8, the Bible says the Devil roams around like a roaring lion. Also in Job 1:7, God asks where he had been, and Satan said roaming about on the earth and walking on it. There have been a lot of theories about how fast Satan can get around. Sorry, the Bible does not give quarter-mile times. What we do know is even if Satan could move from one side of the world to the other in a blink of an eye, it still proves he cannot be on both sides at the same time.

So, because Satan was created as a heavenly being, he does not hold any eternal deity characteristic of God. The Devil is not God, and he will never be God. Do not let him deceive you into believing he even has a chance to win and overpower God. Satan was made so powerful and glorious he has been able to deceive many to believe he is God or that he can defeat God. But it's not true. Satan wants to be God, but all he really can attempt to be is a pitiful copycat and counterfeit.

The Shadow of Satan as an Archangel

We know that Satan is not God or the Son of God, so the question is what or who is he? Tradition has always said Satan is an angel, and even one of the elite angels—an archangel. Many get this because it is said he disguises himself as an angel of light. Well, according to Hebrews 13:2, angels can appear as humans, but that does not mean they are human. Many believe that because of the power of Satan, he must be an archangel. This is all speculation based on what we think an archangel is and what one does. The Bible has a few things to say about angels but, by no means, has the Bible exhausted the subject.

There is a fascination about these spiritual beings called angels. There are questions that the Scriptures do not answer clearly. For example, how do angels win or lose in battle? Can they die? What standard do they follow? Does everyone have a guardian angel? How do angels minister to us as believers? According to Hebrews 1:14 "Are not all angels ministering spirits sent to serve those who will inherit salvation?" There are many other questions that have come up, including whether or not Satan is an angel. There is very little discussion in the Bible about archangels, or even the names of angels, with a few exceptions such as Michael and Gabriel. We can know, most assuredly, that the spiritual world holds a lot of mysteries that we today do not know.

Others have taken the idea that Satan is an angel from Revelation 9:11 where it says, "They have as king over them the angel of the abyss; his name in Hebrew is Abaddon, and in the Greek he has the name Apollyon." Some say this angel over the abyss is Satan. In Revelation 20:1-3, it says:

> And I saw an angel coming down from heaven, having the key of the abyss and a great chain in his hand. And he laid hold of the dragon, the serpent of old, who is the Devil and Satan, and bound him for a thousand years, and threw him into the abyss, and shut it and sealed it over him, so that he should not deceive the nations any longer, until the thousand years were completed; after these things he must be released for a short time.

This would say that an angel other than Satan has the key to the abyss. I think *The MacArthur New Testament Commentary* says it best: "John gives his title as the angel of the abyss. Some identify this angel as Satan, but his domain is the heavenlies (Eph. 6:12), where he is the "prince of the power of the air" (Eph. 2:2). He is not associated with the abyss until he is cast into it (Rev.20:1-3). This angel is better viewed as a high-ranking demon in Satan's hierarchy." This would seem to make sense from the context of Revelation 20, but MacArthur could be stretching it a little by calling this angel a high-ranking demon.

Others have said Satan is a cherub, which is a warrior angel based on Ezekiel 28. The only thing that contradicts with this thought is that the context is referring to the King of Tyre. Some say that since this passage in Ezekiel refers to the Garden of Eden, then it must be Satan. Could the reference about the Garden of Eden be comparing the King of Tyre to Adam, the first man on earth? In Ezekiel 28:2, 9, it refers to this person as a man. Could this passage in Ezekiel refer to the King of Tyre and also a picture of Satan? Sure, but there is no clear definitive proof of whether Satan is an angel. Many are quick to call Satan an angel or an archangel because they have always heard that to be true. Once again, where is the proof from the Scriptures concerning this?

Maybe Satan is an angel but, if anything, Scripture would tend to refer to Satan, this dragon of old, as a created being above the angels. One thing you can know for sure is that the Scriptures do not say anywhere that Satan is an angel or an archangel. The Bible is not clear about Satan and his beginning, or whether he is an angel, but he is definitely not God.

The Shadow of Satan as Lucifer

Once again, tradition has said that Satan's real name is Lucifer, based on the Isaiah 14:12 passage. Isaiah 14:12-15 says:

> How art thou fallen from heaven, O Lucifer, son of the morning! How art thou cut down to the ground, which didst weaken the nations! For thou hast said in thine heart, I will ascend into heaven, I will exalt my throne

above the stars of God: I will sit also upon the mount of the congregation, in the sides of the north: I will ascend above the heights of the clouds; I will be like the most High. Yet thou shalt be brought down to hell, to the sides of the pit. KJV

We read this and we say, what's the problem? The term Lucifer is only in the King James Version. All the other versions say the morning star. In Isaiah 14:4, it says, "That thou shalt take up this proverb against the king of Babylon, and say, How hath the oppressor ceased! The golden city ceased!"

Also if you continue to read that chapter, Isaiah makes it clear this king will not lie in a tomb among other kings because he has ruined his land and killed his people. Isaiah 14:18-20 says:

All the kings of the nations lie in state, each in his own tomb. But you are cast out of your tomb like a rejected branch; you are covered with the slain, with those pierced by the sword, those who descend to the stones of the pit. Like a corpse trampled underfoot, you will not join them in burial, for you have destroyed your land and killed your people.

In the New American Standard Version, it says "you have ruined your country and slain your people." Satan cannot be buried in a tomb, and he does not reign over a country.

This is just another example of something we have always believed because ministers and highly respected Bible teachers have continued to pass this down from generation to generation. Once again, I will ask, when are we going to challenge the things we learn from fallible men and women and become students of God's Word? Calling Satan "Lucifer" is clear proof that you have not studied the context.

Could this be referring to the King of Babylon literally, and to Satan figuratively? Of course it could. But throughout Isaiah, it is referring to judgment and punishment on different nations and cities. Why should we think this is different? Isaiah 15 deals with the judgment against Moab. Isaiah 17 deals with the judgment of Damascus. Isaiah 18 deals with the judgment against Ethiopia. Isaiah 19 deals with the judgment against Egypt, and so on. To say that all these judgments are literal and the first judgment on Babylon is not literal would be a poor interpretation without further proof from the Scriptures. History shows that Babylon was destroyed and has been desolate to this day. That aligns with Isaiah 13:19-22, which says:

> And Babylon, the jewel of kingdoms, the glory of the Babylonians's pride, will be overthrown by God like Sodom and Gomorrah. She will never be inhabited or lived in through all generations; no Arab will pitch his tent there, no shepherd will rest his flocks there. But desert creatures will lie there, jackals will fill her houses; there the owls will dwell, and there the wild goats will leap about. Hyenas will howl in her strongholds, jackals in her luxurious palaces. Her time is at hand, and her days will not be prolonged.

Isaiah 14 is the only place we see Lucifer in the Bible. I am confident from the Scriptures that verse 12 as well as the entire chapter is referring to the King of Babylon, as it says. Could this, in fact, be another thing we have been taught that is not backed by the Scriptures? When are we, as God's people, going to study God's Word fervently on a daily basis? The answers are right there, if we will just read.

Many would rather listen to others instead of reading it for themselves. We live in a time where God's word is so prevalent, especially in our country, we are without excuse if our faith is based solely on what others teach.

CHAPTER 2 WORKSHEET

When you look at your life, do you feel you have been deceived in who Satan really is?

_____

_____

_____

So, who do you believe Satan is?

_____

_____

_____

Do you believe the verse about Lucifer refers to Satan, as some say? Why or Why not?

_____

_____

_____

Have you experienced Satan's power? If so, how?

_____

_____

_____

How do you feel about the power Satan has in the world?

_____

_____

_____

CHAPTER 3

The Existence of Satan

He was a murderer from the beginning, not holding to the truth, for there is no truth in him. When he lies, he speaks his native language, for he is a liar and the father of lies.
— John 8:44

W e know Satan and his followers have been judged. They no longer have their dwelling in heaven, and they cannot be saved. Remember from earlier in our study, we saw that the Scriptures are quite clear when it says angels and spiritual beings are not under the same forgiveness in Christ that we, as believers, are under. In this chapter, we are going to ask some tough questions and work through some complex concepts.

Some of the things we will address in this chapter include the downfall of Satan from the Scriptures, his judgment, and his involvement in today's world. These have been questions that scholars have wrestled with for many years. I want us to see the whole picture to better understand our enemy and his ways. I do not profess to have all the answers to the questions that baffle scholars, but what I do have may give new insight on Satan.

One thing we do know is that Satan is not a rival of God. Satan cannot ever catch God off guard. He knows everything that Satan is doing and what he wants to do. How frustrating it must be for Satan to know that he will never surprise God with anything or ever get one step ahead. How many times has Satan come to God and asked to do a certain thing that God allowed him to do, which only fell into the divine plan of God? Satan only helped God's cause over and over, just as Satan did when he sought to kill the Son of God. When Satan brought suffering on the church, it grew rapidly in quantity and quality. When Satan brought suffering on the apostles, they rejoiced in God knowing that they were counted worthy to suffer for the sake of Christ. To those who truly know and trust God, the suffering which Satan gives out only strengthens the redeemed.

But let's face it, those who are lukewarm and following Jesus because times are good, are brought low by the attacks from the evil one. If Satan has only helped the plan of God all these years, you might wonder if Satan would start doing the opposite of what God would allow. The only problem with that is, God would already know he would do this, so the opposite would help God's plan, as well. I do not know about you, but I want my life to frustrate Satan. I want faith that rejoices in suffering and glorifies God in riches or in poverty, in safety or in tragedy, in disease or in health, always worshipping God for His unfailing love.

Satan as a Spiritual Being

To say that Satan was created as a powerful being is an understatement. The facts are that Satan is so strong and powerful that the Scriptures say a third of the angels fell with him. That means a third of the angels truly believed Satan could give them more than what God was willing, and would ultimately defeat God. I would say with confidence that this is a lot of power God gave him. Just because Satan and even a third of the angels believed this, does not mean it would even be possible for God to fall in power. History as well as the cross of Christ proves our God (Father, Son, and Holy Spirit) is still reigning on His throne, and it proves He always will.

We need to be reminded that Satan was created for a purpose, like all the other heavenly beings and angels. Like the angels who fell with Satan, he apparently had a choice. It does not seem as though there are many choices in heaven. Either you submit to God and his plan, or you do not. I believe Satan knows he made a poor decision.

Angels and heavenly beings are not under the blood of Christ, according to the Bible, so they cannot repent and come back to God.

> For if God did not spare angels when they sinned, but sent them to hell, putting them into gloomy dungeons to be held for judgment; if he did not spare the ancient world when he brought the flood on its ungodly people, but protected Noah, a preacher of righteousness, and seven others; if he condemned the cities of Sodom and Gomorrah by burning them to ashes, and made them an example of what is going to happen to the ungodly; and if he rescued Lot, a righteous man, who was distressed by the filthy lives of lawless men (for that righteous man, living among them day after day, was tormented in his righteous soul by the lawless deeds he saw and heard)—if this is so, then the Lord knows how to rescue godly men from trials and to hold the unrighteous for the day of judgment, while continuing their punishment. — 2 Peter 2:4-10

These verses reveal that God did not spare angels when they sinned. They are not under the forgiveness of Christ, and do not receive any forgiveness. With angels, one strike and you are out. This is another reason we as Christians can be so thankful. We are under the forgiveness and blood of Jesus Christ. Do not take this for granted, because it was not always this way.

In Jude 6, it says: "And the angels who did not keep their positions of authority but abandoned their own home—these he has kept in darkness, bound with everlasting chains for judgment on the great Day." They made a choice to walk away from God, so they are punished.

Jesus says He saw Satan fall like lightning from heaven in Luke 10:18, and John writes in Revelation 12:9 that the great dragon, the serpent of old, was thrown down to the earth along with his angels. If anything, just as in Job 1 when Satan came with some angels, Satan seems to be a spiritual being that was over the angels. Numerous times in the Bible it says, "Satan and his angels."

Satan Cast Down to Earth

One of the most debated mysteries is, at what point were Satan and his angels cast to earth? We see Satan in the form of a serpent in the Garden of Eden, but does that mean he was cast there? Does it mean that was the time of Satan's judgment? The word Devil does not even appear until the New Testament. The name Satan only appears in 1 Chronicles 21, Job, and Zechariah in the Old Testament. So, was Satan even judged during Old Testament times? We do know Satan was on earth and that he tried to stop the seed line of Christ almost every step of the way. We see this in the examples of Noah, Moses, Ruth, and Hezekiah. It is obvious that Satan was at work, but whether he was judged and cast down to earth during this time is still unclear.

There are some Scriptures that are important to read before we form conclusions on this matter. In Luke 10:18-20, it says:

He replied, "I saw Satan fall like lightning from heaven. I have given you authority to trample on snakes and scorpions and to overcome all the power of the enemy; nothing will harm you. However, do not rejoice that the spirits submit to you, but rejoice that your names are written in heaven."

Is Jesus talking about something He witnessed when He was in heaven, or when He was alive on earth? We have always taken this Scripture to mean when He was in heaven, but does that align with other passages? We have a hard time believing Satan could have had access to heaven during the Old Testament years if, in fact, he had already been cast from there. How could God allow this to happen? One thing I have learned through my study and all my experiences is, we are not always going to understand the decisions that God made. We are not always going to have answers for what He allows. For example, why did God allow David to have a life-size idol in his home, according to 1 Samuel 19:13-16:

Then Michal took an idol and laid it on the bed, covering it with a garment and putting some goats hair at the head. When Saul sent the men to capture David, Michal said, "He is ill." Then Saul sent the men back to see David and told them, "Bring him up to me in his bed so that I may kill him." But when the man entered, there was the idol in the bed, and at the head was some goat hair.

It is clearly stated in the law that one should not make any graven images and have no other gods before Jehovah God.

If we continue to look at some other Scriptures like Job 2:1-2, we are able to see that God asked Satan where he had come from. This could have a few possible meanings. It could mean where on the earth because you (Satan) were cast there, or it could mean where have you (Satan) been and what were you doing since you being cast there. According to Satan's answer to the question, it would appear as if Satan did not take the question to mean where on earth, because Satan answers, "From roaming around on the earth and walking on it."

This verse would lead me to conclude that Satan still had access to heaven and the heavenly realms. Satan could have been cast down to earth at the beginning of the world while still having unlimited access to the Father. Does this idea make sense? We know that evil cannot dwell with God, but evil can be before God. If you question this thought, how is it that an unsaved sinner can be in God's presence in prayer and an unsaved sinner can be in God's presence in worship? Did the casting down to earth halt the access Satan had to God?

There are a few possible ways to understand the fall of Satan. The first option is to believe that Satan was cast down when earth was created. The second option is that Satan was cast down during the time of the Garden of Eden. The third option is that Satan was cast down at the beginning of Jesus's life on earth. The fourth option is that Satan was cast down at the death of Christ.

In looking at the very first prophecy of Christ in Genesis 3:15: "And I will put enmity between you and the woman, and between your offspring and hers; he will crush your head, and you will strike his heel," the conclusion could be drawn that there would be a time that Satan will be crushed, and the time had not yet come in Genesis 3. Just because Jesus would crush Satan's head in the future, it does not mean Satan was not judged at this point. Revelation 12 says:

> Michael and his angels fought against the dragon, and the dragon and his angels fought back. But he was not strong enough, and they lost their place in heaven. The great dragon was hurled down—that ancient serpent

called the Devil, or Satan, who leads the whole world astray. He was hurled to the earth, and his angels with him. Then I heard a loud voice in heaven say: "Now have come the salvation and the power and the kingdom of our God, and the authority of his Christ. For the accuser of our brothers, who accuses them before our God day and night, has been hurled down. They overcame him by the blood of the Lamb and by the word of their testimony; they did not love their lives so much as to shrink from death. Therefore rejoice you heavens and you who dwell in them! But woe to the earth and the sea, because the Devil has gone down to you! He is filled with fury, because he knows that his time is short." When the dragon saw that he had been hurled to the earth, he pursued the woman who had given birth to the male child. The woman was given the two wings of a great eagle, so that she might fly to the place prepared for her in the desert, where she would be taken care of for a time, times and half a time, out of the serpent's reach. Then from his mouth the serpent spewed water like a river, to overtake the woman and sweep her away with the torrent. But the earth helped the woman by opening its mouth and swallowing the river that the dragon had spewed out of his mouth. Then the dragon was enraged at the woman and went off to make war against the rest of her offspring—those who obey God's commandments and hold to the testimony of Jesus.

The book of Revelation reveals the vision that John received about this war in heaven. What is intriguing about the term *war* is that it does not seem to be a single event, but it is actually a process. Wars do not usually happen in a few seconds but, sometimes, over a span of years. Consider the war on terrorism being conducted by America on the Middle East right now. Could this war with Satan and his angels have started at the beginning of the earth and ended at the resurrection of Christ? As for the woman in Revelation 12, some believe this is Mary, but the Bible speaks of Israel as being the woman in Isaiah 54:5 and 66:7, Jeremiah 3:6-10, and Micah 4:10 and 5:2-3. The Devil wasn't really after the woman but sought the child.

In Revelation 12:7-12, the future tense is used when making reference to the fact that this dragon would be thrown down to earth. In Revelation 12:11, it says that Michael and his angels overcame him because of the blood of the Lamb. They speak saying, "the accuser of our brethren had been thrown down and woe because the Devil has come having great wrath knowing he has a short time," according to the Revelation 12 passage. Could it be that Satan was cast down because of the blood of the Lamb? Was Satan cast down at the beginning but still had access to the Father until he was crushed by the death and resurrection of Jesus? So, when Satan used Judas to hand over the Son of God, Satan did not realize he was falling into the direct plan of God.

This situation reminds me of our high school basketball team, the Umatilla Bulldogs. The team did not win that often. There was one game in particular where we were down by one point with only five seconds left on the clock. The anticipation to beat our toughest opponent was increasing, especially since we were on our home court. The gym was packed, the crowd was roaring, and the pressure was mounting. Our best player was going to get the ball after the time-out. The plan discussed in the time-out was that the in-bound passer would throw the ball in at half court to our best player, and he would get as close to the basket as he could to shoot before the five seconds were up.

After the time-out, as our starting five players walked on the court, we realized the other team was going to play man coverage. This means that they were going to guard each one of us individually. The referee blew his whistle, and our best player broke in the direction of the goal as the pass came in just as we had planned. He began to dribble toward the basket as fast as he could to make an unbelievable shot during the final second of the game. He began to jump as the buzzer went off to signify the end of the game. As he looked to the coach and other players, he realized he had shot the ball into the wrong basket. He must have been confused about which goal was ours after the intense time-out. I can only imagine what was going through his head as he looked at the scoreboard, which showed that the Umatilla Bulldogs lost by three. He thought he had won the game for his team when, in fact, he lost the game. A hush came over the crowd, and people stood in utter amazement. It was hard not to hang our heads that night.

Do you think this was how Satan must have felt at the death of Christ? He was down by one point in the fourth period and he thought he made the winning shot when, in reality, he had helped the opposing team seal the victory. The scoreboard did not lie that night, just as the empty tomb didn't, either.

In Matthew 4, it was the Devil who tempted Jesus during those forty days. One of the temptations was to give Jesus everything He could see while on the mountain. This was tempting for Jesus because Satan could give all this without Jesus having to suffer for it. If Satan had not been cast down to earth, then he would not be able to offer this to Jesus. The argument is that Satan could not give what was not his to give. If Satan could not really give all this, then it would not be a temptation...but it was a temptation to Jesus.

So, was Satan already cast down to earth at this time? Remember, it was Jesus who said that during His life here on earth He saw Satan fall like lightning from heaven. To say that Satan did not fall from heaven until the cross of Christ or after might be extremely difficult to prove. Falling to earth may not have limited his access to God, but his access might have been limited when God's plan was fulfilled in Jesus Christ, His Son.

The reality is that Satan was cast down to the earth. He lost the war in heaven, which he believed he could win. He was crushed by Jesus on the cross while only bruising Jesus's heel. Satan began his battle with the church already in the first century, and he still intends to win. Jesus says the church will never lose, according to Matthew 16:18: "And I tell you that you are Peter, and on this rock I will build my church, and the gates of Hades will not overcome it." If you are like me, you have witnessed many who have lost that battle with Satan, and there will be many more throughout time who will lose the battle with him because of his deceit. Satan's power is in deception and he only has power in our lives when we give him power over us.

The war has been won but Satan is still fighting battles. We must remember from Matthew 4 that we are in his domain, and we are living behind enemy lines. No wonder the pain and strife we deal with on this earth is so constant; we are living in his territory. There is a lot of evil Satan can give us. He can give us disease, heartache, misery, poverty, and even death, according to the book of Job. But he can also give us wealth, success, popularity, and so much more. Remember, he can only do what God allows, and God sees and knows all. He is the prince of this world until the King of kings comes back to devastate him.

Satan can only give us what is temporary, whether good or bad. Jesus is the giver of the eternal. Even what Satan was trying to give Jesus during the time of temptations was only the temporary. God not only can give you things in this world but in the eternity to come. Do not let Satan deceive you into trading the eternal for the temporary. We would never consciously commit to this, yet Satan deceives so many into doing this without even knowing it. We get sucked right into the here and now, and our eyes lose focus on the real prize of knowing and being with Jesus. The encouragement is that Satan may be strong, but our God is stronger. Satan may come and go, but our God is always there. Satan may be around us, but our God is in us. We may live in Satan's territory, but our home is with the Lord.

> Therefore we do not lose heart. Though outwardly we are wasting away, yet inwardly we are being renewed day by day. For our light and momentary troubles are achieving for us an eternal glory that far outweighs them all. So we fix our eyes not on what is seen, but on what is unseen. For what is seen is temporary, but what is unseen is eternal. —2 Corinthians 4:16-18

This Scripture reminds me that I must keep focused on the eternal, even though Satan wants me to focus on the temporary. We were created for more than this world!

Satan's war against God's people is personal to us because we have witnessed broken marriages, out-of-control children, depression, loneliness, abuse, addictions, monetary pursuits, and even corrupt leadership in the home and church. Satan has deceived wives into believing their responsibilities at home are not glamorous enough. He has deceived husbands into believing they need to provide every desire for themselves as well as for their family. Sometimes it even costs them their marriage and children, and by the time they realize what's truly important, it might be too late. Once again, this is not a matter of women working outside of the home being right or wrong. This is about how Satan deceives us with material things to take our focus away from Christ. What happened to living with simplicity and being content with what God has given us? In our dissatisfaction, we lose sight of what is godly and important.

Years ago, a teenager came to me and said he was struggling because his dad was never home anymore. The teenager knew the reason was because his dad was trying to get enough money to make Christmas morning memorable. What his dad did not know was that the teenager would rather have his dad home for those three months than for one Christmas morning, which did not turn out so great anyway. Satan sure knows how to distract us, does he not?

The point is that Satan is a roaring lion, and he is after the Lord's church. He will not stop until he gets all of us or he runs out of time. We are going to suffer in this life whether or not we are followers of Jesus Christ, because we live in an evil world that is influenced by the prince of darkness.

Satan's Actual Power

So many people live in fear of Satan and his followers. From what the Bible says and from what my own eyes have seen, Satan is in complete submission to the Almighty Father, Son, and Holy Spirit, even though Satan seems to be allowed to cause a lot of evil.

We can see from the instances where Jesus was helping the demon-possessed that it was the demons in submission and fear of Christ. In those stories, Jesus never seems afraid or fearful, but it is the exact opposite for the demons. They shuddered at the sight of Jesus! Despite this truth, people are still afraid of the dark world because it is not visible. What is visible is the power of the dark world displayed throughout our entire world. According to Ephesians 6:12, we learn our battle is against this dark world. I agree that Satan is strong, but he has been defeated and judged. Many of us have this fear of demons and Satan because we have seen his power, which, to some Christians, seems more prevalent than God's power. If we would only step out in faith, go where God wants us to go, and do what God wants us to do, then maybe we would see the abundance of God's power.

When I get my mind off of myself, my problems, materialism, and things which are only temporary, I clearly see the power from God available to me.

We had a Bible study with a group of our teens about witchcraft, mediums, and spiritualists. On this particular night, we talked about the true power that witches and others who pull from evil power have available. The Bible does not say these things do not exist, but what it does say is that these things are evil and an abomination to God. The Bible says that those who practice things like sorcery do not have eternal life. Galatians 5:19-21 says,

> The acts of the sinful nature are obvious: sexual immorality, impurity and debauchery; idolatry and witchcraft; hatred, discord, jealousy, fits of rage, selfish ambition, dissensions, factions and envy; drunkenness, orgies, and the like. I warn you, as I did before, that those who live like this will not inherit the kingdom of God.

We have gotten into questions about psychics and witches, and what we have learned is that there is definitely evil power in the world provided by Satan, demons, and his angels. Psychics can predict your future, but they cannot make your future. What I mean by this is that Satan and his evil empire know us. Imagine if I followed you around everywhere from the day of your birth. I would have a pretty good idea about what mistakes you would make and what path you might choose. Satan and his angels who have been around us, have a pretty good sense of our future and probably would be shockingly close in their predictions. The fact remains that they cannot dictate the future. God is different because when He speaks of it, He speaks it into existence.

Is it not interesting how psychics build your trust by telling you about your past? Of course, Satan knows your past and can reveal it to anyone that God allows him to reveal it to. Christians are getting lured into this, as well, because they see the power and accuracy in it. There are always going to be frauds, but there are many who are drawing power from the dark world. Christians are getting swept into palm reading, where they think there is not any harm, because psychics cannot be too bad if they are helping police solve crimes, right? Once again, Satan is deceiving us into participating in something that is an abomination to God. According to Leviticus 20:6, it says, "I will set my face against the person who turns to mediums and spiritists to prostitute him by following them, and I will cut him off from his people." If you start opening yourself up to the spirits, they will come in!

Remember, it was Saul who went to the witch at Endor and was able to bring back Samuel from the dead. If God allows it, Satan can do it. It still does not prove it is right. Even in the example of Judas, he opened himself up to Satan by pilfering money at times, until he finally did the unthinkable by betraying the Son of God. Satan is looking for any opportunity that you will give him access into your life. Psychics and mediums are a simple way in which we can open ourselves up to evil. I would invite you to research yoga and where that originated and what religions practice this. You just might be shocked! How many things open ourselves up to evil without even knowing it?

Many give access to Satan through drugs. The very word for drugs is pharmakos in the Greek, which is the same word meaning sorcerer or one who uses magical remedies. I experienced this after surgery to remove a brain tumor. I was taking a medication to help with pain. Each night, I was battling demons in the night that would not let me sleep and played tricks on me. It got so bad, I quit taking the painkillers after just two days. Through this strong drug, unfortunately my mind was opened to this evil world.

In our Bible study with the youth, the question came out that if God is so powerful, why do we always hear of Satan's power? We hear about fortune-telling coming true. We see witchcraft and the power behind it. Also, there is the deception that some people have special power to heal like the apostles did, even though they do not, and they are using the money for their personal gain. We hear, or witness, people like Lafayette in the story I told earlier, and how he knew my conversations when he was not around to hear them.

Let me ask you some questions. If Satan can reveal conversations we have to others, can God, who is more powerful, do the same and more for His purpose? Couldn't God reveal the truth to us from His knowledge or reveal truth when someone is not being truthful to us? This thought will come up again as we get into the chapters on the Holy Spirit. If Satan can reveal possible outcomes, does it make sense that God can warn us or prepare us for actual outcomes? The difference is that Satan is predicting, but God knows, for a fact, the outcome.

In Isaiah 8:19, it says, "When men tell you to consult mediums and spiritists, who whisper and mutter, should not people inquire of their God? Why consult the dead on behalf of the living?" It seems clear that God wants you to consult Him and not the spirits about things. If God wants us to consult Him, you would have to conclude that He wants to answer our questions. In the Scriptures, God has given words to His followers. Over and over God speaks, warns, instructs, and even forbids in the Scriptures, as in the example of Elisha the prophet, where God was telling Elisha the very words the king was saying in the privacy of his bedroom.

> The man of God sent word to the king of Israel: "Beware of passing that place, because the Arameans are going down there." So the king of Israel checked on the place indicated by the man of God. Time and again Elisha warned the king, so that he was on his guard in such places. This enraged the king of Aram. He summoned his officers and

demanded of them, "Will you not tell me which of us is on the side of the king of Israel?" "None of us, my lord the king," said one of his officers, "but Elisha, the prophet who is in Israel, tells the king of Israel the very words you speak in your bedroom." — 2 Kings 6:9-12

I believe and have experienced God revealing things to me through His Spirit, including whether or not people are lying to me. A number of years ago in my youth group was a strong youth, a good friend of mine, who was doing so great in his walk with God. He began dating a girl from the college group who was not as strong spiritually, and I knew it would be hard for him to remain pure. After he and this girl had been dating a few months, I had a dream on a Friday night that this guy was not making good decisions in this relationship, and I needed to confront him.

When I woke up, I thought this dream must have been from God. Lying in bed, I rationalized about confronting him because I was so busy. I knew it would hinder our friendship, and the reality was that I didn't want to deal with it. I knew I did not have one-hundred percent proof. Then I began to think it was only a dream, even though the dream was different. I just wanted to go back to sleep and forget the dream ever happened. The problem was that I could not.

I believe to this day it was God who would not let me go back to sleep until I agreed to do what He needed me to do. I kept trying to go back to sleep for over an hour and was getting frustrated. You know how it is when you are lying in bed and you want to go to sleep so much but, for whatever reason, you just cannot. I was fighting God on my responsibility to confront this person. Finally, after about one and a half hours, I finally gave in and told God I would do it, and I fell fast asleep. The next night, I had the same exact dream and, as I awoke, I had learned my lesson from the night before. As soon as I open my eyes from this dream, I whispered quietly to God, "I will do it in the next few days." Then, once again, I fell fast asleep.

What was I to say to this strong friend who was being caught up by lust? Do I tell him, "Oh, by the way, God told me the last few nights that you are being impure, and I want to talk to you about it?" That would go over great in today's world where many believe Christians have little to no power through the Holy Spirit. I prayed before our conversation that Sunday morning, and I just asked the Spirit to lead me. I knew He would because He always does. We sat down, and I told this friend that I was aware he was being impure by having a sexual relationship. I told him that I was not going to tell him how I knew but that I did know one-hundred percent for sure. I asked him to be respectful, trustworthy, and just be honest so we could deal with the situation. He was honest, and God was glorified.

I do not have dreams and visions often, but God gave me a vision about what was going to happen in my ministry job, and everything happened exactly the way I was told.

Some of you may think I am a crazy man who believes God has given me some special power to do extraordinary things. I do believe we have more power available to us as Christians than most like to admit. Here is the truth. I am a sinful man, saved by the blood of Christ, and I have the indwelling of the Holy Spirit. The power I have working in me is the same power other Christians have working in them. We all have the same limits, or measure, of the Holy Spirit, according to John 3:34, where it says, "For He whom God has sent speaks the words of God; for He gives the Spirit without measure." The power of the Holy Spirit becomes more evident when I quit quenching Him in my life and allow His will through complete submission to Christ.

We need to quit doubting God's power and begin trusting that it is within us. Ephesians 3:20-21 says, "Now to him who is able to do immeasurably more than all we ask or imagine, according to his power that is at work within us, to him be glory in the church and in Christ Jesus throughout all generations, forever and ever! Amen." This Scripture says God can do more than we ask or imagine, according to His power at work within us. We always forget to read the last part of this verse. His power is in us. This power of the Spirit is an extraordinary power. How often are you lying flat on your face before God in prayer, while also listening? You do this every day, and you might be surprised at what you start hearing. You will stay more focused on the eternal things, because it is hard to get caught up in greed, or complaining in suffering, when you are on your face before the one who is the one and only true God.

Just to help you out here, you are on your face to know very clearly who is God and who is not. So, you are not bowed low to tell God what you like and do not like, you are there to humble yourself before the one who holds all power and knows His will for you. Don't be afraid of all the things you think about after your prayer. God may just be answering you when you stop and listen for a while. In praying, remember Isaiah 45:9-10 where it says:

> Woe to him who quarrels with his Maker, to him who is but a potsherd among the potsherds on the ground. Does the clay say to the potter, "What are you making?" Does your work say, "He has no hands"? Woe to him who says to his father, "What have you begotten?" or to his mother, "What have you brought to birth?"

This verse tells me I have no right to ask God what He is doing with me or why He made me this way. I should rather rejoice that He is the potter and He is making me and doing in me what glorifies Him.

We have Christians caught up in evil activity because they see the power in it. When will we, as Christians, wake up and understand we have more power than those who tap into the evil power in this world?

This is the reason I can stand before someone who is a witch or who is in the occult and be strong. This is not by my power, but it is by God's power at work within me which is stronger than the power of evil.

I told the youth in this Bible study that if witches only knew what they could do with God's power, they might just reconsider their position. The power of God to have peace in suffering, to love those who mistreat you, and to forgive those who hurt you, is true Divine power that shakes the threshold of hell.

CHAPTER 3 WORKSHEET

What are some new things you may have learned about Satan from this chapter?

_____

_____

_____

When do you believe Satan actually fell from heaven, from these verses?

_____

_____

_____

Do you fear the power Satan has today? Why or Why not?

_____

_____

_____

How can you be deceived by Satan?

_____

_____

_____

Why does God not protect you from the power of Satan at times?

_____

_____

_____

CHAPTER 4

The Existence of Evil Spirits

When he saw Jesus from a distance, he ran and fell on his knees in front of Him. He shouted at the top of his voice, "What do you want with me, Jesus, Son of the Most High God? Swear to God that you won't torture me!" For Jesus had said to him, "Come out of this man, you evil spirit!" Then Jesus asked him, "What is your name?" "My name is Legion," he replied, "for we are many." And he begged Jesus again and again not to send them out of the area. A large herd of pigs was feeding on the nearby hillside. The demons begged Jesus, "Send us among the pigs; allow us to go into them." He gave them permission, and the evil spirits came out and went into the pigs. The herd, about two thousand in number, rushed down the steep bank into the lake and was drowned.

—Mark 5:6-13

There is something about evil spirits which leaves us wanting to know more. We struggle with how they exist. We wonder why Jesus did not throw Legion into the abyss in Mark 5:1-20. We are amazed at the exorcists in Acts 19:13-16:

> Some Jews who went around driving out evil spirits tried to invoke the name of the Lord Jesus over those who were demon-possessed. They would say, "In the name of Jesus, whom Paul preaches, I command you to come out." Seven

sons of Sceva, a Jewish chief priest, were doing this. [One day] the evil spirit answered them, "Jesus I know, and I know about Paul, but who are you?" Then the man who had the evil spirit jumped on them and overpowered them all. He gave them such a beating that they ran out of the house naked and bleeding.

We are also amazed at how the evil spirit leapt on the Jewish chief priests. We are left with questions, such as, are demons and evil spirits the same? Is there demon possession today? If so, how do we cast them out today? What would it take for me, as a Christian, to be demon possessed? What is up with the terminology of water in reference to demon stories throughout the Bible? Well, we are going to attack all these questions and more.

Demons and Evil Spirits

First of all, evil spirits and demons from the Bible appear as one and the same. A good example of this is when a passage is speaking of demons and then refers to them as evil spirits. This is seen in Mark 5:12-13: "The demons begged Jesus, 'Send us among the pigs; allow us to go into them.' He gave them permission, and the evil spirits came out and went into the pigs. The herds, about two thousand in number, rushed down the steep bank into the lake and were drowned." In verse twelve, the Bible says the demons begged and, in verse thirteen, the Bible says the evil spirits came out. From God's Word, we can know that demons and evil spirits are the same. This is seen over and over in the Scriptures, so there is not any doubt they are one and the same.

Demons and Water

It is intriguing when different passages in the Bible refer to demons searching for water. In Job 26:5 "The departed spirits tremble under the waters and their inhabitants," we see these departed spirits are under the water. Is this referencing dead people or evil spirits? But notice that water is included. Also, in the story of the demon-possessed man from the tombs in Mark 5, we see Jesus going to cast out the demons, and they beg to be cast into the pigs. When Jesus sends them into the pigs, they rush down a steep bank into the sea. Once again, they go toward the water. Was this because the demons were trying to kill the pigs or is there something significant about the water and demons? Another example can be found in Luke 11:24-26:

> When the unclean spirit goes out of a man, it passes through waterless places seeking rest, and not finding any, it says, "I will return to my house from which I came." And when it comes, it finds it swept and put in order. Then it goes and takes along seven other spirits more evil than itself, and they go in and live there; and the last state of that man becomes worse than the first.

The unclean spirit goes out of a man and goes through waterless places seeking rest but cannot find it. Why does the Scripture mention waterless places? Is there a reason? Was the reason because the spirit could not find rest since there wasn't any water?

There are some different ideas about why a person's skin and insides burn when they are possessed and what the comparison with demons and water really means. One thought is that there is no significance between demons and water. That the statements are just coincidental. The second thought is demons could live in water. Another thought is demons are already suffering with agony and unquenchable thirst because they do not have the living water. It reminds me of Luke 16:23-24, when the rich man was in torment just wanting a drop of water on his tongue. It says,

> And in Hades he lifted up his eyes, being in torment, and saw Abraham far away and Lazarus in his bosom. And he cried out and said, "Father Abraham, have mercy on me, and send Lazarus, that he may dip the tip of his finger in water and cool off my tongue; for I am in agony in this flame." But Abraham said, "Child, remember that during your life you received your good things, and likewise Lazarus bad things; but now he is being comforted here, and you are in agony."

I tend to agree with the last view because there seems to be some significance.

Some believe that demons are children from fallen angels and women of the world who were killed in the flood. These were the Nephilim (mighty men) discussed in Genesis 6:1-4:

> When men began to increase in number on the earth and daughters were born to them, the sons of God saw that the daughters of men were beautiful, and they married any of them they chose. Then the LORD said, "My Spirit will not contend with man forever, for he is mortal; his days will be a hundred and twenty years." The Nephilim were on the earth in those days—and also afterward—when the sons of God went to the daughters of men and had children by them. They were the heroes of old, men of renown.

The thought of angels and humans having sexual relations is in the book of Enoch. Enoch was found in the Dead Sea scrolls along with parts of the Old Testament, but it was not accepted as Scripture from some of the early church fathers. It is interesting that in Jude 14-15 it says, "Enoch, the seventh from Adam, prophesied about these men: 'See, the Lord is coming with thousands upon thousands of his holy ones to judge everyone, and to convict all the ungodly of all the ungodly acts they have done in the ungodly way, and of all the harsh words ungodly sinners have spoken against him.'" Jude quotes directly from the book of Enoch. Based on this idea, it was the water where these half-angels and half-humans died in the flood. Following this idea, did God have a place reserved for half-angels and half-humans when they died? Also, what would have happened to the angels who impregnated these women? In some parts of the world, many believe spirits live in the water. Many believe the holding place, or what is also known as Hades, is in the center of the earth, and the waters are the abyss. In parts of Indonesia, where the beaches are some of the best in the world, many will not swim there because of this belief. Where did they get this strong belief?

Some have gone as far as to say baptism, or immersion in water, is a big part of this. As one today, by faith, is baptized in the water, could it be then that the demons leave? I know from the things I witnessed in baptizing D.J., when she came out of the water, she was in her right mind. This was something I had yet to see from the months of meeting with her. Demons or evil spirits could have left at that time, but they could have returned if the place where they left was once again unoccupied. If there is any significance between evil spirits and water, it may just go back to the agony that they are already in. This could be the reason why their main purpose is to torment.

Demon Possession Today

I have encountered people who seem to be controlled by evil. Just talking with a sixteen-year-old boy named Todd was proof enough. The parent of a boy from our youth program called me one morning while I was in my office at the church building. This was the day of our church fall festival, as we were getting near the end of October and closer to Halloween. She asked if I could counsel and spend time with this young man if she brought him to my office. Naturally, I agreed. They showed up, and I was very friendly, but he was extremely reserved. I invited him into my office, and told the parent I would call about his transportation home after spending some time with him. I did not realize I would be spending all day with this distraught young man.

At that time I was twenty-five years old, and I believed that I could make a difference in anyone's troubled life. That experience taught me it was up to the person and God, and I was just the instrument.

When Todd walked in my office, my spirit was very disturbed. Something did not seem right. I had felt this feeling before, but why had I gotten this feeling today? We had some small talk, then I started to study the Bible with him. He wanted my office door closed, and I respected that. In dealing with young ladies, I make it a practice never to meet with my office door closed, but with the boy in this situation, I did not see any harm. I started praying for him as we sat on the couch in my office, but he stopped me midway through by grabbing my hands and harshly saying, "No, don't do that!" I respected his wishes even though it seemed very strange. Feeling friendly and concerned, I began talking and studying in hopes of bringing some kind of life to this young man. I remember that every time I asked Todd a question, there would be ten or more seconds of complete silence before he answered. I thought this was a result of abuse or drugs, as I knew this was not normal.

I just continued to be Christ and, as midday got closer, I offered to take him to lunch. By this time, we had spent an hour or so in my office, but I was not getting anywhere. He was not getting it, or even trying to understand what I was trying to teach him. We went to lunch, and afterward, since my wife still at work, I thought a comfortable environment like my apartment would be nice to sit back and play some video games. I had not accomplished much in my office with study, so I figured he needed a friend, not a teacher.

After lunch, as we were in my apartment, it happened! I knew the way he was looking at me was evil. He did not want to play video games, so I just turned on the television. He started telling me how much I had helped him and how he wanted something better in his life. I was so deceived, thinking he was being truthful. Did he need a friend to reach out to him? He came over to give me a hug and made a sexual pass at me. I pushed him away saying, "You just told me you wanted something better in life, and you do this! What are you thinking?"

He apologized and said, "Now you know what my struggle is."

As soon as he said that, my cheerful and friendly wife walked in from work. Without knowing what had just happened, she came in and greeted Todd, saying, "Hi, I am Teresa, Travis's wife. I hope you are making yourself at home."

He acted as though nothing had happened, and I gave Teresa a look to let her know that he was making himself a bit too comfortable. She did not get the hint, though, and went to our bedroom to take a shower.

While Teresa was in the shower, Todd got up and started pacing around while I was seated on the couch. At this point, I was ready to take him home and call it a day. He went around a corner in our apartment, and I got up, only to find him trying to get in the bathroom while my wife was showering. Thank goodness my wife always locks the door when people are over.

I grabbed him, and it took all my strength to not hit him. I demanded, "What are you doing? My wife is in there!"

He apologized and immediately tried to hug me again. I told him it was time for us to leave. I took him back to the living room and grabbed the phone to work out transportation. As I was on the phone, he got up again and headed for the kitchen. I could not reach anyone at the phone number I had. I asked him if he wanted a drink before we left, doing everything to be Christ to him. As I spoke, I heard the Holy Spirit tell me very clearly to get up and go to the kitchen. I leapt off the couch and ran into the kitchen. I found Todd reaching for the biggest butcher knife in our knife holder. I grabbed his hand and, through the power of God, made him put it down. I believe to this day that he was going to try to kill me and my wife.

If I had not figured it out by now, this boy was demon possessed. I could see it in his eyes, and I knew it when he walked through my office door. At the beginning of the day, I didn't want to believe it. I wanted to grab him and pray the evil spirits out of him, but I did not. I honestly did not know what to do. We left, but I had no place to take him. I finally got hold of a parent who knew his mother, and she told me to bring him to the fall festival. Great idea. Let me just put him near young, vulnerable children. After I explained things somewhat on the phone, I found out where he lived and took him home, never to see him again. Looking back and reflecting on my study, I believe this young man was controlled by evil.

These things always seem to happen to me. It has been obvious from one experience to another that demon possession is real, and it happens today.

I want to go back to the questions I posted earlier in the chapter. Absolute possession and demonic oppression are a little different from one another. Complete possession as we see in the Bible seems very rare, but as with D.J., it does exist. I believe the situations we see today are more like what happened to Judas, where Satan got more and more access to a part of Judas's life, and Satan could then come and go within him.

Let me add that I do believe in demonic influence or oppression, which is different than demon possession. I believe many Christians deal with evil influence regularly in their lives. I believe the difference between demon possession and demon influence or oppression is when dealing with Christians whose bodies are temples of the Holy Spirit. I see from the Scriptures that God cannot dwell with evil. Therefore, the evil spirits or demons cannot dwell where the Holy Spirit dwells. That demons cannot dwell in a Christian does not mean demons do not influence Christians or torment Christians the way Satan can. The influence can be there, but if the Holy Spirit dwells within, it is only the influence Christians can experience. From what I have seen and experienced, that is bad enough.

According to the Bible, as well as those who have now separated themselves from satanic cults, there are different spirits whom you can invite in. In Acts 16, it talks about the spirit of divination that a slave girl had since childhood. Can there be demons of lust, anger, pride, greed, and even homosexuality? Within the occult, many speak of what is called "high spirits." These are evil spirits who are silent and secretive. Those in the occult world believe many so-called church leaders have these spirits if they are involved in continual sin or if they are false teachers. D.J. believed the ministers who got caught molesting children were victims of high spirit involvement and possession.

Evil Organization

I will share some of the things those in cults have taught me about the names of these evil spirits. I am including this in the book to open your eyes to what the people involved in the occult believe. I am not saying these names and concepts are true, but I do think it is insightful. From my experience dealing with people in satanic cults, it seems the dark world is more visible to them because of the power they receive from Satan, so they have witnessed things those outside the occult world have not.

Is there such a thing as a demon hierarchy? Well, some cults believe there are certain months in the year when an evil spirit is at its strongest. They believe there are ten types of demons. The first are called the Falter spirits, and these are spirits that alter destiny. Next there are Poltergeists, which are spirits who cause mischief. Then there are Incubi and Succubi, which are spirits who stimulate lust and perversion. Marching Hordes are spirits who bring war and fighting. Familiars are evil spirits that assist witches as well as provide information about the dead and the living. Then there are ones called Nightmares, which are spirits who give messages through dreams and disturb sleep. There is also a spirit called Lilith. This spirit can take over a woman or child of either sex and cause that person to be irresistible to men. She breaks up marriages, hurts the woman or child she is in, and often lures the men to either destruction or death. This reminds me of the woman in Proverbs 7:10-23:

> Then out came a woman to meet him, dressed like a prostitute and with crafty intent. She is loud and defiant, her feet never stay at home; now in the street, now in the squares, at every corner she lurks. She took hold of him and kissed him and with a brazen face ...Come, let's drink deep of love till morning; let's enjoy ourselves with love! My husband is not at home; he has gone on a long journey...With persuasive words she led him astray; she seduced him with her smooth talk. All at once he followed her like an ox going to the slaughter, like a deer

stepping into a noose till an arrow pierces his liver, like a bird darting into a snare, little knowing it will cost him his life.

Lilith is now a name that some believe was the name of the first created woman before God created Eve from Adam's rib. She was rebellious according to these thinkers, and left Adam because of her lack of submissiveness. I do not believe that is true, but I do find it interesting that the name is used to refer to that particular woman. Where did they get the name?

Next are Disguised Demons, and they are often hard to detect because they can even hide in churches and high positions. The last two are demons that attack Christians and demons that tempt you, lure you, and trick you into witchcraft.

When I first heard about this demon hierarchy, not knowing whether it was true or not, I thought it made good sense. Whether there are demons who have specific functions or not, I have witnessed Satan's involvement in dreams, lust, and demons of mischief.

If all this was not enough, there is more. From my talks with people involved in the occult and those who have escaped satanic cults, I've learned there are also main spirits. Satan is, of course, the head spirit. Then, under him, are the main spirits. They are the strongest of the spirits and assign missions to all the other spirits. The first main spirit is known as Beelzebub or Belial. This spirit is arrogant and often so closely related with Satan that almost every religion refers to them as one and the same. Beelzebub and Belial are both referred to in the Bible.

But when the Pharisees heard this, they said, "It is only by Beelzebub, the prince of demons, that this fellow drives out demons." — Matthew 12:24

Do not be yoked together with unbelievers. For what do righteousness and wickedness have in common? Or what fellowship can light have with darkness? What harmony is there between Christ and Belial? What does a believer have in common with an unbeliever? — 2 Corinthians 6:14-15

The next main spirit is called Leviathan, which attacks a Christian's religious beliefs. I have been told this main spirit is responsible for causing things like car accidents right before Christmas and the destruction of religious symbols. Also, there is the main spirit called Asmodai, which rules over lust and marital strife. Berith heads up murder and blasphemy. Next is Astaroth, which is nicknamed the "Python spirit" for its ability to slowly squeeze the life out of a person. This one leads the spirits of laziness and vanity. This main spirit causes you to just give up and stop fighting, whether it is in spiritual ways, practical ways, or physical ways. This would be, for instance, a Christian who does not read the Bible or develop a relationship with God because of laziness, or a cancer patient who does not feel like driving to his or her chemotherapy appointment. Verrin is the main spirit over impatience. Gressil is the next that reigns over impurity, uncleanness, and nastiness. This one causes the people they are possessing to do embarrassing and offensive things like going naked in public, urinating on the cross, and things of that nature. Then there is Sonnilon, which heads up hate and rage. This is a very powerful spirit that often stays around a person even after it has been cast out. Lilith is the name of the main spirit who is lustful and works a lot like a Venus flytrap. It is very deadly, sneaky, and dangerous. Olivier is a fierce, envious, and greedy spirit. This spirit is never quenched and drives the person it inhabits to addiction, obsession, madness, and/or death. Pithius is the head of the liar spirits. Merihem causes pestilence-like or addictive behavior which is easily picked up by someone else. Finally, there is the main spirit called Abaddon. This spirit loves war as well as evil against good.

These names amazed me. If there was some truth to this, then the evil world was a lot more organized than I had ever thought. This would take us back to the words of Jesus when He said we better watch and pray so that we do not fall into temptation. Satan and his followers are not roaming the earth like chickens with their heads cut off. They are extremely organized in their tactics as well as conniving in their methods. Satan's organized tactics are reflected in the ways satanic cults have been structured.

In my search for spirits in the Scriptures, here is what I found. There are different spirits referred to throughout the Scriptures. There are spirits of divination which include witchcraft, foretelling the future, and so on. There are spirits that are not of God, called tormenting spirits, stubborn spirits, angry spirits, bitter spirits, lying spirits, timid spirits, deaf and mute spirits, crippling spirits, and haughty or prideful spirits. If that is not enough, the Bible speaks of spirits of dizziness, spirits of distress, spirits of despair, spirits of prostitution, spirits of impurity, spirits of stupor, spirits of error, and the spirit of the Antichrist.

Would you have ever thought throughout the Scriptures and over time, mankind would have battled so many spirits? Have you seen any of these in your life? I have always wondered if the people Jesus healed were people who were ill, diseased, or crippled by a spirit. Jesus did not heal every disease or illness, and even in the story of the man at the pool of Bethesda in John 5, there is nothing that said Jesus healed any of the others waiting there for healing. One example actually says the woman had been bound by Satan in her illness for eighteen years. In Luke 13:16 it says, "Then should not this woman, a daughter of Abraham, whom Satan has kept bound for eighteen long years, be set free on the Sabbath day from what bound her?" This is just a thought to get you thinking.

While smuggling Bibles into Cuba, my family and I met a pastor and his wife way up in a mountain community of a couple thousand people. I know God sent our team to them to deliver Bibles and supplies, especially when we learned this entire community had only two Bibles. The people in this church would tear out pages to take home with them from one old Bible in order to memorize and learn of God's Word. You can imagine the joy when we showed up with brand new Bibles for everyone in the church, as well as for some people searching for the Lord. We thought we were an encouragement to their faith, but what they gave us encouraged our faith. The pastor and his wife shared their testimony with us. This is another example of evil being defeated by God.

> The man named Jose and his wife Patricia were not always Christians. In fact, Jose was heavily involved in evil and was considered a witchdoctor. He got terribly sick and he could not heal himself, and the others in his cult could not heal him either. Jose battled with such excruciating pain that he could not sleep and was ready to take his own life. During this time, a missionary had met Patricia and she became a believer in the Lord. She knew her husband would be opposed, so for a period of time, she kept her faith to herself. She would cry out to God saying, "Please Lord, save my husband and help him to see the truth. Let him learn of Your power and goodness and turn from evil." As every day would pass, Jose would be more and more in pain and unrest. Jose told us about a day when he went high up in the mountains to take his life to escape the misery. Jose said, "As I was way up on that mountain, he pointed out the back of his shack, and cried out, 'If your there, reveal yourself to me!'" He said he did not even know to whom he was crying out.

Then Jose heard the voice of one who could change his life and his eternity forever. The words he heard were, "I am here!" Then Jose asked, "What is your name?" The voice replied, "I am Jesus! Go to the nearest church, and the man there will tell you about me." Jose said the voice was not in his head but was the voice of a man. So, Jose left immediately and sought the nearest church which was a ways away. The pastor had Bible Study with Jose and taught him about Jesus. Jose went home and told this miraculous story to his wife. At first, Patricia was speechless about whether or not it was really true. She knew she had prayed for her husband, but when Jose said, "I heard HIS voice," she knew he would not be making it up. Patricia said, "Jose did not know of Jesus before this." She then told Jose that she was a believer, as well, and had been praying for him. They went back to the pastor together and were both baptized in the river.

As we continued to listen in amazement and see their sincere tears, they showed us the picture of their baptism. The story was not over, because God's power was just beginning in their life. Jose said, "That night, I went to sleep, slept through the night and woke up the next day pain free." Jose continued, "I did not know much, but this community did not have a church, so we made our house into a church and I became the pastor."

Just as the Bible speaks of all these spirits that cause us to focus on evil, the Bible also refers to spirits that are from God. This may give testing the spirits a whole new meaning and understanding. The Bible speaks of a willing spirit, a quiet spirit, a spirit of wisdom, a spirit of knowledge, a spirit of counsel, a broken or humble spirit, a spirit of grace, a spirit of holiness, a spirit of unity, a spirit of gentleness, a spirit of power, a spirit of love, a spirit of self-discipline, and a spirit of truth. This is not the one Holy Spirit, but these are the spirits referred to in the Scriptures that we ought to take hold of and possess. I encourage you to study this further and to test the spirits in your life to see if they are from God. In 1 John 4:1-6 it says,

> Dear friends, do not believe every spirit, but test the spirits to see whether they are from God, because many false prophets have gone out into the world. This is how you can recognize the Spirit of God: Every spirit that acknowledges Jesus Christ has come in the flesh is from God, but every spirit that does not acknowledge Jesus, is not from God. This is the spirit of the antichrist, which you have heard is coming, and even now is already in the world. You, dear children, are from God and have over-come them, because the one who is in you is greater than the one who is in the world. They are from the world and therefore speak from the viewpoint of the world, and the world listens to them. We are from God, and whoever knows God listens to us; but whoever is not from God does not listen to us. This is how we recognize the Spirit of truth and the spirit of falsehood.

Test every spirit by the very Words of God. Notice I did not say the words of man or the words of your minister or pastor. I also did not say test the spirits based on your traditions or your church's creed or beliefs. The Bible says that we as Christians can test the spirits ourselves, and any spirit in or around us that does not submit to Jesus Christ and His Words must be removed. For example, if there is within you a spirit of anger or a lying spirit, then take that spirit to the feet of Jesus and His Word and know that Colossians 3:8-9 says, "But now you must rid yourselves of all such things as these: anger, rage, malice, slander, and filthy language from your lips. Do not lie to each other, since you have taken off your old self with its practices."

No matter why you are involved in lying or anger, God clearly says we must rid ourselves of these things and not do them. This is why it is important to read God's Word and humble ourselves in prayer, so we are confronting ungodly attitudes in our life on a regular basis.

Can a Christian Be Possessed?

There is much debate over whether a Christian can be possessed. I have heard that because there is a difference between body, soul, and spirit, your physical body can be possessed even though your spirit belongs to God. I struggle with that idea. Do we all have the potential to let evil control aspects of us?

Take, for example, a young man who has given in to pornography, and it now consumes his thoughts and actions. We can be sure that evil is there and that we have to battle it regularly. A key in Christianity is never to allow anything to control you, whether it is visible to others or not. Accountability to God and confessing our sins to one another will help guard against demon possession or demon influence. Do not ever allow yourself to be addicted to anything because, through these addictions, you might be opening yourself up to be controlled by evil spirits.

I have to tell you the story of a young man we will call John. Within the first month of the release of the first edition of my book *Walking in Shadows,* John found my office number and called me. I had met John a few times, but by no means were we close. I did not know much about him, so he started off by telling me he needed to talk to me about my book.

Thinking he was a critic, I said, "What part of the book can I try to help you with?"

He said, "I want you to know I bought your book the other day because I knew you a little, but to be honest, I did not have any intention of reading it." He went on to tell me about his beautiful wife and his two children, and how he has been so blessed by God. He told me that for the last few years, he had been in and out of church, and had been living in a fog where he lost control over his life. He said, "Even though God has blessed me so much, it was as though I was making decisions without being in my right mind, and I cannot understand this."

I asked him why he started reading my book, and he said he was just led to pick it up one day and start reading. He had got to the part in the book about the organization of evil, which puts names and purposes to each of the major spirits. He said, "This is where things started to change for me." He reluctantly continued, "I do not know why I am telling you all this, but I had plans to cheat on my wife this weekend with a lady I recently met. I have been involved in pornography for quite some time, and I believe demons of lust and perversion are all around me." He went on, "As I continued to read your book, I decided to pray and ask God to take these spirits away from me. Then it happened—my face began to burn, and my eyes were watering. I did not know if I was crying or what, as my face was so flush. And then I thought clearly for the first time in months," he said. "I cannot believe what I was about to do. I cannot believe I was going to destroy everything."

I told him, "I think it is amazing how God has opened your eyes, because you would have ripped the hearts out of your wife and children. This could have been the choice that destroyed your faith, which you might never have recovered from."

John said, "I sat down with my wife, and I was completely open and honest with her. Tears were shed, but I stayed away from the worst mistake I could have ever made."

At that moment, I was so proud of this man for hearing the voice of God, but also for being open and honest. Satan had to be cringing. He'd had John in the palm of his hand and on the brink of physical and eternal disaster. Satan had failed to realize that God would give John a way to escape the snare, and the strength to do it. I could not help but say a silent prayer to God during this conversation to thank Him for saving this young man. Praise God for His love and faithfulness to us.

We continued talking about some practical ways he could rid his life of pornography and never allow himself to go back to that terrible position again. I recommended that he immediately get involved in some accountability with other men in his church. Just because Satan was defeated in this one battle did not mean he wouldn't be back.

God was doing powerful things with those who wanted to follow Jesus Christ wholeheartedly in spite of the attempt by Satan to destroy the book and the author.

Then there is the question of whether children can be possessed. I admit I struggle with this one. We see from the example of Jesus being born into this world that just because children are born into a sinful world, does not mean they are sinful. If this were the case, then Jesus was sinful, as well, simply because of His birth. We know from 2 Corinthians 5:21 that Jesus did not know sin. How can children be possessed if they are pure and innocent? According to Matthew 18:1-6, Jesus says, "Unless you are converted and become like little children, you cannot enter the kingdom of heaven." This passage also says, "But if anyone causes one of these little ones who believe in me to sin, it would be better for him to have a large millstone hung around his neck and to be drowned in the depths of the sea."

So, can someone cause a child to sin and therefore be controlled by evil?

In Mark 9:21 it says, "Jesus asked the boy's father, 'How long has he been like this?' 'From childhood,' he answered." The demon-possessed boy's said he'd had the evil spirit since childhood. According to the Scriptures, apparently a child could be possessed. Matthew 2:8 says, "He sent them to Bethlehem and said, 'Go and make a careful search for the child. As soon as you find him, report to me, so that I too may go and worship him.'" This verse in Matthew uses this same word to refer to Jesus as a child when the Magi were looking for Him while following the star. In this situation, the term *child* most likely refers to the first one or two years of Jesus's life. The word can also mean ages seven to fourteen, depending on the context. The context in Mark 9 could refer to either one. I believe if the Bible gives examples of demon possession with children, then we know it did happen then, and therefore can happen now.

As to how or why it happens, the Scriptures never say. We could speculate, but what would that really accomplish? The reality is that there are children who are a part of the occult worship where they invite evil spirits into their lives at young ages. Somehow, God allowed this. Jesus has power over the evil spirits and, if God allows this, it is only because He has the power to undo it later. Remember, this is Satan's playing field and, therefore, he is scheming after children as well as the rest of us. Which this leads us to the next section about how a person casts out demons.

Casting out Demons

Since our battle is more with the influence of demons, we ought to discuss ways to keep evil spirits from influencing us as well as those we love. To begin with, there is the importance of repentance. We must first repent of anything that is grabbing hold of us and giving Satan more access and control. A key reason for daily prayer before God is because we constantly need to be in God's presence to be reminded how unworthy and unholy we are on our own. Unrepentant sin can allow Satan to gain more of an advantage or foothold in our life. If we do not confront ungodly attitudes and behaviors, we will always feel as if Christianity is powerless against evil.

I believe we do not really understand repentance the way we should. Repentance today seems to be a simple phrase in our prayers even when our hearts remain unchanged. Have we striven against sin to the point of shedding blood, as the Hebrew writer states? Repentance is a true change of heart that will last. The fruit of repentance will be seen in a change of action to follow. I love the teaching of repentance from the parable of the prodigal son. Repentance to this son was not only coming home and saying the right words, but the willingness to just be a slave in his father's household. This tells me that repentance brought forth humility where this son did not feel worthy to be a son. When you look at yourself, do you believe you deserve heaven, or would you be grateful if you were a slave to all the righteous in heaven for all eternity? Just knowing that you do not even deserve to be a slave in heaven means you are getting it.

> When he came to his senses, he said, "How many of my father's hired men have food to spare, and here I am starving to death! I will set out and go back to my father and say to him: Father, I have sinned against heaven and against you. I am no longer worthy to be called your son; make me like one of your hired men." — Luke 15:17-19

In dealing with evil spirits today, I believe the Bible will give us the answers, but we must read slowly and carefully so we do not miss anything. I had always heard the story in Mark 9:25-29 where the man with the deaf and dumb spirit could only come out through prayer and fasting:

> When Jesus saw that a crowd was running to the scene, he rebuked the evil spirit. "You deaf and mute spirit," he

said, "I command you, come out of him and never enter him again." The spirit shrieked, convulsed him violently and came out. The boy looked so much like a corpse that many said, "He's dead." But Jesus took him by the hand and lifted him to his feet, and he stood up. After Jesus had gone indoors, his disciples asked him privately, "Why couldn't we drive it out?" He replied, "This kind can come out only by prayer and fasting."

The belief today is that we do have the power of God to cast out spirits, but it will be through prayer and fasting. This is what I was taught, and it makes sense, right? When I spent more time studying that story in its proper context, I realized the reason the demon could not be cast out was because the demon could not hear the voice of the disciples. The demon could not hear the voice because it was deaf. Jesus was able to speak to the deaf spirit because of faith in the power of God. So, in all likelihood, this does not apply to us at all today, unless we are confronting and talking to deaf spirits.

So, what is true? If there are demon-possessed people today, how can they be released from that terrible evil presence? From my experience, it makes sense that if you invite them in, you have to kick them out. And without God's power, that is not possible. Possession today may come through people inviting or allowing the spirits to control specific aspects of their life. Then before they know it, the demons try to control their entire life.

Is there any evil controlling your speech, actions, or thoughts? If so, God did not intend for you to live this way.

Surrender your life to Christ. Repent of your sins according to Acts 2:38: "Peter replied, 'Repent and be baptized, every one of you, in the name of Jesus Christ for the forgiveness of your sins. And you will receive the gift of the Holy Spirit.'" Confess Jesus as Lord because you believe with all your heart, according to Romans 10:9: "That if you confess with your mouth, 'Jesus is Lord,' and believe in your heart that God raised him from the dead, you will be saved." And be clothed with Christ, according to Galatians 3:26-28: "You are all sons of God through faith in Christ Jesus, for all of you who were baptized into Christ have clothed yourselves with Christ. There is neither Jew nor Greek, slave nor free, male nor female, for you are all one in Christ Jesus." I cannot deny as a witness that the evil spirits left D.J. at her baptism. You can be free from demon possession by giving your life to Christ, but demonic influence may never leave, and that is okay. One day, I will never have to deal with evil again because they will all be thrown into the lake of fire forever. God, give us the strength to be influenced by You rather than by evil.

Coming to Jesus is about sacrifice and surrender. It is about not being ashamed of Christ, but declaring Him as Lord of your life. The Bible teaches that if I surrender my life to Jesus, He now takes the lead. The more I decrease, the more He increases in control and power. Baptism is a picture of that spiritual transformation from death to life.

CHAPTER 4 WORKSHEET

What are some new things you have learned about evil spirits from this chapter?

_____

_____

_____

What potential demon from the section "Evil Organization" seems to trouble you the most?

_____

_____

_____

How do you feel knowing the evil realm is closer than you previously may have thought?

_____

_____

_____

What potential destruction would Satan like to bring to you and your family?

_____

_____

_____

What can you be doing now to preserve the faith of your friends and family?

_____

_____

_____

CHAPTER 5

The Existence of the Holy Spirit

You, dear children, are from God and have overcome them, because the one who is in you is greater than the one who is in the world.
—1 John 4:4

I cannot go into depth about evil spirits without explaining the Holy Spirit. People are drawn to things such as witchcraft, the occult, and even healing services, as a way of finding power. Some are looking to abuse power, while others are seeking to receive this power to do good. People understand a lot can happen—both good and bad—if they have more power outside of themselves. So, the pursuit begins even as teenagers. Not realizing the strength one can have from God, evil power seems, quite frankly, to be more.

Why is this? If we are Christians, we know God is more powerful than Satan. The problem is that the world does not see the power Christians have because Christians do not fully experience the power they have been given through the Spirit. If Christians could only tap into the power of the Holy Spirit, we would all walk around victorious and strong instead of depressed and defeated.

Do you want to learn how to use the power God has given to you? In the last chapter, we learned the difference between possession by evil spirits and influence from evil spirits. As a Christian, I cannot be possessed because where the Holy Spirit dwells, Satan or evil spirits cannot. Going back to the story of D.J., the only reason I had confidence and spoke the way I did was because of the Holy Spirit.

You might ask, who is the Holy Spirit? Is He my conscience? What has He done for people? How do I know if I have Him? Can I feel Him inside? It all comes down to, What can He do for me today?

In this chapter, we will look closely at each of these questions and, once again, see how the Bible answers them.

Who is the Holy Spirit?

We must answer this question before we can go any further. If the Holy Spirit is having a conscience, then how is His power equal to or greater than the power of evil? Answering this question accurately is a key to having the confidence, as Christians, to go out and boldly live by faith.

Jesus does not leave his followers empty-handed. He gives them His Spirit, which will be with them until the end. Jesus was only able to be with His disciples for approximately three years because of His submission to God's plan. Even then, while Jesus was on earth, they did not have Him all the time, every second of the day. Through God's plan of giving the Spirit, they will have God within them all the time because He will live in their hearts. This is actually better, because He will not only teach them and guide them, but He will also counsel them and speak through them. Reading in the book of Acts, we find the apostles finally understood all they had learned when they received the Spirit. They fully comprehended God's plan and could see why things happened the way they did with Jesus, as well as what the purpose was for the kingdom, or church.

Receiving the Holy Spirit can make a dramatic difference in our lives! The Bible teaches in 1 Corinthians 13 that we do not have full knowledge right now, but only see parts of the whole. It says, "We only see in a mirror dimly but one day face to face." This means that even though we have the Holy Spirit, on earth we only have the partial knowledge given to us.

While Jesus is not here in physical form with us, it is all right because He can be with us in spiritual form through His Spirit. God is not being flesh around us, but God being Spirit within us. Now that is a divine concept!

How do we know that the Holy Spirit is, in fact, part of the Godhead? Once again, our answers do not come from people but from the source of the solid truth—God's Word. There are some, including many Jehovah's Witnesses, who do not believe in the Trinity because the word is not mentioned in the Bible. I have to admit the term Trinity is not used in the Bible, but the words Godhead and Deity are used. Also the very name of God mentioned in the first verse of the Bible is the name Elohim, which is translated as "God" but is plural. We were created with a body, soul, and spirit. Some say Jesus represents the body, the Father represents the soul or mind, and the spirit represents the Holy Spirit. This is how we were created in His image. Believing in the Trinity or Godhead does not contradict when the Scriptures speak about God being one. The word "one" which is used in Deuteronomy 6:4, is the Hebrew word *eched*. This is the same word used in Genesis 2, where it is referring to man and woman as one flesh. There are many evidences that God manifests Himself in three separate persons. These three include: His Name Elohim from Genesis 1:1, 11:7. The second evidence is that in 21 of the 27 books of the New Testament make reference to the Godhead. Matthew 28 even says that we are to baptize people in the name (singular) of the Father, Son, and Holy Spirit. Each of these separate persons of the Godhead are specifically called God and each have the attributes of Deity in the Bible.

The four major qualities that define God were discussed earlier in the chapter about Satan, and now we will prove the deity of the Holy Spirit. The Holy Spirit is spoken of as eternal with no beginning or end in Hebrews 9:14, where it says, "How much more, then, will the blood of Christ, who through the eternal Spirit offered himself unblemished to God, cleanse our consciences from acts that lead to death, so that we may serve the living God?"

The Holy Spirit is omniscient (all-knowing) based on 1 Corinthians 2:10, where it says, "But God has revealed it to us by his Spirit. The Spirit searches all things, even the deep things of God."

Also from the Scriptures, it can be seen that the Holy Spirit is omnipotent (all-powerful). An example is in Micah 3:8, where it says, "But as for me, I am filled with power, with the Spirit of the LORD, and with justice and might, to declare to Jacob his transgression, to Israel his sin."

Then, the final quality which defines the deity of the Spirit is that He is omnipresent (everywhere), according to Psalms 139:7-10, where it says,

> Where can I go from your Spirit? Where can I flee from your presence? If I go up to the heavens, you are there; if I make my bed in the depths, you are there. If I rise on the wings of the dawn, if I settle on the far side of the sea, even there your hand will guide me; your right hand will hold me fast.

This explains how the Holy Spirit can live in one Christian and also live in another at the same time. The love that God sent His Son, and now the love He demonstrates by living inside of us as Christians, make you wonder how anyone could ever say that God created us to leave us. If anything, God created us to be with us.

Even though the Holy Spirit is one-hundred percent God, He is spoken of through the Scriptures in characteristics that define a human being. The Holy Spirit is always referred to in the masculine form in the

Scriptures, so He should be referred to as a "He," not an "It." Some of the characteristics that the Holy Spirit holds are:

- He speaks—"The Spirit clearly says that in later times some will abandon the faith and follow deceiving spirits and things taught by demons" (1 Timothy 4:1).

- He witnesses—"When the Counselor comes, whom I will send to you from the Father, the Spirit of truth who goes out from the Father, he will testify about me" (John 15:26).

- He teaches—"But the Counselor, the Holy Spirit, whom the Father will send in my name, will teach you all things and will remind you of everything I have said to you" (John 14:26).

- He guides—"But when he, the Spirit of truth, comes, he will guide you into all truth. He will not speak on his own; he will speak only what he hears, and he will tell you what is yet to come" (John 16:13).

- He leads/forbids—"Paul and his companions traveled throughout the region of Phrygia and Galatia, having been kept by the Holy Spirit from preaching the Word in the province of Asia" (Acts 16:6).

- He possesses mind—"And he who searches our hearts knows the mind of the Spirit, because the Spirit intercedes for the saints in accordance with God's will" (Romans 8:27).

- He has knowledge—"For who among men knows the thoughts of a man except the man's spirit within him? In the same way no one knows the thoughts of God except the Spirit of God" (1 Corinthians 2:11).

- He has affections—"I urge you, brothers, by our Lord Jesus Christ and by the love of the Spirit, to join me in my struggle by praying to God for me" (Romans 15:30).

- He possesses a will—"All these are the work of one and the same Spirit, and he gives them to each one, just as he determines" (1 Corinthians 12:11).

- He can be grieved—"And do not grieve the Holy Spirit of God, with whom you were sealed for the day of redemption" (Ephesians 4:30).

- He can be resisted—"Then Peter said, 'Ananias, how is it that Satan has so filled your heart that you have lied to the Holy Spirit and have kept for yourself some of the money you received for the land'" (Acts 5:3).

- He can be quenched—"Do not put out the Spirit's fire" (1 Thessalonians 5:19).

- He can be blasphemed—"Anyone who speaks a word against the Son of Man will be forgiven, but anyone who speaks against the Holy Spirit will not be forgiven, either in this age or in the age to come" (Matthew 12:32).

These are just a few of His characteristics. Later in this chapter, we will look more closely at a few of these in order to better understand Him.

How Do I know if I Have Him? Can I Feel Him?

There is a story of a young man climbing down the stairs to a traditional baptistery in the front of the church. As usual, the church members would sing a few songs as the person who had decided to give his or her life to Christ was made ready. This particular young man had been studying the Bible and by no means did he have all the answers. What he did know was that Jesus died for him, and that he was sinner. He knew that, because Jesus conquered death and was resurrected, He was qualified to be this man's Savior. Actually, He was qualified as the unblemished Lamb to be the Savior of the world.

The preacher, in his baptismal robe and waders, joined the young man in the water and went over what he was going to say. As the singing continued and the curtain remained closed in this small traditional church, the preacher said, "I am going to ask you if you believe that Jesus is the Son of God. Then, after your answer, I will take your confession that Jesus is your Lord or Master. Once that is completed, you will be ready to be baptized. I will say, 'I baptize you in the name of the Father, the Son, and the Holy Spirit for the forgiveness of sins, and you will receive the gift of the Holy Spirit as it says in Acts 2:38.'"

This young man had been told he was going to receive the Holy Spirit, but he asked, "How will I know I have the Holy Spirit?"

As the final verse of the song was sung, the preacher realized that he did not have much time left before the curtains were opened and the lights shone down. So the preacher said, "Don't worry, you will just know."

The young man asked, "Will I feel it?"

The preacher replied in a whisper as the curtains were opened and the lights started to shine, "Trust me, you will just know."

The preacher began by introducing the young man to the congregation, and proceeded to ask him if he believed that Jesus is the Son of God.

The young man answered in faith and the preacher proceeded to do all that he had explained earlier. After the preacher ended with the phrase, "You will receive the gift of the Holy Spirit," the man put his hands over his nose, and the preacher baptized him in the traditional way of putting his hand behind the young man's back and laying him back under the water.

Then a miracle seemed to happen! In all the years the preacher had baptized people, he had never seen this before. While the young man was underwater, his eyes popped wide open, and he became stiff as a board. Because the congregation was looking on from their seats, they could not see what was happening. The preacher did not want to make an issue about it, so he pulled the young man upright and to his feet. The people applauded, the singing continued, and the curtain began to close. The preacher was bothered by what he had just witnessed. The preacher thought, *I didn't experience this when I was baptized. I had always taught you will just know you have the Holy Spirit because the Word of God says so.*

As the two began walking up the stairs, the preacher asked, "What happened in the water? In all the years of preaching and baptizing, I have never seen anything like it."

The young man, rubbing his head and looking a little dazed, responded, "As you took me back into the water to baptize me, you rammed my head into the stairs of the baptistery."

Needless to say, a person will know they have the Holy Spirit when they do what God asks them to do. If God commands a specific way to receive His Holy Spirit, then you can know that if you follow exactly what He says, you will receive the Spirit He promised. The Spirit has been involved throughout all of the Scriptures, but the indwelling of the Spirit was something better after Jesus ascended to heaven and the day of Pentecost took place.

Is there more than one way to receive God's Spirit? Maybe, but you can stand before God in faith because faith comes by hearing the Word of

God. According to Romans 10:17, "Consequently, faith comes from hearing the message, and the message is heard through the word of Christ." The Holy Spirit is God living inside us and, if we are going to be the dwelling place of God, we must be forgiven. We receive the Spirit when we, by faith, change our hearts and are baptized into Jesus for forgiveness of sins. According to Acts 2:37-39:

> When the people heard this, they were cut to the heart and said to Peter and the other apostles, "Brothers, what shall we do?" Peter replied, "Repent and be baptized, every one of you, in the name of Jesus Christ for the forgiveness of your sins. And you will receive the gift of the Holy Spirit. The promise is for you and your children and for all who are far off—for all whom the Lord our God will call."

Now many want to debate baptism, but I just want to do what the Bible says so I can be confident that I have listened to God and not man. These verses in Acts 2 confirm to me that when people responded by faith to Christ, they repented and were baptized for forgiveness. Whether or not this means they were never forgiven before, or whether before they had been forgiven from past sins and now they were being forgiven of all future sin, I do not know. What I do know is that the Bible says it, and I believe it!

The verse says, "This promise is for you and your children and all who are far off." This statement would seem to apply to us, as well. Jesus received the Holy Spirit when He was baptized. The Bible also speaks of receiving the Holy Spirit when they believed what they heard in Galatians 3:2, where it says, "I would like to learn just one thing from you: Did you receive the Spirit by observing the law, or by believing what you heard?" From this passage, the context would seem to be discussing the receiving of the Holy Spirit to work miracles.

One other passage speaks of receiving the Holy Spirit when we ask. The passage is in Luke 11:13, where it says, "If you then, though you are evil, know how to give good gifts to your children, how much more will your Father in heaven give the Holy Spirit to those who ask him!" This could be another way to receive the Holy Spirit. But receiving the Holy Spirit to make His home in our lives, and the giving of the Holy Spirit at times in our lives for an immediate purpose, could be different, as well. We know from the example of Jesus and the Acts 2 passage that we can be confident when we believe by hearing in faith, being baptized, and asking to receive Him, we will receive the gift of the Holy Spirit.

Many are looking for something visible to know for sure they have received the Spirit. Being forgiven of sin is similar to this. There is not a sin gauge which tells a person God does not see their sin anymore and that their sins are forgiven. You cannot hook up to a gauge which tells you there are zero sins showing. That is ridiculous. We know we are completely forgiven when we put our trust in Jesus as the Messiah and our Savior, and obey what God asks us to do. The Holy Spirit is a gift that God gives because of faith. We do not deserve the gift of the Holy Spirit just as we do not deserve the gift of God's saving grace. Because God is faithful and can be trusted, we can have complete confidence that our sins are taken away, never to return to us again, as long as we walk in the direction of God by faith. In the same way, we can have confidence in loving Christ and following God's Word in order to receive His Spirit. We will see the effects and power of the Spirit as we learn to totally submit to the Spirit. The fruit of the Spirit in a changed life is a great way to know we have Him. We will discuss this in greater detail in the next chapter.

Sign Gifts and the Indwelling

God no longer dwells in temples made with hands. He now dwells within His church and within individuals of that church. Each Christian is the temple in which the Holy Spirit dwells, according to 1 Corinthians 6:19-20, where it says, "Do you not know that your body is a temple of the Holy Spirit, who is in you, whom you have received from God? You are not your own; you were bought at a price. Therefore honor God with your body." The word *you* in this verse is singular, so it refers to each person individually. There is a Scripture where the word *you* is plural, referring to the church as the temple of God. This is found at 1 Corinthians 3:16-17, where it says, "Don't you know that you yourselves are God's temple and that God's Spirit lives in you? If anyone destroys God's temple, God will destroy him; for God's temple is sacred, and you are that temple." So whether we, as Christians, are alone or gathered together, we are considered to be the temple of God. We are the indwelling of God.

Many confuse the supernatural sign gifts of the Spirit with the indwelling gift of the Spirit. There is one Holy Spirit, according to Ephesians 4:4-6, where it says, "There is one body and one Spirit—just as you were called to one hope when you were called—one Lord, one faith, one baptism; one God and Father of all, who is over all and through all and in all." There is one Spirit but many gifts.

The Spirit given to the apostles in the first century was not only the indwelling of the Spirit, but it was also the supernatural sign gifts of the Spirit. These gifts of the Spirit I am referring to is the actual gift assigned by the Holy Spirit for the purpose of being a sign to unbelievers. I do believe in the power given by the Spirit to any Christian in which God could cause something supernatural to occur around, or through them, in His Will. I see a difference in the Scriptures, and I will explain this later in this section. The supernatural sign gift was given during that time for a purpose. The people who lived during the first century did not have the complete written Word of God. The Scriptures they studied were of the Law and the Prophets. This teaching about Christ and His words were spoken through the apostles by the Holy Spirit. According to John 15:26, it was directly from God.

Remember, the verses in John 14-17 were spoken only to the apostles in a private setting. This does not mean the principles in that passage cannot apply to us today, but the Holy Spirit does not teach us all things the way He did with the apostles in writing the Scriptures. According to John 14:26, it says, "But the Counselor, the Holy Spirit, whom the Father will send in my name, will teach you all things and will remind you of everything I have said to you." How is the Holy Spirit going to remind us of what Jesus said when we were not alive to hear from Him? Today, we are taught by the Spirit through the Word of God whether read, spoken, or listened to. If the Holy Spirit taught us all things, then we would never disagree about truth with others who have the Spirit. He would not teach me one thing and you another. As we learned earlier, He is God, and God does not lie or contradict Himself. God is light, and He is truth.

Even during the time of the first century, there were many false teachers like the gnostics who did not believe Jesus had come in the flesh. In Matthew 24, Jesus also speaks of false teachers who were claiming to be Christ. If you lived during this time, how would you know what was true and what was false? That was the purpose of the supernatural sign gifts of the Spirit. According to Mark 16:20, the signs and wonders were to confirm the Word. This was not necessarily the New Testament, which had not yet been completed, but the spoken Word.

If I was searching for salvation in the first century and someone told me that I must kill myself in a holy manner in order to have salvation through Christ, how would I know if they were right, if I did not have the Bible? What if another claimed to have truth, and I was told to believe in Christ and have my sins washed away to insure salvation, what would I think and what should I do? Both people are claiming to speak truth, but my salvation and eternity depend on real truth, according to Proverbs 4:12, where it says, "There is a way that seems right to a man, but in the end it leads to death."

Let's say I have a grandmother who is sick and she has been battling a disease for years. Only one of these people claiming to have truth could raise her up and completely heal her. That would make my decision of who is with God quite a bit easier. If there was not any sign gift of the Spirit, then there would not be any confirmation of what is true. That is why they needed that confirmation directly from God in the early stages of the church.

The first question is, how did the people receive a supernatural sign gift of the Spirit? The apostles received the power on the day of Pentecost when the tongues of fire came on them in Acts 2. This was the beginning of the church. This event was prophesied by the Old Testament prophet, Joel. The apostles were God's chosen people who were to be the foundation stones of the church, according to Ephesians 2:19-22:

> Consequently, you are no longer foreigners and aliens, but fellow citizens with God's people and members of God's household, built on the foundation of the apostles and prophets, with Christ Jesus himself as the chief cornerstone. In him the whole building is joined together and rises to become a holy temple in the Lord. And in him you too are being built together to become a dwelling in which God lives by his Spirit.

The apostles had all of the supernatural sign gifts, and they were also given the power to pass these gifts on to other Christians in order to confirm the Word.

It is clear not all Christians had the same gifts as each other, but the Holy Spirit gave to each as He had determined.

> Now to each one the manifestation of the Spirit is given
> for the common good. To one there is given through the
> Spirit the message of wisdom, to another the message of
> knowledge by means of the same Spirit, to another faith
> by the same Spirit, to another gifts of healing by that one
> Spirit, to another miraculous powers, to another proph-
> ecy, to another distinguishing between spirits, to another
> speaking in different kinds of tongues, and to still anoth-
> er the interpretation of tongues. All these are the work of
> one and the same Spirit, and he gives them to each one,
> just as he determines. —1 Corinthians 12:7-11

When churches teach that everyone must have the gift of tongues, this is in conflict with the Scripture which says not all speak in tongues.

We see from the Scriptures it was only the twelve apostles who were performing these signs and wonders until they laid hands on the seven men in Acts 6. Notice from these few verses that it was the apostles who were performing miracles at the beginning of the church. After laying hands on these men, we see Stephen and Philip performing great signs and wonders.

Also in the Scriptures, we can see it was only the apostles who laid their hands on Christians to receive a sign gift the Holy Spirit would determine. An exception to this was in Acts 10, which relates the story of Cornelius. This was an example of a time in which God gave a supernat-ural gift of the Spirit to those who were not even Christians. The pur-pose for this seems to have been to convince the circumcised believers that the Gentiles could also be saved. To Jews, like Peter's companions, the only way they would agree to accept and baptize a Gentile was if it was clear from God this was His will. Cornelius and those other Gentiles who heard began speaking in tongues the way Peter had in Acts 2. When they witnessed the baptism of the Holy Spirit on the Gentiles that Jesus spoke of, and that the apostles experienced on the day of Pentecost, this was proof enough for these Jews that it was from God and not from man. It took an experience like that in Acts 2 to convince these circumcised believers that Gentiles could also be saved.

All the other examples, as in Acts 8:14-19, show that even men like Philip could not pass on these supernatural sign gifts:

> When the apostles in Jerusalem heard that Samaria had accepted the word of God, they sent Peter and John to them. When they arrived, they prayed for them that they might receive the Holy Spirit, because the Holy Spirit had not yet come upon any of them; they had simply been baptized into the name of the Lord Jesus. Then Peter and John placed their hands on them, and they received the Holy Spirit. When Simon saw that the Spirit was given at the laying on of the apostles's hands, he offered them money and said, "Give me also this ability so that everyone on whom I lay my hands may receive the Holy Spirit."

Simon the sorcerer wanted the power to pass on the gifts, but he was sinful in desiring this power. Even Simon knew this gift was given by the laying on of the apostle's hands. They had to call Peter and John in order to receive these supernatural sign gifts. The apostles were needed in order to pass on these gifts. It would be absurd to send for the apostles if there were others who could have been called. Why bother the apostles who were so busy doing kingdom work? Also, later in Acts 8, Philip never laid his hands on the Ethiopian eunuch because he could not pass on the gifts, even though he himself had the gift of healing. It would have been nice for this man to return to Ethiopia with signs and wonders, but that did not appear to happen because none of the twelve apostles were present.

If the apostles were the only ones who could pass on the sign gifts of the Spirit, then what would happen after all the apostles died? It would mean the sign gifts, which were done by the Christians to confirm the Word, would end as soon as the last person who received the gift died. What this means is, if John lived until AD 96 or AD 98, as many scholars believe, and he laid his hands on a thirteen-year-old girl who lived until she was seventy or so, the supernatural sign gifts would be in the world until AD 150, give or take a few years. By then, the Word of God would have been completely written and copied numerous times. At this point in history, the Word of God was being compiled into what we have today in the Holy Bible.

A former Pentecostal preacher made a claim all over the Internet, calling to come forward the true healers, according to Mark 16:17-18, where it says, "And these signs will accompany those who believe: In my name they will drive out demons; they will speak in new tongues; they will pick up snakes with their hands; and when they drink deadly poison, it will not hurt them at all; they will place their hands on sick people, and they will get well." It is called the One Million Dollar Miracle Challenge. He claims that no Pentecostal faith healer has ever tried to perform a miracle with us watching over them. He said if a faith healer can survive a bite of a snake chosen by him, then he will win the money and prove to all the skeptics that they have this power at their disposal today. He knows, since coming out of that movement, that no one will step up. In a number of years, no one has yet stepped forward. Let no one claim this is not for the right reason, because anyone could do any of these things to confirm the claims they have spoken. All this man was asking was for someone who knows they are empowered to step forward.

Do not be misled in this section of the book. I believe supernatural things can and do happen today. I do believe in miracles, because I know God has not quit working powerfully since the first century. I have personally witnessed supernatural things, and it was obviously the power of God. I have met sincere people who have spoken of miraculous things. I believe the sign gifts of the Spirit that were given to the apostles and first-century Christians were used to convince unbelievers and confirm the Word. But today this is not needed because we have the complete written Word. There are areas of the world where miracles are seen more frequently because the Word of God is scarce. Let's face it, from some of my personal experiences as well as from the Scriptures, to deny supernatural power from the Holy Spirit would be absurd. The specific supernatural sign gifts of the Spirit, those given by the apostles, had purposes during the infancy of the church which are hidden today.

Things are not the same now as the first century with the twelve apostles and Christians. I do not see these sign gifts of healing happen in the same form as in the first century by men like Paul. I do not see handkerchiefs or aprons taken by men today to the faithful and faithless sick. The healing back then was one-hundred percent of the diseases and illnesses, and one-hundred percent recovery. The man who was crippled in Acts 3:2-8 received complete healing when his legs were strong enough to walk and leap, even though he had not ever walked:

> Now a man crippled from birth was being carried to the temple gate called Beautiful, where he was put every day to beg from those going into the temple courts. When he saw Peter and John about to enter, he asked them for money. Peter looked straight at him, as did John. Then Peter said, "Look at us!" So the man gave them his attention, expecting to get something from them. Then Peter said, "Silver or gold I do not have, but what I have I give you. In the name of Jesus Christ of Nazareth, walk." Taking him by the right hand, he helped him up, and instantly the man's feet and ankles became strong. He jumped to his

feet and began to walk. Then he went with them into the
temple courts, walking and jumping, and praising God.

He was never taught to walk, so part of the miracle was that it had been
as if his body had always walked. His muscles were trained and strong
enough even to leap. Healings were always complete.

Not only were people being healed by handkerchiefs from Paul, according to Acts 19:11-12: "God did extraordinary miracles through Paul,
so that even handkerchiefs and aprons that had touched him were taken
to the sick, and their illnesses were cured and the evil spirits left them."
The dead were also being raised in Acts 20:9-10, where it says, "Seated
in a window was a young man named Eutychus, who was sinking into
a deep sleep as Paul talked on and on. When he was sound asleep, he fell
to the ground from the third story and was picked up dead. Paul went
down threw himself on the young man and put his arms around him.
'Don't be alarmed,' he said. 'He's alive!'"

Today, I do not see healing like what happened with Peter in Acts
5:15 where it says, "As a result, people brought the sick into the streets
and laid them on beds and mats so that at least Peter's shadow might fall
on any of them."

You see examples of healing and raising the dead performed by only a
few men in the Scriptures. Think of the chaos if Christians had the power to raise the dead or heal. These gifts were performed as a sign when
the Holy Spirit allowed. During that time and even in the Old Testament,
apostles and prophets never made a profit from healing someone. They
understood that the power was in Christ and not of them. Therefore,
God was to receive the praise, honor, and glory for all the power displayed. I love the story in 2 Kings 5, where through Elisha the prophet,
God healed Naaman completely of leprosy. Elisha would not take any
gift from Naaman, but Elisha's servant, Gehazi, was greedy and wanted
some of the gifts. Because of the greed, Gehazi caught up with Naaman

and told him that his master, Elisha, changed his mind and would accept some of the gifts. Because Gehazi did this evil act he, as well as his future generations, were struck with leprosy. It appears that no one in Scripture ever received gifts or money for raising the dead, and when Gehazi tried, he was punished.

I think it is clear in God's Word people are not to ever profit on the power of God. There are many "faith-healers" who are very rich in the world today. They are living a luxurious life because of miracles God is doing. The true miracles people experience and witness today are not from any man or woman, preacher or priest, but because of God's power working through their faith, whether they are in a full stadium or in the privacy of a home.

The question for us today is, do you need to see a supernatural occurrence to come to faith in Christ? Or does a person have everything one needs to believe in Christ from the complete written Word of God? According to John 20:30-31, we have all we need to believe Jesus is the Christ from His Holy Scripture.

If you want to look further into the sign gifts, let us take a look at a passage which shows the laying on of hands and the receiving of tongues.

> While Apollos was at Corinth, Paul took the road through the interior and arrived at Ephesus. There he found some disciples and asked them, "Did you receive the Holy Spirit when you believed?" They answered, "No, we have not even heard that there is a Holy Spirit." So Paul asked, "Then what baptism did you receive?" "John's baptism," they replied. Paul said, "John's baptism was a baptism of repentance. He told the people to believe in the one coming after him, that is, in Jesus." On hearing this, they were baptized into the name of the Lord Jesus. When Paul placed his hands on them, the Holy Spirit came on them,

and they spoke in tongues and prophesied. There were
about twelve men in all. —Acts 19:1-7

Paul planned to pass on the sign gift of the Spirit to Christians so they
could confirm the Word in which they would speak. He asked them if
they received the Holy Spirit when they believed. He did not ask them if
they received the indwelling of the Spirit when they believed. That would
be a given if they believed and had been baptized into Christ. Obviously,
because they had not even heard of the Spirit years after Christ's resurrection, they had not been baptized in the name of Christ. So, as a matter
of priority, Paul had them baptized in the name of Jesus. Then he laid his
hands on them so they might receive a supernatural sign gift to confirm
God's Word. When they received the gift, they spoke in tongues to confirm to Paul that they had, in fact, received at least one sign gift of the
Spirit.

Many have questions about tongue speaking, and I cannot address
every aspect of this topic, but I will clarify one thing. The gift of tongues
where the apostle spoke and everyone heard him in their native language according to Acts 2 was a sign gift. The tongue speaking where
your spirit prays and your mind is unfruitful is different than the sign
gift of speaking a language miraculously. I believe most would agree that
we do not see people speaking foreign languages miraculously by the
Holy Spirit without any training. Some claim to have a prayer language,
but even this is not an actual spoken language. To be able to go to China
on a mission and speak so others could hear and understand in their
native language would be amazing. In many ways, when we translate
Bibles into other languages, the Bible is read in their native tongue. It is
not done miraculously as a sign gift, but it still takes the hand of God.

Do not be discouraged if you did not receive a sign gift as many
did in the first century. We have the Word of God, and we can read it
and study it anytime, and there is power in it. I would rather have the

complete Word of God and the indwelling of the Spirit than the supernatural sign gifts from the Spirit that the first-century Christians had in the church's infancy. It is the indwelling of the Spirit that leads, guides, and gives us power to live victoriously. Because we have the indwelling of the Spirit today, there are miracles and wonders which still happen, but not because we have received a sign gift. It is because the power of the Holy Spirit is still impacting the world for Jesus.

While I was on a mission trip helping refugees in the jungles of Thailand, I met a women in her early-to-mid twenties who was there helping, as well. The people called her Birdie and she had been helping these refugees for about a year. She was from Sweden and had come to serve the displaced people who were from the tribes in Myanmar. I asked her how long she planned on staying, and she told me of a new venture God was calling her to. Birdie told me about a trip to the Middle East she had recently returned from where God had confirmed to her that she needed to go. While she was in the Middle East, her team had to be careful of where they went and who they talked to. One night on the trip, Birdie had a dream. She told me, "I had a very vivid dream of a woman wanting me to come to her house. In the dream I saw the name of the road, all the houses down her road, and her front gate. I even saw this Muslim woman's face!" Birdie went on to say, "In the dream, Jesus told me to go to her house and through our translator, teach her about me." The next day, Birdie told her team and translator, and the translator knew the road. That day, Birdie went to meet this woman, and as she got to the same gate she had seen in the dream, the translator called out, "Is there anyone inside?" A lady came out, opened the gate, and invited them inside saying, "I have been expecting you." The lady explained she had a dream of this young woman who would come and tell her about Jesus. The lady was Muslim, but that would soon change as the Holy Spirit was at work supernaturally once again. It is exciting to have God living inside us and working through us.

CHAPTER 5 WORKSHEET

Do you have the Holy Spirit at work in your life? If not, what are you going to do about it?

_____

_____

_____

What are some new things you have learned about the power of the Holy Spirit?

_____

_____

_____

How is the Holy Spirit's power greater than that of Satan's power?

_____

_____

_____

How can you hear from the Holy Spirit right now?

_____

_____

_____

What does it look like to live in the power of the Holy Spirit today?

_____

_____

_____

CHAPTER 6

God's Power in us

Now to him who is able to do immeasurably more than all we ask or imagine, according to his power that is at work within us, to him be glory in the church and in Christ Jesus throughout all generations, forever and ever! Amen.
—Ephesians 3:20-21

Leading of the Spirit

Earlier, we looked at some of the characteristics which define the person of the Spirit. Some of these were self-explanatory. I want to focus on a few that might need some explanation in order to help us free the Spirit in our lives as Christians. Let me first focus on how the Holy Spirit can lead or forbid based on Acts 16:6.

In the fall of 1995, while I was in the Adventures in Missions (AIM) program in Lubbock, Texas, I was told there was a girl named Carolyn who wanted to study the Bible and become a Christian. This is the same Carolyn I mentioned earlier in the book who was pursued by the man, Lafayette, who was in the satanic occult. The friend who told me about this girl knew the area where Carolyn lived, but he did not know her exact address. My friend did not even know her last name. At nineteen, I was energetic and ready to take on the world. No last name, no address, no problem. After classes that day, I decided I was going to go to the "other side of the tracks" to the projects of Lubbock by myself. I got to an area where I had never been before, driving my small, black sports car and having my Bible ready to find Carolyn.

As I sat in my car for a few minutes, I remember praying, "Lord, you know where this teenage girl lives, and I pray your Holy Spirit will guide me to her as well as others who are searching for you. I trust in you, and I know you want her saved." I got out of the car and began walking through this drug and gang-infested area. I was probably the only white person within a two-mile radius. No sooner had I gotten out of the car and began walking down the street that I heard a few gunshots in the distance. After that, I saw a big car stop and five people came out of nowhere to gather at the trunk of the car, pay money, grab what they needed, and run. It all happened in five seconds, but of course I saw nothing, right? An older man was outside his small home on the block, so I went up to him and we began talking. I needed to make some friends quick. Naturally, he was wondering what I was doing walking the streets in that area, which gave me a perfect opportunity to share Christ.

After talking a few minutes with this older man, I continued on and saw some low-income duplexes with a teenage boy outside pushing a shopping cart. So, I asked him if he knew a girl named Carolyn.

Before I even got the words out of my mouth, he ran inside the duplex, yelling, "Carolyn! Carolyn! There is a white guy right outside who is here to see you!"

As I watched what was going on, I have to say I was surprised God had led me to her so quickly in the midst of all these apartments and duplexes. As I was invited inside, I was overcome by the smell of rotten food. This little one-bedroom duplex housed six people. I looked around and greeted her brother, who was a fourteen-year-old with the intelligence of a first grader. As I got to know him, I realized he had the kindest heart. I could tell after meeting her parents that they were slow, as well. Carolyn's dad was almost blind, with cataracts covering both eyes.

Everyone there was wearing clothes that were so thin you could practically see through them. For this family to ever have the resources to buy new clothes was only a fantasy.

As I waited, they offered me food and drinks, but I would not accept these because it easily could have been the only meal for them that day. As Carolyn came out, she could not stop smiling. She said I was an angel sent by God. I knew I was not an angel, but I eventually came to understand that I was His messenger that day. In fact, it was the Holy Spirit who led me to this girl within thirty minutes of my arrival to the area. He guided me through the valley of shadow and death to a seeking teenager to whom God was keeping His promise. This reminded me of Matthew 7:7-8, where it says, "Ask and it will be given to you; seek and you will find; knock and the door will be opened to you. For everyone who asks receives; he who seeks finds; and to him who knocks, the door will be opened."

I know it could only have been through the direction of God that I found this girl who later gave her life to Christ. Because of this experience, I never again have doubted the Holy Spirit's guidance. Because of this knowledge and true understanding from the Scriptures, mission trips are a little different for me because I trust in the direction of God.

I have learned not to push through doors and try to do whatever I want. I believe God wants us to live by the Spirit, not just ask God on the big decisions. This begins with having the attitude that I want to know God's will. I have got to want what God wants more than what I want. I used to pray asking God to do this and do that. Now, I do not want to convince God of anything. I want God to align me with what God wants me to do, no matter what the cost. God knows what is best, so I must be all right with whatever He wants if I live my life for Him. This later became tough, when I was diagnosed with a brain tumor in 2017, and had to walk that road.

Let me give you an example of trusting God and seeking His will. If I am out looking for a job, do I want the job based on my knowledge and the wisdom that I think is best, or do I want the job that God knows is best for me?

I have learned through experience that what I think is best is not always that good, after all. That new car I thought I could afford seemed great at the time, until I lost my job and realized I should have sought His will and direction. I could have been deceived and led by greed when I said God had blessed me with a new house when my other was just fine, and now I am limited more financially. I think we can all agree that we have made selfish decisions led by greed and materialism which has cost us dearly.

What I have learned is that I am not pushing through any doors and, if anything, I am praying certain doors close if they are not in God's will for me. I now spend time praying about that conversation at work, and instead of forcing that conversation, I now allow God to reveal the right timing and whether He wants me to have it all. If the opportunity does not arise throughout the day, I do not force it because I know today must not be the day. I let God work out the timing. I have been amazed at how God has led me by His Spirit. Some days, my boss that I need to talk with just comes in and says, "Is there anything on your mind today that we need to talk about?" God clearly opened the door and wants me to communicate. Other times, our schedules never meet, but I see how it gets worked out, anyway, so no conversations were needed. It is amazing how God works if we will not bust through doors and say what we are emotionally charged to say. It is time for us as Christians to start allowing the Holy Spirit to truly lead our lives. Many say they allow the Spirit to lead, but only in things they cannot lead themselves. This can cause us to grieve the Holy Spirit.

Grieving the Spirit

The next characteristic I would like to explain in more detail is found in Ephesians 4:30, and is about grieving the Holy Spirit. The word *grieve* means to bring sorrow or sadden. This is the idea that we can actually bring sorrow to God, who lives inside of us through His Holy Spirit.

How can we make the Holy Spirit sad, or how can we make Him sorrowful? I would answer with a question, which is, how do we make God sad since the Holy Spirit is God? I think it would start by not listening to the Holy Spirit inside of us. The voices in our mind get so loud, and we live in this fast-paced world where we want it now and we want to know now. It gets really difficult to hear the Holy Spirit. The best way to listen is just to take a time of silence and quietness. At times, I lie face down and put on my noise-cancelling headphones to pray. After I pray, I lie there and listen. I believe the Holy Spirit is constantly speaking and leading us, but maybe we do not hear because we do not want to know what He is saying. Would you rather know what God is saying, even if you do not like it at the moment, or would you rather bear the consequences of rushing your decisions?

If you struggle with this question, ask the many teens I have worked with over the years who did not want to listen to God when it came to dating. They pushed through doors, and they now have the burden of the consequences of doing what they wanted to do instead of waiting on God's perfect will for them. I would tell those who wanted true love so badly, who would have low standards and rush into a relationship with the first guy or girl interested in them, that God says love is patient. According to 1 Corinthians 13, the very first word used to define love for us is "patience."

We also make God sad by allowing our flesh to win in our thoughts, our speech, and our actions, instead of allowing the Spirit to win. This is nothing new. From the beginning, flesh has been battling God all the way back to when Eve wanted knowledge in the Garden of Eden. I am reminded of the Spirit's words through the apostle Paul in Romans 7:14-20:

> We know that the law is spiritual; but I am unspiritual, sold as a slave to sin. I do not understand what I do. For what I want to do I do not do, but what I hate I do. And if I do what I do not want to do, I agree that the law is good. As it is, it is no longer I myself who do it, but it is sin living in me. I know that nothing good lives in me, that is, in my sinful nature. For I have the desire to do what is good, but I cannot carry it out. For what I do is not the good I want to do; no, the evil I do not want to do—this I keep on doing. Now if I do what I do not want to do, it is no longer I who do it, but it is sin living in me that does it.

Even an apostle of Christ dealt with what we have all experienced. There is this battle going on, and the strongest influence in our life will win. Galatians 5:17-18 says, "For the sinful nature desires what is contrary to the Spirit and the Spirit what is contrary to the sinful nature. They are in conflict with each other, so that you do not do what you want." The Bible also says in Galatians 5:25 that it is not enough to just live by the Spirit but to also walk or keep in step with the Spirit. We have a responsibility to keep in step, or we will be left behind.

If our flesh is always going to battle our Spirit, then how can we be assured the Spirit will win more times than not? I think it starts by crucifying our own passions and desires. Galatians 5:24 says, "Those who belong to Christ Jesus have crucified the sinful nature with its passions and desires." I also believe in a mindset that submits to what God wants in our life instead of what we want. According to Romans 8:5-6, "Those who live according to the sinful nature have their minds set on what that nature desires; but those who live in accordance with the Spirit have their minds set on what the Spirit desires. The mind of sinful man is death, but the mind controlled by the Spirit is life and peace." Because of this submission, we are controlled by God's Spirit, as seen in Romans 8:9, "You, however, are controlled not by the sinful nature but by the Spirit, if the Spirit of God lives in you. And if anyone does not have the Spirit of Christ, he does not belong to Christ."

If you believe you are grieving the Spirit and are not listening well, try lying face down on the floor when you pray. After you are finished, just lay and listen to whatever comes to your mind.

Quenching the Spirit

Do we realize that a Christian can get rid of the Holy Spirit in their life? The less we allow the Spirit to freely reign in our lives, the less control He has. We can actually get to a point where the Spirit has no influence in our life. That is when the Spirit knows He must leave a person's heart because He is no longer invited to stay. The key to being controlled by the Spirit begins with not quenching the Spirit or putting out the Spirit's fire, as discussed in 1 Thessalonians 5:19. The word *quench* invokes the idea of extinguishing. The purpose of a fire extinguisher is to put out fires.

When I was a young boy, fire extinguishers fascinated me. I was always told not to touch them and to view the little pin in the handle as if it were the pin in a grenade. If you pulled the pin, Mom always insinuated bad things would happen. Because I was told never to mess with them, the curiosity continued to grow until I finally had my chance. Never before had I even held a fire extinguisher. Years later, as an adult in the back of a thrift store where a few youths and I were volunteering, we found what appeared to be an unused fire extinguisher out back near the dumpster. Like a child all over again, I had to check to see if it was live. I pulled the pin and aimed, not knowing what would really happen. When I pulled the trigger, it happened—absolutely nothing! How could it be? It felt full, the pin was out, and I had pulled the trigger. Was I doing something wrong? Thank goodness the pyromaniac teen from our youth group was there to show me that the trigger was broken. Now it was obvious why this extinguisher had found its way to the dumpster. I knew that my time for extinguishing fires or anything else would have to wait. It was probably a good thing it did not work because, as a young youth minister, I might have gotten into real trouble. I was aiming it right at the members of the youth group!

How do we keep the Spirit's fire burning strong and keep from putting the fire out? Just as with a physical fire, the spiritual fire of the Holy Spirit needs to be fueled. For a physical fire, you need to add oxygen, dry wood, and possibly some lighter fluid or gasoline to get it blazing. The longer a fire burns, the hotter it gets, especially if you give it more fuel.

At a retreat I led for high school boys in the Ocala National Forest a few years back, we started playing with the fire like most kids want to do late at night. This was a night when I could have used a fire extinguisher that worked. It all started when some of the group threw various things into the fire to see what would burn. Tradition had been to shake up a can of Coke, put it top down in the burning hot fire, and wait for it to take off like a rocket into the air. That night, the tradition continued. I have learned that teens get mad when you break tradition, so I couldn't do that to them. Next thing I knew, after the Coke rocket had been launched, a full bug spray can was tossed upside down into the fire, preparing for takeoff. Everyone started to scatter, yelling, "Bug spray!" at one o'clock in the morning. The burning bug spray can ignited and took off straight into the air with a loud pop, while cheers erupted from the teens. It was as though we had created the very first rocket to fly. Let's just say we did not have mosquito problems that night. I firmly drew the line when one of the teens started to grab the small propane canister from our grill. Some of us had not lost all sense, thank goodness.

And yet, next thing I knew, I saw someone off near the fire pouring gasoline out of a metal gallon jug. I did not know it was gasoline until later, but I could definitely tell it was extremely flammable. At this point, I wondered where our chaperones were because I really needed their help—and that of a working fire extinguisher. As I ran close to the fire, the huge blaze ignited the jacket of the boy pouring the gasoline. I yelled, "Hit the ground and roll," and soon realized it was our "responsible" chaperone rolling on the ground. This ex-highway patrol officer had brought the gasoline and added it to the blaze which had now set him on fire. I am happy to say it all calmed down after that, with no injuries and no forest fire. There were only a few complaints from the hillbillies in the next campsite over, which actually scared me more than the fire. It was a retreat that none of us will ever forget.

Needless to say, that fire was hot and large because it received plenty of fuel to stay burning. Likewise, the Holy Spirit living inside of us wants us to experience a well-fueled fire all the time. If the Spirit is to win daily against the flesh and sinful nature, it will be because we allow Him to burn. Do not ever forget that the Spirit is always strong. It simply is a matter of whether or not we will let Him burn strong all the time in our lives. We are either the fuel or the extinguisher. It is our free choice to fuel the Spirit's fire or to extinguish it from our life.

Let us look at what feeds our flesh. Anything bad we see on television, at the movies, on the Internet, in the mall, at the beach, in video games, and so on, feeds our flesh. Anything bad we hear from music, phone conversations, jokes at the office, the sexual experiences and impressions of others, the names we are called, and everything else bad we hear feeds our flesh. Anything bad we touch or feel can feed our flesh, as well. Pretty much using our five senses to experience evil is contributing to feeding our flesh. Our flesh is being fed all the time every day. This is why our flesh wins the majority of the time for most of us. It is still no excuse because Jesus lived in this evil world and did not conform to it. Even though Jesus was the Son of God, He felt it necessary to constantly keep the flame burning.

We have got to make some bold decisions when it comes to our faith, and when it comes to raising our children in the Lord. Our boys growing up were not allowed to watch much television because of the garbage being shown. I am amazed that even though you monitor what programs your children watch, the commercials are getting worse than the shows. We have a rule in the house that if a sexual girl or a half-dressed girl comes on the TV, we are all to turn our heads. If we do not turn our heads each time, then watching TV will be prohibited in our home. We practice this same thing at the beach, in the mall, and everywhere else we go. The toughest thing to explain to our boys is why women from the church wear immodest clothing. I just explain, "Some people are not taught that Christians ought to be different than the world, including what they wear." This is why we need to help teach people what messages they are sending when they live as the world lives.

I am crazy to think that if my boys are subjected to these types of things growing up it will not affect the way they view girls as they get older. Part of the problem is that the lines of right and wrong, appropriate and inappropriate, are becoming gray in our culture as we base what we think on how we feel. I do not believe they are gray in God's Word. In Psalm 101:2-4, it says, "I will be careful to lead a blameless life—when will you come to me? I will walk in my house with blameless heart. I will set before my eyes no vile thing. The deeds of faithless men I hate; they will not cling to me. Men of perverse heart shall be far from me; I will have nothing to do with evil."

We have got to fuel the fire of the Spirit even more than we feed our flesh. We must fuel our Spirit with spiritual things. Philippians 4:8, says, "Finally, brothers, whatever is true, whatever is noble, whatever is right, whatever is pure, whatever is lovely, whatever is admirable—if anything is excellent or praiseworthy—think about such things." I think this verse says it best. It begins in your mind. A person's thoughts turn into actions, and their actions turn into habits.

Our goal is not just to have the Spirit, but also to live by the Spirit, according to Galatians 5:16, where it says, "So I say, live by the Spirit, and you will not gratify the desires of the sinful nature." How many people have the Spirit, and then how many people live by the Spirit? Some of the obvious things that fuel the fire of the Spirit include attending a true Bible-taught church regularly; not just reading, but studying the Scriptures daily (check out Rick Warren's book on Bible study methods); conducting an intimate prayer life; having an accountable partner of the same gender; and making time for uninhibited worship, Christian music, Christian friends and relationships, and Christian books, as long as they are not a substitute for the Word of God.

Years ago, there were a few youths in my group who would come to my apartment after school to work out in our apartment fitness room. I remember telling those youth to work their spiritual bodies harder than they do their physical bodies. I remember practicing that in my own life. You cannot tell if I have worked out my physical body from reading this book, but hopefully, you can see that I exercise my spiritual body. Our spiritual bodies will last forever and, to say it bluntly, our physical bodies will burn up. I told these youth to focus on the most important things, and I was trying to be an example for them.

Can we ever expect the Holy Spirit's fire to stay ablaze in our life by going to church for two hours or less per week? Can we expect our flesh to be strong when we feed it all the time in the world? When working with teenagers, I see why they push down, or are extinguishing the fire of the Spirit. Many do not ever study the Bible. They put worthless things before their eyes. Teenagers look at so much pornography in movies these days. Yes, a ten-second to ten-minute sex scene is pornography.

It feeds your mind the same way. They know the words of every popular song and every great line in a movie but can quote little to no Scripture. Oftentimes, they began extinguishing the fire of the Spirit out of fear of being different, or fear of being criticized. I do not believe these are teenage issues but, rather, Christian issues.

Satan has deceived us into putting the Spirit's fire out of in our lives, but blaming churches and others for why we fall prey to the flesh. It becomes everyone else's fault that we do not see the Spirit at work. We hear the Spirit's voice telling us to repent openly of our sins, to lift our hands up in praise, to drop to our knees in prayer, to speak to this person about Christ, or to go give a hug to that person in distress but, time and time again, we do not let Him be free and act.

Have you ever wondered what worship might look like if true Spirit-led worshippers who were defeating their sinful natures came together to be free in their praise? It would not cost a thing, and it might just be the most encouraging "church" you ever experienced. If you want better worship, then be a more prepared and better worshipper. The more we fuel the Spirit, the more we will begin to love what God loves and hate what He hates.

Blaspheming the Spirit

A characteristic which confuses many people is one taken from the story in Matthew 12:32 about blaspheming the Holy Spirit. Is there really one unpardonable sin? Can a person really murder, rape, molest children, and blaspheme Jesus, and still be forgiven but have eternal consequences for blaspheming the Holy Spirit one time? Does this make much sense, or do we need to understand this further?

In Matthew 12, the term blasphemy means to speak against. It is understood that the miracles Jesus did while on earth were through the power of the Holy Spirit. The context involves people accusing Jesus of casting out demons by the power of Beelzebub, the ruler of the demons. The idea of blaspheming the Holy Spirit is to give credit for those things which are done clearly by the Holy Spirit, to evil instead. Mark 3:28-30 says, "I tell you the truth, all the sins and blasphemies of men will be forgiven them. But whoever blasphemes against the Holy Spirit will never be forgiven; he is guilty of an eternal sin." He said this because they were saying, "He has an evil spirit." From this context, it seems that blaspheming the Holy Spirit also involves claiming that a miracle did not come from the Holy Spirit through Jesus but from an evil spirit. If this was something we had to be careful about, would it not be spoken about throughout all the Scriptures? Wouldn't there be warnings in every letter to the churches warning against this or how to deal with people who actually blasphemed the Holy Spirit? Could this be something people could only do when Jesus was casting out a demon? The emphasis is on Jesus doing the miracle.

In another gospel, the Bible speaks about how this is something that can be done after Jesus's initial time on earth. In Matthew 12:32 it says, "Anyone who speaks a word against the Son of Man will be forgiven, but anyone who speaks against the Holy Spirit will not be forgiven, either in this age or in the age to come." From looking at all the gospels that speak of this story, and the contexts surrounding the story, it appears as if blaspheming the Holy Spirit is saying that Jesus was using the power of an evil spirit to perform His miracles. Could "this age" be the time of Christ on earth, and the "age to come" when He returns to reign? If so, I believe blaspheming the Holy Spirit could happen only when Jesus was present, performing miracles.

Regardless of the exact meaning, we need always to speak well of the Holy Spirit and be careful about anything we say about Jesus and His power.

What Can the Holy Spirit Do For Me Today?

Many churches have gone to extremes. One of these extremes is to say the Holy Spirit indwells Christians, and that is about it. If this were the case, it is no wonder Christians seem weak and defeated. The other extreme is that the Holy Spirit makes all of your decisions and causes you to be out of control and, as some say, caught up or drunk in the Spirit. Remember, the Holy Spirit is God and will always act as God inside you. He will never go beyond the Word of God or cause you to do anything that would displease God. If you say the Holy Spirit causes you to be disorderly and unedifying in worship, then the Spirit you claim cannot be the Holy Spirit because God will not go against what He has said in 1 Corinthians 14:33, 40, where it says, "For God is not a God of disorder but of peace. But everything should be done in a fitting and orderly way."

The Holy Spirit is a gift that is given to Christians to ensure our eternity with God. We see that the Holy Spirit is a deposit or guarantee, according to Ephesians 1:13-14. "And you also were included in Christ when you heard the word of truth, the gospel of your salvation. Having believed, you were marked in him with a seal, the promised Holy Spirit, who is a deposit guaranteeing our inheritance until the redemption of those who are God's possession—to the praise of his glory." I always say God's judgment will not be very difficult. If you have the Holy Spirit, you have eternal life, and if you do not have the Holy Spirit, you have your sins, which means you have eternal destruction by your own choice.

You were created to live for God. A V8 car was made to run on eight-cylinders. Anything less than that would not fulfill what the car was capable of doing. I believe many Christians are not living the way they were intended to live because they are not using the power they have been given.

I once owned a 2003 Ford Mustang Cobra show car that had 750 horsepower. Just to put this horsepower in perspective, a Dodge Viper has a little over 500 horsepower, and a Lamborghini has around 550 horsepower. The motor was custom built, and the estimated time from zero to sixty was 3.5 seconds. The top speed was estimated at just over 200 mph. I sold the car because I was not able to use the car for the purpose it was made, which was to be shown at car events all year. In the two shows I entered it, I won first place. It was built to run on the race track, but I never was able to do that. To be honest, it scared me to put the pedal to the floor and go all out. It was made to get out on the highway and fly, but I drove on 45-mph roads almost every time I drove it. It was not used to its capacity.

When it comes to the Holy Spirit, this is how I see today's Christians. First, let us make sure we have Him by being obedient to God's Word and, second, let us use the power that has been given to us to truly experience God and thrive in this world for Him. Many of us are walking around admitting defeat when the power is right there for our use. We are driving 45 mph in our faith when we have the capability of driving 200 mph. We are looking to medications for spiritual healing instead of seeking Christ. We are searching everywhere for spiritual healers and counselors when the greatest physician and most wonderful counselor lives within us. We leave the 200-mph driving to those we think are just crazy while we sit back and complain about why God is not moving in our lives. We wonder why counseling and other things are not working, when we are not ready to be completely led by the Spirit.

Trust Him like you never have before. Free Him to take you to speeds you have never experienced before, and hold on for the ride!

Filled with the Spirit

Ananias was a man who laid his hands on Saul, also known as Paul, to regain his sight and be filled with the Holy Spirit. There seems to be a difference between receiving a sign gift and being filled with the Spirit. There are different passages in Acts where a person would be filled with the Spirit on occasions, like Stephen, who was known as a person with the quality of being filled with the Spirit before the apostles even laid their hands on him for him to perform signs.

There are examples throughout the book of Acts about people speaking boldly when filled with the Holy Spirit. The word "filled" in many of these verses means "just having been filled."

- Acts 6:5-6—"This proposal pleased the whole group. They chose Stephen, a man full of faith and of the Holy Spirit; also Philip, Procorus, Nicanor, Timon, Parmenas, and Nicolas from Antioch, a convert to Judaism. They presented these men to the apostles, who prayed and laid their hands on them."

- Acts 4:23-24—"On their release, Peter and John went back to their own people and reported all that the chief priests and elders had said to them."

- Acts 4:31—"After they prayed, the place where they were meeting was shaken. And they were all filled with the Holy Spirit and spoke the word of God boldly."

- Acts 11:24—"He was a good man, full of the Holy Spirit and faith, and a great number of people were brought to the Lord."

- Acts 13:9-11—"Then Saul, who was also called Paul, filled with the Holy Spirit, looked straight at Elymas and said, 'You are a child of the Devil and an enemy of everything that is right! You are full of all kinds of deceit and trickery. Will you never stop perverting the right ways of the Lord? Now the hand of the

Lord is against you. You are going to be blind, and for a time you will be unable to see the light of the sun.'"

It seems to mean that we, today, can also be filled with the Holy Spirit on occasion and receive the boldness and power at that time. Are you taking advantage of this when you have that meeting at work, when you are called on to serve and lead in the church, or when your friend is struggling in life and he or she comes to you? If you fear the times you are called on to lead or share, you just might be trying to do things yourself. Next time, try asking to be filled with the Spirit and step out in faith confidently for God to accomplish what He wants to accomplish.

Helps with Our Weaknesses and Intercedes for Us

Because we no longer have to fear our salvation with our heart right before God when we are struggling, the Holy Spirit is there to help us, not condemn us, according to Romans 8:26-27: "In the same way, the Spirit helps us in our weakness. We do not know what we ought to pray for, but the Spirit himself intercedes for us with groans that words cannot express. And he who searches our hearts knows the mind of the Spirit, because the Spirit intercedes for the saints in accordance with God's will." Do you understand this says He helps us in our weaknesses? He is not there to kick us when we are down, but to help us up when we fall. God's Spirit is there to help us! What an encouraging thought when we make poor choices, and we are calling out for help.

The Spirit of God not only helps us, but He also intercedes on our behalf with God. Making intercession has to do with speaking on our behalf to better express the things we find difficult. Have you ever prayed, and as you prayed, you just sat there because you did not know what to say or how to say it? I see the Holy Spirit as the translator of my heart.

This is the reason the condition of our hearts matter. Have you ever heard the phrase, "Your heart does not lie?" I believe this phrase is only true in this context.

Back in 1998, I went on a trip to Romania to consider the possibility of planting churches there. I had an opportunity to preach a few times at the small church already established in one of the cities there. Because the people spoke Romanian and I spoke English, I had to preach through the use of a translator. What an experience! This was a first for me. It was like having a few seconds after every sentence to form my next thought. They told me my lesson would be twice as long with a translator, but the people would feel short-changed if I shortened the sermon. That was a sweet song to my ears. For when I preach, I usually lose all concept of time because my heart is full of so much from the Lord. I knew this was a special place if they wanted to hear God's Word and time was not an issue. Going long in Romania would not be the difficult part. Like the apostle Paul in Acts 20, I could take them all the way to midnight if they allowed it. The difficult part would be waiting for my interpreter to finish because I have a tendency to get in a zone—also known as allowing the Spirit to speak.

After being in Romania for one day, I started to preach. As I spoke, the interpreter translated everything I was saying. My preaching sentence was five words, but the interpreter said ten words. It took a great interpreter to correctly translate what I was saying in terms the congregation could understand. It would be someone who knew the heart of the message I spoke. You have to trust your interpreter in these situations to relay the true message of Christ. Well, after the lesson, people responded, and some new people were ready to study more about the good news of Jesus. The interpreter must have done well. In a similar way, the Holy Spirit already knows what our heart wants to say. He just says it with tones and words that are appropriate to the Almighty. He is the ultimate interpreter because He not only interprets what I say, but He also speaks when I cannot find the words.

Overcoming Sin

The Holy Spirit also helps us in overcoming sin, according to Galatians 5:16-17: "So I say, live by the Spirit, and you will not gratify the desires of the sinful nature. For the sinful nature desires what is contrary to the Spirit and the Spirit what is contrary to the sinful nature. They are in conflict with each other, so that you do not do what you want." Just in living by the direction and leadership of the Spirit, we will sin less. Also, the more submissive we are to the Holy Spirit, the less we will sin. If we ever get to the point where we are completely submissive to the Spirit, we will not sin. This is the place Jesus was at when He was on the earth, and this should be the goal for all Christians. The abundant life Jesus told us we can have on earth depends on our submission to the Spirit. John 10:10 says, "The thief comes only to steal and kill and destroy; I have come that they may have life, and have it to the full." The less we sin, the fewer the consequences. The fewer consequences we have, the better our lives.

Satan deceives us into thinking abundant life is in sin. He tells us that Christianity is about following rules and laws that keep us from having fun. As we grow in our maturity in Christ, we have the wisdom to see that sin is not great. We see that doing it God's way is so much better. Just ask the Christian teenage girl who had an abortion because of sexual immorality and could not face her dad, who was an elder of the church. Ask the man who lost everything but his money when he won the lotto and was driven by greed. Ask the teenage driver who was street racing over 100 mph and crashed into the back of a car, realizing the person he killed in the car ahead of him was his own mother. Ask the young man at the hospital if the party was fun after he got his stomach pumped due to alcohol poisoning. These examples are all true. The answers will all come back the same. Sin was not fun and, if they had it to do all over again, they would do it differently.

We must learn to believe sin is evil and wrong. If our beliefs and knowledge do not come from listening to God's Spirit and God's Word, then we will be continually justifying and rationalizing that how we live is right. The problem with this is we have received our reward in full, here and now. You have the power to overcome any and all of the sins in your life when you are ready to be controlled by God's Spirit. Quit fighting traditions, denominations, and even your own will. Fully submit to live every day and make every decision within the parameters of God's will and according to His Word. Maybe this is why most do not ever seem to overcome sin. They rely on their work to change instead of doing the work of the Holy Spirit.

Live in Unity

We have misunderstood the idea of unity for years. The unity the first century church had, according to Acts 4:32-33, was a unity of heart and mind. Somehow, we today think it is up to us to make unity and fellowship. But once again, we have listened to men and neglected the Word of God. Our responsibility is to preserve the unity, according to Ephesians 4:3: "Make every effort to keep the unity of the Spirit through the bond of peace." For this Scripture, the New American Standard Version says, "to preserve the unity." Where do we get the right to break fellowship with a church down the street unless God has already broken fellowship? Unless it is clear to us that God has not given salvation to those people by His Word, we are to preserve unity in the bond of peace. We are to promote peace even if we differ on some things or even if we have different methods of worshipping God. Whatever happened to preserving the unity? The Spirit enables us to live in unity when we are under His influence. It makes you wonder about the number of Spirit-led churches that exist. We must be about preserving unity instead of trying to break unity at every turn with those who follow Jesus, even if they do things a little differently than we do.

Let us consider the church at Corinth. If this church was down the street from your church today, you would have already written them off as lost. These Corinthians were getting drunk at their gatherings; they were having sexual relations with family members; wives were not being submissive; their meetings together each week were out of control; and they were divided over who they were following. Yet, Paul still addressed them as the church and saints in Corinth, according to 1 Corinthians 1:2: "To the church of God in Corinth, to those sanctified in Christ Jesus and called to be holy, together with all those everywhere who call on the name of our Lord Jesus Christ —their Lord and ours."

Did you notice they were also called the sanctified or the set apart? We do not even want to talk about this because we do not have any answers except that we might be too harsh. We have divided over a lot less than this. We have separated ourselves from other Christians on the basis of steeples on church buildings, kitchens in church buildings, holiday practices, traditional or contemporary worship, a cappella or instrumental worship, songbooks or projectors, and so many other unreasonable things I do not have enough room in this book to list them.

If disunity from one church to another were not wrong enough, many are dis-unified within their own churches. I have learned this firsthand serving as a minister for almost fifteen years. I must admit there were times when Satan was trying to divide me from the Lord's church. Because of perceptions, assumptions, and gossip, walls were built up by others against me. I would like to say I responded perfectly at every turn and against every accusation, but it was really difficult when falsehood prevailed and emotions were high.

I had an opportunity to step away from the situation and just read the gospels of Jesus, and I learned some things about how to respond to accusers. There were some obvious sins which needed to be confronted in a few people who had gotten out of control. Some of these sins included gossip, outbursts of anger, and bitterness. In spite of all that, I needed to do everything I could to preserve the unity. No matter what had been said and what had been done, these were my brothers and sisters in Christ. This was the family God had blessed me with, and making the right choices was something I could only control for myself. I assure you, it was only by God's Spirit I could do this. My desire to expose their sins would destroy the people involved because I was the last person who should confront them about what they had done to contribute to the conflict.

After reading the gospels, I realized Jesus humbled Himself at every step of the way. Humility is not about getting walked on, but stems from a spirit of love. God led me to do my best to make things right with these people. I went to the entire family and apologized for anything I had done to upset them, and for anything I had done out of pride or defense. I asked that they forgive me for anything I had done to bring heartache to them or their family.

When you know others are guilty, it is hard to put them above your own feelings. This family left the church, and it broke my heart, because disunity displeases God. It was obvious that bitterness consumed them toward many in the church, including bitterness toward me, but I knew I had done everything I could to preserve the unity. It just isn't right that many people today who have a problem with someone else in the church just pick up to go to another church down the street. We are unified with them, too, and if you are holding on to bitterness or malice, you should be called to deal with that, no matter which church you attend. It is far too easy today to run from conflict in an ungodly manner. It is easy in the church today to run away and bring all the baggage to another part of the body and, because of this, the whole body is weakened and becomes unhealthy.

I believe Ephesians 4 explains to us the lines of fellowship. The more you understand the one body, one hope, one faith, one baptism, one Lord, and one God and Father, the more you will get to the heart of fellowship. There are some things from God's Word that do matter eternally, but a kitchen in a church is not one of those things.

I challenge you to study the meaning of fellowship from the Scriptures. The point is that God makes unity, it's not up to us to break it. There are some things God makes clear from the Scriptures so we can be confident when it comes to fellowship. If a person does not believe Jesus is God and that He is the only way to the Father, then this person is not my brother or sister in Christ. John 14:6 says, "Jesus answered, 'I am the way and the truth and the life. No one comes to the Father except through me.'" Acts 4:10-12 states,

> Then know this, you and all the people of Israel: It is by the name of Jesus Christ of Nazareth, whom you cruci-fied but whom God raised from the dead, that this man stands before you healed. He is "the stone you builders rejected, which has become the capstone." Salvation is found in no one else, for there is no other name under heaven given to men by which we must be saved.

This is why we need to stand strong against other religions in which people deny the deity of Christ. Those people are not saved unless God compromises His Word, which is impossible for God to do. Do not count on it!

I see clearly from the New Testament and the teachings of Jesus that each sinful person must choose to surrender his or her life to Christ. We are saved by grace through faith according to Ephesians 2:8-9: "For it is by grace you have been saved, through faith —and this not from your-selves, it is the gift of God—not by works, so that no one can boast."

Fellowship also consists of a person having a relationship with God. They must know Him and be known by Him. Second Thessalonians 1:6-10 says:

> God is just. He will pay back trouble to those who trouble you and give relief to you who are troubled, and to us as well. This will happen when the Lord Jesus is revealed from heaven in blazing fire with his powerful angels. He will punish those who do not know God and do not obey the gospel of our Lord Jesus. They will be punished with everlasting destruction and shut out from the presence of the Lord and from the majesty of his power.

None of the three things mentioned—Jesus as God, surrendering your life, or a relationship with God—can save us in and of themselves. The demons believe Jesus is God. That never saved them. So many have claimed to have a relationship with God, or some call Him "Allah," but that never saved them. Many claim to have a relationship with God, but a true relationship can only come through the blood of Christ. We come in contact with that blood because of faith, and we act on that faith as we are baptized (immersed) into Christ.

God is the judge and He has determined unity, and I can know this from His Word. Before we set out, ready to judge others where we do not have authority, let us judge ourselves and allow the Word of God to judge our hearts. The authority we have does not come from a person or a church, but our authority comes from God's Word. If we are living in a thriving relationship with God through His Spirit, we will be more about love than condemnation, anyway. We will be more about teaching than breaking fellowship. We will be more about listening than arrogantly thinking we have all the answers. If you want the grace that abounds through His Spirit, then humble yourself because God opposes the proud but gives grace to the humble.

Enables Us to Bear Fruit

The fruit of the Spirit is spoken of in Galatians 5:22-23, where it says, "But the fruit of the Spirit is love, joy, peace, patience, kindness, goodness, faithfulness, gentleness and self-control. Against such things there is no law." First of all, the images used to picture the fruit of the Spirit are not a good representation of what God meant. The fruit of the Spirit is not different fruits, but one fruit with many parts. For example, an apple has many different parts, including the skin, core, seeds, stem, etc. The fruit of love is a part of the fruit of faithfulness, and the fruit of peace is a part of the fruit of joy. We could even say that love is the core.

The fruit of the Spirit is produced by the Word of the Spirit. The Spirit is either producing this fruit in our lives, or He is not. God is not asking us to go out and get this fruit, but be planted and rooted in God, and then the fruit will be produced. He is asking us to receive the Holy Spirit and allow Him to bear fruit in us.

Fruit carries with it the idea of growth, so it takes time for fruit to grow into full blossom. If we live by the Spirit, our lives will continue to produce this fruit. As we continue in producing fruit, we will reap the harvest of having the fruit. A self-controlled life is full of joy and love, having patience with ourselves and others. It almost seems like heaven, does it not?

On the other hand, people can appear to have this fruit even though they do not have the Spirit of God. The fruit is self-produced instead of overflowing out of them from their submission to the Spirit of God. People can have the characteristics of fruit without the Holy Spirit, but it is self-produced and usually based on circumstances and emotions. In other words, this would be a situation where a person desires to do something, or it is expected of them. If this is the case, this is not the Spirit bearing or producing fruit.

If we are trying to have the fruit of the Spirit, we are not being led. This is a problem with Christians today. They are focusing so hard on trying to love, have joy, and be patient that if they were only rooted and planted in God alone, they would not have to try so hard. These things would just happen. Christians get so down on themselves when the fruit of Spirit is not produced. They begin thinking of ways they can add more self-control to their lives or have more kindness in their families, but they are going about it the wrong way. Learn to love God more than anything. Learn to love His Word as David did in Psalm 119:47-48: "For I delight in your commands because I love them. I lift up my hands to your commands, which I love, and I meditate on your decrees." Over and over in that chapter, David says how much he loves God's law and commands. What did he know that we do not? He learned how right God's Word is as he held his son, born because of his adultery with a married woman, to only have God take his son away.

The Holy Spirit enables us to bear fruit when we are living in the Spirit. When we are living by the Spirit and this fruit is produced, we will not have to try to obtain these qualities. These qualities will just bubble out of our life in the Spirit.

The fruit does not determine whether you have the Spirit, but whether you are living by the Spirit. It would be wrong to assume that someone does not have the Spirit of God when these qualities are not visible, just as it would be wrong to assume someone has the Spirit because a few of these qualities are visible. New Christians are just beginning to learn how to allow the Spirit to lead them. As a new Christian is planted and rooted in God, the fruit will begin to grow and become more visible. This is called discipleship, and it is why we are called by Jesus to make disciples and not just have people express their faith.

Those people who have been Christians for years should have been maturing and, by now, the fruit should be visible. Hebrews 5:11-14 says:

> We have much to say about this, but it is hard to explain because you are slow to learn. In fact, though by this time you ought to be teachers, you need someone to teach you the elementary truths of God's word all over again. You need milk, not solid food! Anyone who lives on milk, being still an infant, is not acquainted with the teaching about righteousness. But solid food is for the mature, who by constant use have trained themselves to distinguish good from evil.

Because so many Christians have not been living by the Spirit, this fruit is not being produced. Therefore, their homes, workplace, streets, and even churches are not Spirit-led. We ought to be training new Christians to learn how to be led by the Spirit instead of learning how to have peace. The peace the Spirit gives us surpasses all comprehension, as seen from Philippians 4:7, and therefore it cannot be learned. If someone claims to be able to explain the peace of God, then they do not have the peace of the Spirit, because that peace is indescribable. We are trying to be submissive to our desires while adding in some peace at times. The Holy Spirit enables us to bear fruit if we will only submit completely to Him. There is wisdom in God telling us to pray at all times in the Spirit. Do not expect to have this fruit overflowing in our lives if we are not living every day connected to His Spirit.

Concluding Thoughts on the Holy Spirit

By no means do I think the only way the Holy Spirit works is by what has been mentioned. By having God live inside of us, God can warn us of things, teach us things, and even help us discern things, because of the power of the Holy Spirit. Remember, miracles and supernatural things still happen today, but the sign gifts, which were given by the apostles in the first century, were for a purpose during the time the New Testament was being written, and the beginning of the church.

If Satan can tell people things about what others have said, is it not possible that Jesus can do the same through His Spirit? Is it unreasonable to think God could not help us discern the truth when people are speaking to us, if He so desired? I believe there are times when faith is needed and given by the Spirit. I believe there are miracles still happening all over the world.

The conclusion is that God has more power than Satan, and Christians have more power through the Spirit than evildoers have with the evil spirits. The message through this chapter has been constant. Fully submit to God and His will daily, allow the Holy Spirit to be free to do and say what He so desires, and learn to listen and live by the Spirit. Then, and only then, will you unleash the power inside of you that raised Jesus from the grave. Ephesians 1:18-21 says:

> I pray also that the eyes of your heart may be enlightened in order that you may know the hope to which he has called you, the riches of his glorious inheritance in the saints, and his incomparably great power for us who believe. That power is like the working of his mighty strength, which he exerted in Christ when he raised him from the dead and seated him at his right hand in the heavenly realms, far above all rule and authority, power

and dominion, and every title that can be given, not only
in the present age but also in the one to come.

His great power of raising Jesus from the dead is for us who believe. May
you, in Christ, receive this power which, in turn, will change your existence and the existence of others.

CHAPTER 6 WORKSHEET

What comfort does God bring when you realize these truths about the Holy Spirit?

_____

_____

_____

What do you need the most right now in your life from the Holy Spirit?

_____

_____

_____

What could be quenching the Holy Spirit in your life?

_____

_____

_____

How do you allow the Holy Spirit to be free in your life?

_____

_____

_____

What does a Spirit filled, fruit bearing Christian look like?

_____

_____

_____

The Shadow of Purpose

*For while we are in this tent, we groan and are burdened, because we do not
wish to be unclothed but to be clothed with our heavenly dwelling, so that what is
mortal may be swallowed up by life. Now it is God who has made us for this very
purpose and has given us the Spirit as a deposit, guaranteeing what is to come.*
—2 Corinthians 5:4-5

If Satan can only get us to forget why we are on this earth, he will have
already won many battles. As I look at my own past, because I have
dealt with teenagers in youth ministry, I see the real depth of deception.
I counsel continually about relationships between guys and girls. I counsel about colleges and future plans. I counsel about money and how to
handle it. All these things are great, but was this why we were created?

In 2017, I was diagnosed with a brain tumor. I had never spent one
day in a hospital and I had never gone to an emergency room unless
I was there to see and pray with someone else. After I wrote my first
book in 2007, I was aware Satan would be upset. My books expose the
truth of Satan and the ways he deceives. I asked my wife if we wanted to
publish this book because I knew Satan might retaliate, and my whole
family needed to be on board and ready. I began rapidly losing hearing
and having numbness in my face. The headaches I had were different
and they got worse. I finally got a MRI at the hospital which confirmed

a tumor. Based on the kind and size of the tumor, the doctor said it had been growing for 10 to 12 years. It had been 10 years since I published my first book.

As I was preparing to go down this long and hard road, I discussed finances and insurance with my wife as I always did, just in case something were to happen. You never want to think about those things, but the reality of experiencing Satan's attacks was imminent, and you never know how that will play out. The fatality rate of the surgery was 1 in 200, but I still wanted to prepare for going to be with the Lord. I will discuss in the chapter entitled "The Shadow of Suffering" all the questions in suffering that even my boys experienced.

Before the surgery, I wanted my family to know I loved my marriage, my family, and my life. I wanted them to know God had blessed me with a great wife and partner, healthy and adorable children, an awesome job, a financially comfortable life, and so many other things. I wanted them to be clear that those blessings were not why I was created. I was not created to marry, have children, work a good job, and be comfortable financially, but I was ultimately created to be with God for all eternity. All those other things are good, but that is not why I was created. I told Teresa, my wife, if I were to die through this, my reason for existence would be fulfilled. My only request was that she and my boys would also fulfill their purpose and join me in heaven one day.

As surgery time came and God had not removed the tumor, I wrote each of my boys and my wife a letter to read while I was in surgery. The surgery was supposed to be 5 to 6 hours, but went on for over 10 hours. In my recovery, I dealt with some very difficult things as you can imagine. I dealt with demonic activity as I took pain killers (so I stopped taking them after 2 days), facial paralysis (which came back to 90% normal after 6 months), loss of hearing in one ear, and so much more that comes from a surgery of this kind. I made a joke and told my family that if I wake up from surgery and am still on the earth, I will say, "Ah man, I am still here?" My eternal purpose will have to wait. God has use for me here a little longer.

Is it not amazing how many Christians today live their lives as if this world is why they were made? Can this be part of the deception of Satan to keep us from staying focused on Christ? How many of us have fallen into that trap? How many ministers fall into that trap as they teach their congregations that material blessings and success will come to those who are faithful? Many in America are hearing that message and filling stadiums, but the poverty-stricken around the world have experienced it to be false teaching.

I believe many American Christians are caught up in this world because many of their spiritual leaders are, as well. We have rationalized Jesus's words about simplicity for long enough. With greedy hearts we have accumulated more and more, built bigger and bigger barns (houses), and are justified because our ministers live the same way. I confess that I have needed to make serious changes in my life in this area. I was raised in America, too, and have seen and heard ministers justify their lifestyles. I became what I had learned. I fell into the trap of wanting to look rich—from the gold watch to the nice sports car.

Now I am learning from Christ and not the example of man. He has a whole different way, and it begins with understanding our purpose. I challenge you to read the gospels and learn about what is most important in this life. The Holy Spirit made some radical changes in my heart, and now God is causing my appearance to mirror the treasure in my heart. I would rather give more than receive more. I would rather have what I need and give to others the extra I have. I would rather support missions instead of supporting my greed. God forgive us if we have put our eyes on things of this world and not on Him. I refuse to be a Christian where people see an example of rationalized greed and materialism, but want to set an example of storing up treasures in heaven by investing in people.

What I will tell you now, I tell you because I want you to know the faithfulness of God if we strive to live completely for Him and His purpose.

Not long ago, I was challenged by the Scriptures many of us have heard or read before in Matthew 25:31-46:

> When the Son of Man comes in his glory, and all the angels with Him, He will sit on His throne in heavenly glory. All the nations will be gathered before Him, and He will separate the people one from another as a shepherd separates the sheep from the goats. He will put the sheep on His right and the goats on His left. Then the King will say to those on His right, "Come, you who are blessed by my Father; take your inheritance, the kingdom prepared for you since the creation of the world. For I was hungry and you gave me something to eat, I was thirsty and you gave me something to drink, I was a stranger and you invited me in, I needed clothes and you clothed me, I was sick and you looked after me, I was in prison and you came to visit me." Then the righteous will answer Him, "Lord, when did we see you hungry and feed you, or thirsty and give you something to drink? When did we see you a stranger and invite you in or needing clothes and clothe you? When did we see you sick or in prison and go to visit you?"
>
> The King will reply, "I tell you the truth, whatever you did for one of the least of these brothers of mine, you did for me." Then He will say to those on His left, "Depart from me, you who are cursed, into the eternal fire prepared for the Devil and his angels. For I was hungry and

you gave me nothing to eat, I was thirsty and you gave me nothing to drink, I was a stranger and you did not invite me in, I needed clothes and you did not clothe me, I was sick and in prison and you did not look after me." They also will answer, "Lord, when did we see you hungry or thirsty or a stranger or needing clothes or sick or in prison, and did not help you?" He will reply, "I tell you the truth, whatever you did not do for one of the least of these, you did not do for me." Then they will go away to eternal punishment, but the righteous to eternal life.

I quoted this entire passage because I wanted you to see it and examine it. If you skipped it or skimmed it, go read it again. Jesus says when He returns, He is going to divide up the people based on these things. If He is telling us this in advance, then I better take note of what He is saying. He is giving me a heads-up.

So, I began to evaluate myself on each of these. Am I feeding the hungry, giving drink to the thirsty, clothing the naked, visiting the sick or those in prison, and inviting in strangers? The truthful answers were sad. Okay, in my life, I have given some food and clothes. I have visited a few sick, but Jesus is going to ask me this when He returns, and He is not looking for a couple of deeds over forty-two years of my life. I realized I am not ready and I can do more.

With this new conviction, I began to pray on how God would help me do this. There are millions of people around the world that do not have clean drinking water; what am I doing? Do I trust God enough to invite a stranger in my home in today's climate of crime? Am I here on this earth to live to one hundred years old, or to be salt and light to everyone?

I have come to the conclusions that we are so rich, we are wasteful. While millions are dying because of the lack of clean water, we are taking five-gallon jugs of water and Gatorade and pouring it on the heads of coaches when we celebrate a big game. With many in the world dying of hunger every day, we are spending our money on feeding our pets. We are helping our animals eat well while watching men, women, and children of our own humanity die of starvation. Just because we do not see people dying next to us does not mean we ought to turn our heads and believe it does not happen.

The church needs to wake up and get focused on what God is calling us to do. Do not get me wrong, because if you have a pet, you are probably mad at me right now. I have a pet also. I am not saying we need to get rid of our pets, but what I am saying is we are very rich, and Jesus has told us very clearly what is important. Each person is important to God, and it breaks His heart when Christians become so self-focused that they neglect their purpose on this earth and their purpose for eternity.

I mentioned earlier that I began praying about how God could use me. I purposefully began praying about how I could provide clean water to people around the world. I cannot solve this problem, but I can do my part. The very day I began to pray for God to show me an opportunity to give in this way, across my desk came a Christian camp I was taking my youth to that year, where the special contribution would go to build a well, providing drinking water to a remote village.

Do you think God wants us to be involved in things like this? Once I decided I wanted God to lead me in this, it happened immediately. I was so excited that we purposefully put away money for this contribution to help those dying of dehydration, along with Christians who are thirsty. These opportunities are all over the world, and God is just waiting for us to wake up, take our minds off ourselves, and get to work.

Why do I need twenty blankets in my home when people are sleeping in the cold? Why do I need things I never use when the money could be used to help Christians and other people around the world? I realized we did not need six bikes when we are a family of four. We packed up our car on numerous occasions and sold our things, where the entire amount of money was given to the opportunities God provided.

I don't usually pawn items in the pawn shop, but I do go to look for good deals. That day, I needed money for something God was calling me to do. The clerk asked me if I really needed the money. I told him more than he knows. He asked me if I wanted to pawn my gold necklace since the value of gold was at an all-time high. I took it off and asked him to appraise it. He offered me $200 for it and, without any hesitation, I sold it. How could I have a gold necklace when missionaries needed my support? That $200 was given to missionaries in Kazakhstan.

Please understand I am not writing this to boast about myself but to boast about the Lord. If anything, I am ashamed it took me thirty-five years to get focused on what is really important. But I praise God for His faithfulness and His Spirit-led direction from His Word. I am reminded of humbling verses in Luke 17:7-10:

> Suppose one of you had a servant plowing or looking after the sheep. Would he say to the servant when he comes in from the field, "Come along now and sit down to eat"? Would he not rather say, "Prepare my supper, get yourself ready and wait on me while I eat and drink; after that you may eat and drink"? Would he thank the servant because he did what he was told to do? So you also, when you have done everything you were told to do, should say, "We are unworthy servants; we have only done our duty."

Sometimes we look at those who are servants of Jesus Christ feeding the hungry, teaching in the prisons, or even praying over the sick; and we say what great faith they have. Should we not rather look to them and know they are just doing what they were created to do on this earth? I am only allowing God to make me into the man He created me to be. He is the potter and, therefore, He deserves the praise for what He creates.

A good way to determine if the world has its claws in you is to ask yourself whether or not you would want to die today. Are there too many reasons you would plead with God for allowing you to live longer rather than going today to be with Him? My thought to the question in the past would have been, well, what about my wife who needs her husband, or what about my twin boys who need their dad? After having a brain tumor in 2017, my thoughts of death were closer than ever. Today, I am working on true faith in God, knowing if God took me home to be with Him, He would take care of my wife and my boys because He loves them even more than I do, which must be a lot of love. I do not desire disease, heartache, or poverty for me or anyone, but I am not afraid of any of them. If I must learn what it means to be content in riches and in poverty, good health and poor health, then so be it. My faith in God will never waver based on how much I have or how healthy I am.

There was a man in the church I looked up to in so many ways who ended most every prayer with the statement, "We look forward to being with you for eternity." It encourages me to know his desire is to go be with God, and sooner is better. His son died of a brain tumor leaving a wife and children. I know a father losing his son cannot be easy. No father expects to bury his child. This church leader was a great example of peace through it all. He might have been slightly envious, of course, in a good way if I can say it like that, because his son reached the fulfillment of life before his father. The only way a person can live like this and believe in the midst of a tragedy is if one knows one's eternal purpose. Can we say every day this prayer of looking forward to being with God for eternity, being reminded that we were not created for this world? Our attitude should be like the Apostle Paul in Philippians 1:21-24:

> For to me, to live is Christ and to die is gain. If I am to go
> on living in the body, this will mean fruitful labor for me.
> Yet what shall I choose? I do not know! I am torn between
> the two: I desire to depart and be with Christ, which is
> better by far; but it is more necessary for you that I re-
> main in the body.

My mind goes to the story of Lot and his family. The story is about how God would save Sodom and Gomorrah if there were just ten righteous people. Abraham, Lot's cousin, could not even find ten righteous people. So, because of God's justice, He was going to rain fire and brimstone from heaven to destroy the cities. A few angels came to Lot, and the Scriptures say they grasped them out of the city because of God's mercy on them. Lot and his family were told by God not to look back. As they were walking from the city, Lot's wife looked back and was turned into a pillar of salt. To this day, there is a salt mountain outside of the ancient city of Sodom. When you study the term *looking back,* you will see that it means Lot's wife looked intently or gave careful consideration for those people. She was not separated from the influence of the worldly people in that city. The world had sunk its claws deep into her, pulling her down even to death.

Satan works at trying to get the world to pull us close to it without us even knowing. The claws sink in, and we dress like the world, talk like the world, mark our bodies like the world, and even act as much like the world without people thinking we are worldly. We do not fool unbelievers. They see us just as worldly as they are, and sometimes unbelievers have better morals and higher standards than some professed Christians.

Why battle these worldly things? What words we are "allowed" to say should not even be a topic to discuss if we know we are separate from the world. Whatever happened to following 2 Corinthians 6:14-18, where it says:

> Do not be yoked together with unbelievers. For what do righteousness and wickedness have in common? Or what fellowship can light have with darkness? What harmony is there between Christ and Belial? What does a believer have in common with an unbeliever? What agreement is there between the temple of God and idols? For we are the temple of the living God. As God has said: "I will live with them and walk among them, and I will be their God, and they will be my people. Therefore come out from them and be separate," says the Lord. "Touch no unclean thing, and I will receive you. I will be a Father to you, and you will be my sons and daughters," says the Lord Almighty.

Our God's name is holy, and He has called us to be holy. Holiness does not happen by accident, and it is something you cannot fake for long. Many Christians today have blended so well with the world that it is hard to pick them out in a crowd, in your workplace, or in your schools. It is no wonder God did so much keeping outside influence away from His chosen people. Yet His people intermarried and followed after those of the world. Samson is a great example of the pain in marriage when you try to do things your own way based on how you feel. Samson had two separate marriages at different times with women who were Philistines (enemies of the people of God) and ended up unhappy, blind, and weak because of their influence and deceptions. There is more discussed about the holiness of God in the Scriptures than any other attribute. We better take notice and realize our God is holy and His people must also be holy.

In my conversations with teenagers, I remind them that having active faith and a relationship with God, as a Christian, is important. If God blesses their physical lives with a spouse, children, health, education, and financial success, then it is not to distract them from the eternal reason they were created. Enjoy these things, because they are gifts from God. Paul said it well in Philippians 3:7-11:

> But whatever was to my profit I now consider loss for the sake of Christ. What is more, I consider everything a loss compared to the surpassing greatness of knowing Christ Jesus my Lord, for whose sake I have lost all things. I consider them rubbish, that I may gain Christ and be found in him, not having a righteousness of my own that comes from the law, but that which is through faith in Christ— the righteousness that comes from God and is by faith. I want to know Christ and the power of His resurrection and the fellowship of sharing in His sufferings, becoming like Him in his death, and so, somehow, to attain to the resurrection from the dead.

Paul counted all the things he could boast about as a loss or rubbish compared to gaining and knowing Christ. Knowing Christ is far more important than any other pursuit right now.

Parents, here is a side note for you. Remember that your child's education, financial success, worldly status, acceptance by their peers, and so on mean nothing to their eternity. Raise them to love Christ and to do everything, whether word or deed, for Him. Colossians 3:17 says, "And whatever you do, whether in word or deed, do it all in the name of the Lord Jesus, giving thanks to God the Father through him." If they get numerous degrees and are financially stable but do not have Christ, the mission and purpose was unaccomplished. Teach them how to discipline themselves to grow in Christ through study, prayer, meditation, fasting, being with the church, serving, and giving.

Start at a young age. As soon as our boys learned to read, they woke up every morning and read a children's Bible story. Now they read directly from the Bible each day. As soon as they learned to write, they began writing prayers to God in a journal each morning. Many may say this is crazy, but I see it as an essential training that affects their future and eternal purpose. I can tell them to do these things, but my children are going to do as I do. You have heard the phrase, "Do as I say, not as I do." Your children will grow up and do as you do. You must be intentional in raising your children in the Lord, because Satan is intentional about destroying them and their faith. My boys have accused me of studying and praying all the time. Thank God for what they see and know about their dad and His love for God. In this, I pray they do as I do.

There was an invitation at the end of a lesson I once heard and I also have used it in my years of ministry. The illustration starts out where the minister asks the members of the church where they see themselves ten years from now. Giving them some time to think about their answer, the minister will give his general thoughts for them as well as himself. Then he will ask them, where do you see yourselves twenty years from now? Again the minister gives them time to think. Then, he will ask them what about thirty years and so on, all the way to one hundred years. You can assume everyone, including the youngest there, will not be alive one hundred years from now. The illustration then continues by the minister telling them the only thing that will matter one hundred years from now is whether you had a true relationship and love for Christ. The minister will then conclude by asking them, "One hundred years from now, what decision will you have wished you made today that would have affected your eternity forever and ever?" This illustration gets you to think as well as understand that success, education, and even families are great on this earth, but these do not change the reasons we were all created.

We were created to love and have a relationship with the everlasting God for all eternity. That is what will matter when we are dead and gone from this earth.

If you can teach your children how to have a relationship with God, it might help them understand and live the purpose for which they were created. We talk about this all the time with our children. We talk about what we would think or what would happen if one of us died. I have asked questions like:

- Would you blame God if Dad died?

- Would you love God even if He did not stop a tragedy?

- Would you still follow God if you were the only one left in our family?

- Would you die for God if given the opportunity?

We even read and tell martyr stories about children who died for their faith throughout history. I do not know where God will lead us in this life, how much time I have left on the earth, or whether persecution will ever be experienced by Christians in America during our lifetime, but I do not want any of us to be unprepared. I do not want us to have such a hold on the world that we can't let go; and I also do not want us to be deceived about our purpose on this earth. To a Christian family and those who follow Jesus Christ wholeheartedly, death is not the end but eternity is what we have waited our whole life to enter into. So we must celebrate!

If you can live this relationship with God in front of your children and with your children, it will help them understand and live the purpose for which they were created. May we make the decision today to be with our Father for all eternity, thus fulfilling our purpose in this temporary world!

CHAPTER 7 WORKSHEET

What did you learn about God's ultimate purpose?

_____

_____

_____

What distractions do you have which tempt you away from God's purpose?

_____

_____

_____

How have you dealt with tragedy in your life thus far?

_____

_____

_____

How do you live in a temporary world but have an eternal mindset?

_____

_____

_____

How can God use you to bless others who are struggling with their purpose?

_____

_____

_____

The Shadow of Suffering

Consider it pure joy, my brothers, whenever you face trials of many kinds, because you know that the testing of your faith develops perseverance. Perseverance must finish its work so that you may be mature and complete, not lacking anything.
—James 1:2-4

Why does suffering happen to Christians if we have a God who loves us? What does the Bible teach about what God can allow Satan to do? Why does God allow divorce, terrorist strikes, betrayal, and so forth? If God can protect us, then why doesn't He always? Where is the love of God when children are killed or abused, when they are molested or kidnapped? Many people have blamed God and lost their faith and trust in God because bad things happen to them. What do you say to a person who questions God and asks why did God allow a loved one or a friend to die? If I have great faith and believe wholeheartedly God can heal, why does He not always heal? So many questions are asked, and many just say they do not have any answers. I believe we do have answers, but we must understand our purpose, why we were created, and the gift of choice.

In this chapter, we are going to answer some of the tough questions not many want to answer, but we are also going to take a deep look into what the Bible says about suffering. Many are told God always protects

His people, blesses His people, and will never allow harm to His people. These are deceptions and false teachings that can be very damaging, and cannot be supported by the Bible. Many teach prosperity and monetary success for God's people. If anything, the Bible says we are all going to suffer on this earth whether we are good or bad. We as Christians are called not just to believe but to suffer for the name of Jesus, to persevere in tribulations, and to not be surprised when suffering occurs but to be joyful in our trials and tribulations. Should we be teaching people the truth about Christianity? Christianity is about suffering and sacrifice for His Name's sake while we are on this earth. We do not hear this taught much, but if we did, maybe we would have less fallout in the church when the troubles do come. The Bible says even Jesus learned obedience through the things He suffered.

I believe many Christians who are taught a false sense of security are on rocky soil when it comes to Jesus's teachings and will get scorched when trouble comes. This is seen in the Parable of the Sower when Jesus explains the seed on the rocky soil in Mark 4:16-17: "Others, like seed sown on rocky places, hear the word and at once receive it with joy. But since they have no root, they last only a short time. When trouble or persecution comes because of the word, they quickly fall away." Too many are taught today that Christianity shields you from disease, poverty, and tragedy, which is just not true.

Suffering happens on earth because we live in an evil and fallen world where people make evil choices. God does protect, but He has an eternal purpose that may not include each of us living to one-hundred-twenty years old. His plan is more important than my life span, and if my heart's desire is to be with Him eternally, then I must trust Him since He is the one and only God. It takes a spiritually mature person to see it as a privilege to be considered worthy to suffer for Him. The apostles, after witnessing the resurrection and ascension of Jesus, were excited to suffer, as written in Acts 5:40-42:

His speech persuaded them. They called the apostles in and had them flogged. Then they ordered them not to speak in the name of Jesus, and let them go. The apostles left the Sanhedrin, rejoicing because they had been counted worthy of suffering disgrace for the Name.

Let me tell you how God opened our eyes years ago and allowed suffering to become personal to a teenager in our youth group named Ian. Ian was a young man in high school and had dreams of being a politician in the future. He was not a real big guy, standing about five feet ten and weighing about a hundred-forty pounds. I first met Ian a year or so before his accident when he was brought to church by a few girls in our youth group. He came to church, and we made a connection immediately. Ian began coming over to my apartment with some other high school teens from our youth group for video games, swimming, weight lifting, and, of course, dinner made by my wife, Teresa. He was very close to Teresa and me, and we wanted to see him come to Christ.

In his junior year of high school, Ian signed up to go on a spring break trip with Christians instead of his worldly friends. Our youth group juniors and seniors chose this trip to Clearwater Beach for their spring break to hang out, get a tan, and be with church friends, without the spring break temptations of Daytona Beach, Florida. I took care of all the hotel details, and we loaded up cars and took off on our three-hour trip to Clearwater. Ian was in the front seat next to me as we were traveling. This would be a great opportunity to talk to him about his faith. The subject of dying came up, and it hit me as I said while driving, "Imagine we were to get in a wreck right now, and our heads hit the windshield. I wonder if as our heads were hitting the windshield, our eyes would go from the physical car to a new dimension of eternity." As I continued driving down Interstate 4 between Orlando and Tampa, to make my point I took my hands off the wheel for a split second. Using my hands as the windshield in front of my face, I proceeded to act as if my face was going through my two hands and entering a whole new world. It was a great analogy, but probably driving was not the best time to use it.

I do not recommend this way of driving to my readers, but my point would later prove to be thought provoking. That same night, Ian came up to me and wanted to give his life to Christ and be baptized in the hotel pool. I never want fear to be the motivating factor in coming to Christ in faith or obeying Christ, so I talked with him a little while that night. We called Ian's parents, who were not real sure at the time about the decision of faith to follow Christ, but allowed us to take his confession and baptize him that night. We took pictures and, needless to say, it was a great spiritual start to our spring break trip. After we returned home from the trip, Ian's parents and younger sister started going to our church, as well. God continued to work powerfully in Ian and his family.

Go forward ten months. Ian had continued to grow in his faith, but as a senior in high school, temptation was at a peak in this young man's life. Every Wednesday night after our youth night, we would go to Borders bookstore down the street for coffee and to hang out with Christian friends. Usually we were there for forty-five minutes to an hour. This night appeared to be like none other, except this night would change Ian's life forever. This night Ian was taking home a younger guy in our youth group named Donny. Donny could not drive yet and wanted to come out with us, so Ian, being a caring and selfless guy, agreed to give Donny a ride home at nine o'clock after our fellowship. Ian had to get on a freeway to take Donny home. Less than a mile after he got on the toll road, Ian decided to stop and help a young man whose car was broken down on the side of the road. This was the kind of thoughtful young man Ian was. They pulled over on the dark road and got out to help the man in distress.

I was leaving Borders, and my wife had already arrived back at our apartment. As I walked out of Borders talking to the other kids, we saw flashing blue lights, and heard helicopters hovering in the sky not far from where we were. We realized from all the commotion that an accident had taken place on the toll road. Never imagining it involved two of our youth, I received a cell phone call from my wife. You can probably guess the news was the last thing I expected to hear. Ian had been hit by a car going nearly a hundred mph.

I jumped in my car and drove to the scene, not knowing what I would find. My stomach lodged in my throat and the feeling that this was some kind of terrible mistake weighed on my mind. As I arrived at the scene of the accident, I saw Donny, and he ran over to me crying. I jumped out of my car as the helicopter was taking flight with the body of Ian barely holding onto life. We waited at the scene for his parents, who were en route to the location. I asked Donny what had happened.

Trying to gather himself, he said in tears, "We stopped to help this man with car trouble, and we were walking by the back of Ian's car. This other guy was flying down the road, lost control of his car, and hit Ian. He then hit Ian's car, causing it to just graze my leg." Donny was crying even harder as he said, "I couldn't find Ian! The guy we had stopped to help and I started searching everywhere on the road, on the grass, and we still could not find him!"

I reassured Donny, saying to calm down a little, that everything would be all right. He showed me where they eventually found Ian, fifty to one hundred feet away and down the side of the dark embankment in the weeds. Donny said, "He was moaning and mangled in the ditch. Blood was all over his body and covering his face, and I could barely recognize him. He was so swollen from the impact of the car. I did not know what to do."

I asked Donny the question I was not sure I wanted answered. "Was Ian still alive and conscious when they left with him for the hospital?"

Donny answered, "I think I heard them say he was in shock, but I did talk to him when I first found him, and he was breathing then."

Just then, Ian's parents and sister showed up, and we looked at Ian's wrecked car, which was so crunched the entire hatchback and backseat were gone. I went to his parents and tried to be some source of comfort as they listened to Donny's explanation of what had happened.

You sure cannot be trained for situations like this. I had not stopped praying since I heard the news. I knew it would be a miracle if Ian survived, but it was not likely. From the look of the wreckage and knowing the impact on Ian's vehicle was the same impact Ian bore, it left major doubt about his survival. We all left the scene of the accident and drove to the hospital. My wife and some women from church met us there. We knew it would be a long night, which might have proven to be the worst of my life.

We arrived at the hospital and found Ian's family. I asked, "Have you heard any update?"

His mom answered, "They are preparing him for immediate surgery." And, trying to finish the sentence as a mom with faith, she said, "And the doctors have given Ian a five percent chance to live."

The doctor came out and said his parents could come see him while they were rushing him off to surgery. His mom could not bear to see him, and his dad asked them if I could come, since I was his minister.

The doctor said, "Yes, but you have to hurry!"

We took off down long hallways and up elevators. I never thought I would have to experience this in ministry. What do I do and what do I say? The elevator doors opened, and there was Ian, on his way to surgery, lying on a blood-soaked gurney. I could not imagine a person looking like that and still being alive. Apparently they had cleaned him up some, but his body still appeared to be twice his normal size because of the swelling. I did not know a body could swell that much.

The doctor said, "You have a few seconds as we go to the next floor for surgery."

Ian's dad began talking to him, and I began to beg God out loud in prayer for Ian's life and for the surgery. The doctors were not waiting for my prayer. As the elevator doors opened, they wheeled him out. My prayer was abruptly ended, and his father and I were left standing in the elevator, watching him go off to surgery, having only our faith to pull us through the next few hours.

We headed back to the waiting room with those terrible images in my head of my friend barely holding onto life. Ian's dad was strong while we sat, waited, and prayed. You did not need to tell any of us to pray, because we hadn't stopped for hours. There was not much to say, and what could you say? Ian's life was in the Almighty God's hands now. Would God spare his life? Only God knew at that time.

After many hours of surgery and worrying about whether or not Ian would live through it, the chaplain and one of the doctors came out to talk to the family. Because I had never been in this situation before, I did not know if this was a bad sign. Ian had made it through the surgery, but he was nowhere close to being out of the dark yet. Each hour he remained alive would give him a better chance for survival and recovery.

The next few days I spent most of my time at the hospital. As the news spread, our church took care of the food and miscellaneous needs for the family. If Ian survived, it would be a long and hard journey. The femurs in both of his legs and many other bones throughout his body had been broken.

For the following weeks, we had prayer sessions at my apartment for Ian. We packed our apartment with teens wanting to pray, study, and comfort each other. The unity our youth experienced during this time was spectacular. For weeks, there wasn't any bickering or cliques within the youth group. Because of our love for Ian and his family, we put our selfish needs and desires aside and focused on theirs. We functioned as a team, or should I say, God's team. We all encouraged, comforted, and answered the numerous questions asked by many. We learned what it meant to mourn and have God comfort us.

As time went by and Ian began to slowly recover, I helped the family take care of the insurance with the car, which was a total loss, of course. We all got talking about how Ian's parents found out the accident had occurred. Ian's mom told us she was called from Ian's cell phone the horrible night of the accident, but she didn't know who had called her. She figured it must have been a fireman on the scene, but it was a mystery because the call had come right after the accident. Ian's mom could hear Donny in the background calling for Ian, trying to find him, before anyone else had arrived on the scene. The person told Ian's mom, "Ian has been in an accident on the Greenway near Aloma Avenue in Oviedo, and don't worry, he is going to be all right." Could it have been the person they stopped to help? But how did he get Ian's cell phone, and how did he get Ian's home phone number?

Dealing with all the insurance of Ian's car, we learned his cell phone had been found untouched in the backseat, covered in wreckage and completely unreachable.

Who made that call, and who said he would be all right? God was in control of the entire situation from the very beginning. Ian has recovered and won a lawsuit to cover doctor bills and more. He will never play sports the way he once did, and he lost a lot, including the end of his senior year in high school, but he did graduate.

We are going to suffer in this life, and Satan is out to destroy us and our families. This story reminds me of how God knows all that is happening and reassures us He has never left us. God does not always prevent suffering, but He always will walk us through it if we keep our eyes on Him. This did not happen to Ian because of God's punishment or because of God leaving Him for a second; this happened because we live in a world where people make bad choices. The man whom Ian and Donny had stopped for ended up coming to the hospital and began seeking God as Ian recovered. Ian was able to share Christ with Him, and God was able to work His good once again through irresponsible and ungodly choices by people in the world. It is a given that both Ian and Donny's lives were changed forever.

Satan's power in Suffering

We discussed earlier in the book that we are on Satan's playing field and we are living behind enemy lines. Satan can do some terrible things on this earth if God allows. We learn a lot from the book of Job in the Old Testament about what Satan can do to followers of God on this earth. According to the book of Job, Satan tried to get God to harm Job, but God cannot be tempted by evil and so He put limitations on what Satan could do, only because God had trust in His servant, Job. In Job 1, God allowed Satan to do anything he wanted to Job, but Satan could not touch him. Let us take a look at that chapter and determine what Satan had the power to do.

> One day when Job's sons and daughters were feasting and drinking wine at the oldest brother's house, a messenger came to Job and said, "The oxen were plowing and the donkeys were grazing nearby, and the Sabeans attacked and carried them off. They put the servants to the sword, and I am the only one who has escaped to tell you!" While he was still speaking, another messenger came and said, "The fire of God fell from the sky and burned up the sheep and the servants, and I am the only one who has escaped to tell you!" While he was still speaking, another messenger came and said, "The Chaldeans formed three raiding parties and swept down on your camels and

carried them off. They put the servants to the sword, and I am the only one who has escaped to tell you!" While he was still speaking, yet another messenger came and said, "Your sons and daughters were feasting and drinking wine at the oldest brother's house, when suddenly a mighty wind swept in from the desert and struck the four corners of the house. It collapsed on them and they are dead, and I am the only one who has escaped to tell you!" —Job 1:13-19

From these verses, we learn Satan was allowed to kill Job's servants through a group of people, cause fire to fall from heaven and kill Job's sheep, which could have been for food, clothing, sacrifice, and wealth. And if all that was not bad enough, Satan caused a mighty wind, possibly tornadoes, to kill Job's children and destroy the house. Did you know Satan had the power to do all this? Job proved his faith to be genuine and sincere, as he did not curse God. The events of Job 2 appear to have been years later. Sometimes we read it as if it happened the next day, but that is not what it says. It actually starts out by saying, "On another day the angels came to present themselves before the Lord, and Satan also came with them to present himself before Him."

Let us now take a look at the next attack by Satan on Job.

Then the Lord said to Satan, "Have you considered my servant Job? There is no one on earth like him; he is blameless and upright, a man who fears God and shuns evil. And he still maintains his integrity, though you incited me against him to ruin him without any reason." "Skin for skin!" Satan replied. "A man will give all he has for his own life. But stretch out your hand and strike his flesh and bones, and he will surely curse you to your face." The Lord said to Satan, "Very well, then, he is in your hands; but you must spare his life." So Satan went out from the presence of the Lord and afflicted Job with painful sores from the soles of his feet to the top of his head. —Job 2:3-7

From this we learn God allowed Satan to do whatever he wanted to the body and health of Job, but God did not allow Satan to kill Job.

Satan had the power now to strike Job with a disease and illness. Why would God allow this to happen to such a faithful servant like Job? Was God ultimately responsible for what happened to Job, his family, his servants, and his wealth? This may come as a shock to you, but the answer is yes, God was responsible. God could have not allowed this to happen. If anything, it appears as if God suggested that Satan consider Job. Could God prove to Satan that a human who had never seen God, be more devout through love than Satan himself?

Do we serve a God who sets us up, or does God know so much more than we do? God is concerned about this life for us, but God is ultimately concerned for the souls of man as He looks to eternity. Once again, we were created to be with God for all eternity. God has always been concerned more for the soul than our welfare on earth. We saw the Father in Jesus Christ as He healed the paralytic, but first he would say your sins are forgiven. Forgiveness cleansed the soul, and physical healing was worthless without spiritual healing. Jesus first took care of the soul of man.

Since they could not get him to Jesus because of the crowd, they made an opening in the roof above Jesus and, after digging through it, lowered the mat the paralyzed man was lying on. When Jesus saw their faith, he said to the paralytic, "Son, your sins are forgiven." Now some teachers of the law were sitting there, thinking to themselves, "Why does this fellow talk like that? He's blaspheming! Who can forgive sins but God alone?" Immediately Jesus knew in his spirit that this was what they were thinking in their hearts, and he said to them, "Why are you thinking these things? Which is easier: to say to the paralytic, 'Your sins are forgiven,' or to say, 'Get up, take your mat and walk'? But that you may know that the Son of Man has authority on earth to forgive sins…" He said to the paralytic, "I tell you, get up, take your mat and go home." —Mark 2:4-11

If all Jesus was concerned about was physical healing, then what He did would only be temporary, but Jesus was concerned for the eternal. Forgiveness of sins improves the quality of life here on this earth, but secures eternity forever with God.

Why Does God Allow Suffering?

Why would God allow abuse, molestation, tragedy, and disease, especially in children? A lady named Sue came to my office one day and asked me some very tough questions. I was so thankful for the Holy Spirit and how He spoke through me that day. Sue had heard that I had been teaching about Job in my class. She began to tell me about her life and the sexual abuse that began at the age of five. She said in tears that it went on for many years before the relative moved away. As you can imagine, she had many questions about God. She had lived with this secret for many years and had always wondered why the God of love would not have stopped this. She would cry out each night, saying, "Please God, make this all stop and make him quit hurting me!"

She asked me, "Why did God not answer, and why did He not care?"

This woman had tried to have faith all her life and had battled this tragedy since childhood. What do I say? What could be said? It was then the words came to me from God by His Holy Spirit.

I replied, "God was with you all along and has even brought you to this day. He did not turn his head from what was done, and it broke His heart every time He witnessed the abuse. You are His daughter, and I would not want to be this man, as he must stand before God after violating God's daughter. God allowed this to happen in your life, and I believe He would have jumped in and stopped the abuse, calling fire down from heaven, if this world were all there is. But it is not! You were not created for this world, but you were created to be eternally with our God and our Creator. God knows what He has in store for us is so much better and we will never have to suffer in the ways we do now."

She said every lesson she had ever heard always said we do not know why bad things happen, and that never helped her faith. Overjoyed, she smiled and jumped up to give me a hug to thank me. I knew it had not been me, but God's love and encouragement to her. We later talked about the ways God can work out the good through wounded people. Sue has a calling to work with abused children. She is a strong woman, and she can't wait to be with her God. She mentioned how she pities this abuser and how she will not live her life as a victim but as an overcomer.

That is what the power of God can do in a person's life. I do not believe every question was answered for her that first day, but I do know our God hates evil and will punish those who do evil to His sons and daughters.

In this study, remember the worst Satan can do is to kill you. If I do not fear death but rather see death as an entrance into eternity with God, then I will celebrate the deaths of all those who love the Lord. If Satan took away my children, as he did with Job, it would not be easy, but I would not forget the Word of God in Isaiah 57:1-2, where it says,

"The righteous perish, and no one ponders it in his heart; devout men are taken away, and no one understands that the righteous are taken away to be spared from evil. Those who walk uprightly enter into peace; they find rest as they lie in death."

Satan can take everything physically away from me, including my own life, but he can never take my soul. My soul is bought by the Lord, and it is my choice who it is I follow. I want to live life always as God's son, no matter what happens to me or those to whom I am close.

How God Uses Suffering

I know God uses suffering to get people to look to Him. There is no doubt God is responsible for the suffering in the world. He didn't always cause it, but He has allowed it. Suffering brings many people to their knees, where they will call out to God for help. Let's face it, when things get beyond our control in life, we tend to look to a higher power. Therefore, God uses the suffering He inflicts or the suffering He allows in order to save our souls. Some may not like this truth about God, but where else are we to turn? Don't we know He loves us enough to do all He can do to keep us from an eternity in hell?

I saw this firsthand years ago when a young man in our youth group was diagnosed with a brain tumor. I learned a lot from this young man named John, who was sixteen years old at the time. He was not very involved in the youth group. He came to church for social reasons, and had the attitude that no one liked him or cared about him. I did not see that to be true, but it appeared to me as a minister that John came in with a negative attitude, and the attempts that were made to help him grow spiritually, fell on deaf ears.

When he was diagnosed with a deadly brain tumor, our youth group devoted themselves to praying for him. When the time came for his surgery and for him to travel up north to a specialist, we sent cards and stayed involved in his life. Let me relate what this young man experienced while there. God was fighting for John to take Him seriously. He wanted to show John that He was there every step of the way. John was scared before the surgery, knowing he could die or something could go very wrong. This was completely outside John's control; he knew it was up to God. The night before his surgery he struggled to sleep. His mind was racing with what could happen. He said he had the realization that he may not be saved if he died, and that thought scared him. Like many who had been in situations like this before John, he began telling God that his life would be different if God spared his life and brought him back to complete health. Even though John was pouring out his heart before God, he still needed confirmation that God was with him in the darkest hour of his life. He wanted to go into the surgery with absolute peace.

As John was getting wheeled to the prep room, he came across a painting he believed God wanted him to see. Could this be the sign John needed from God? It was a painting which showed doctors performing surgery on a young man, but Jesus was behind the doctors watching over them. For the first time in this process, John believed that Jesus was going to be watching over him, too. After praying for peace and trust, he had received this powerful sign.

The surgery came, and before he knew it, he was in recovery. There had been some complications that were not expected, but John remembers waking up in the recovery room with joy that he had made it through surgery. Jesus had been with him and had chosen to spare his life. While recovering in the days to follow, John was in a hospital room across from a younger boy. As he lay there, the sounds of what happened next would be engraved in his mind forever. The boy in the room across from him set off a bunch of alarms. The nurses and the doctors came and rushed him off, only to find the boy had died and they could not revive him. John saw the boy's mother wailing at the loss of her son, and John realized at that moment, she could have easily been his own mom.

Life changed for John because he now had a new appreciation for life. As he returned to central Florida and fully recovered, he got immediately involved in our youth group and into leadership. I had lunch with him and heard his amazing testimony. He was a young man who had been profoundly changed.

He said, "I now see every day as a gift from God, and so I am not going to waste my time on things that do not really matter. I realized that the youth group I thought was pushing me away was, in fact, the same youth group who supported me all along, and I had allowed Satan to deceive me into thinking no one cared."

Once John came back and got involved, he grew in his relationship with God so much he became one of the best leaders we have ever had in the youth program. He went from having bad friends and a bad attitude to leading a Bible study group and helping connect others who thought as he once did. John has gone on to marry a lovely and pure Christian girl who was also in the youth group I led. I officiated their wedding, and it was one of the most beautiful moments when they exchanged their vow to purity rings on their wedding day.

Because John saw every day as a gift, he did not waste his time. At his high school homecoming, he and others in our youth group saw the dancing and environment get out of hand. John was the first one to tell them all he was leaving the dance. It was his homecoming and a special memory in high school, but to John, that day was a gift from God that could not be wasted. When a youth asked him why he was leaving, he responded, "Life is too short to waste time here watching this."

With that leadership, the rest of our youth group left the homecoming dance, too, to go do something else. I definitely saw a true transformation in his life because of how God used suffering to reach him. Now, John has graduated high school and wants to get a print of the picture of

Jesus over the surgeons that gave him peace in the midst of a storm. John rejoices that suffering came because it positively affected his eternity.

Suffering can wake us up if we run toward God instead of running away from God, and if we thank God instead of blaming God. God did not create us to suffer; but in and through suffering, we can be the people God purposed us to be.

Suffering as a Christian

Let us now take a deeper look at the suffering a Christian can expect. On this earth, we cannot get away from suffering. Even the perfect Christ was not exempt from suffering. The Bible says that I am going to suffer no matter what, so I might as well suffer for the sake of Christ. In 1 Peter 3:17 it says, "It is better, if it is God's will, to suffer for doing good than for doing evil."

Here are some key verses about suffering and trials throughout the entire Bible that are self-explanatory:

- Psalms 34:19—"A righteous man may have many troubles, but the Lord delivers him from them all."

- Matthew 10:22—"All men will hate you because of me, but he who stands firm to the end will be saved."

- John 16:33—"I have told you these things, so that in me you may have peace. In this world you will have trouble. But take heart! I have overcome the world."

- Acts 14:22—"Strengthening the disciples and encouraging them to remain true to the faith. 'We must go through many hardships to enter the kingdom of God,' they said."

- 2 Corinthians 1:5—"For just as the sufferings of Christ flow over into our lives, so also through Christ our comfort overflows."

- 2 Corinthians 6:4-10—"Rather, as servants of God we commend ourselves in every way: in great endurance; in troubles, hardships and distresses; in beatings, imprisonments and riots; in hard work, sleepless nights and hunger; in purity, understanding, patience and kindness; in the Holy Spirit and in sincere love; in truthful speech and in the power of God; with weapons of righteousness in the right hand and in the left; through glory and dishonor, bad report and good report; genuine, yet regarded as impostors; known, yet regarded as unknown; dying, and yet we live on; beaten, and yet not killed; sorrowful, yet always rejoicing; poor, yet making many rich; having nothing, and yet possessing everything."

- Philippians 1:29—"For it has been granted to you on behalf of Christ not only to believe on him, but also to suffer for him."

- Philippians 3:10—"I want to know Christ and the power of his resurrection and the fellowship of sharing in his sufferings, becoming like him in his death."

- 1 Thessalonians 3:4—In fact, when we were with you, we kept telling you that we would be persecuted. And it turned out that way, as you well know.

- 2 Timothy 1:8—"So do not be ashamed to testify about our Lord, or ashamed of me his prisoner. But join with me in suffering for the gospel, by the power of God."

- 2 Timothy 2:3—"Endure hardship with us like a good soldier of Christ Jesus."

- 2 Timothy 3:10-12—"You, however, know all about my teaching, my way of life, my purpose, faith, patience, love, endurance, persecutions, sufferings—what kinds of things happened to me in Antioch, Iconium and Lystra, the persecutions I endured. Yet the Lord rescued me from all of them. In fact, everyone who wants to live a godly life in Christ Jesus will be persecuted."

- 1 Peter 5:10—"And the God of all grace, who called you to his eternal glory in Christ, after you have suffered a little while, will Himself restore you and make you strong, firm and steadfast."

All these Scriptures refer to Christians suffering and that it is inevitable on this earth. If you think Christianity will keep you from suffering hardships, you are disregarding the Word of God. We are not guaranteed physical blessings of wealth, health, long life, or many other things. I follow Jesus Christ because no one else and nothing else can get me through the hardships that will come in this life. I will suffer in this life because of people's choices of sin, my own choices of sin, and because Satan is my enemy. I need to expect suffering and realize that the more threat I am to the evil forces, the more opposition I will encounter. I had to learn to not be afraid of a short life, poverty, and disease. I will be victorious in any of these because my eternal purpose is to be a child of God who will dwell with God forever. Therefore, I will praise Him in the good and in the storms of this life. I will thank Him for the plenty at times and the periods where I am without. I will always worship Him no matter what happens, because He is in control and I know He will only do what is best for me.

Rejoicing in Suffering

It is hard enough enduring the storms and living in the aftermath of the storms of this life; how does God expect us to rejoice and be thankful for these hardships? Once again, let's take a look at some Scriptures on this before we answer this question:

- Matthew 5:10-12—"Blessed are those who are persecuted because of righteousness, for theirs is the kingdom of heaven. Blessed are you when people insult you, persecute you and falsely say all kinds of evil against you because of me. Rejoice and be glad, because great is your reward in heaven, for in the same way they persecuted the prophets who were before you."

- Luke 6:22-23—"Blessed are you when men hate you, when they exclude you and insult you and reject your name as evil, because of the Son of Man. Rejoice in that day and leap for joy, because great is your reward in heaven. For that is how their fathers treated the prophets."

- Acts 5:40-42—"His speech persuaded them. They called the apostles in and had them flogged. Then they ordered them not to speak in the name of Jesus, and let them go. The apostles left the Sanhedrin, rejoicing because they had been counted worthy of suffering disgrace for the Name. Day after day, in the temple courts and from house to house, they never stopped teaching and proclaiming the good news that Jesus is the Christ."

- Heb 10:32-34—"Remember those earlier days after you had received the light, when you stood your ground in a great contest in the face of suffering. Sometimes you were publicly exposed to insult and persecution; at other times you stood side by side with those who were so treated. You sympathized with those in prison and joyfully accepted the confiscation of your property, because you knew that you yourselves had better and lasting possession."

- James 1:2-4—"Consider it pure joy, my brothers, whenever you face trials of many kinds, because you know that the testing of your faith develops perseverance. Perseverance must finish its work so that you may be mature and complete, not lacking anything."

- 1 Peter 1:6-9—"In this you greatly rejoice, though now for a little while you may have had to suffer grief in all kinds of trials. These have come so that your faith—of greater worth than gold, which perishes even though refined by fire—may be proved genuine and may result in praise, glory and honor when Jesus Christ is revealed. Though you have not seen Him, you love Him; and even though you do not see Him now, you believe in Him and are filled with an inexpressible and glorious joy, for you are receiving the goal of your faith, the salvation of your souls."

We must change our thinking and expect suffering. This does not mean we go out and cause suffering for us and our families. A lot of suffering we experience comes from us and our bad choices. Remember the story Jesus told about the rich fool, and how this fool was concerned so much about his stuff that he did not know he would die that night.

If we could only learn to live a life of contentment, we might have more peace and less stress. The more we spend on our stuff, the more we have to lose. The more we have to lose, the more our stuff begins to own us. If we would only invest in our children and if we would only be concerned about others and providing for them, we just might receive the abundant life that Jesus speaks about in John 10. Life abundantly is not what we have been told it is. Abundant life has less to do with what I have and more about being sheep to the true Shepherd. It is not about wealth, success, education, marriage, friendships, and health but, rather, abundant life is living in the arms of God under the authority of Christ. Why would I ever want to be anywhere else?

One of my favorite verses on suffering is 1 Peter 4:12-16:

> Dear friends, do not be surprised at the painful trial you are suffering, as though something strange were happening to you. But rejoice that you participate in the sufferings of Christ, so that you may be overjoyed when his glory is revealed. If you are insulted because of the name of Christ, you are blessed, for the Spirit of glory and of God rests on you. If you suffer, it should not be as a murderer or thief or any other kind of criminal, or even as a meddler. However, if you suffer as a Christian, do not be ashamed, but praise God that you bear that name.

I must be reminded as sufferings come, and they will, that God counts me worthy to suffer for Him, and in that I will rejoice. Many people do not suffer well. You can tell when a person is usually suffering because they want you to be able to tell. Many get attention and pity from others during suffering, and they like it so much, I have known people to fake illnesses in the church. God forgive the lady who took so much from people in our church claiming she had cancer, when it was all a lie. I believe we need to be helping those who rejoice in suffering, and those who suffer well as Christians. A great Scripture to memorize is where it says, "Rejoice always; pray continually; and give thanks in all things for this is the will of God in Christ Jesus." This attitude will help us suffer well for the glory of God.

I believe suffering may be summed up in Romans 8:17-18, where it says, "Now if we are children, then we are heirs—heirs of God and co-heirs with Christ, if indeed we share in His sufferings in order that we may also share in His glory. I consider that our present sufferings are not worth comparing with the glory that will be revealed in us." There is no doubt I want to share in the glory of Jesus, so may we suffer well and look toward eternity with God.

Jesus's Peace in the Storms

Have you ever wondered if anything rattled Jesus? The demons did not frighten Him, the storms did not scare Him, and death itself did not bring out selfishness in Jesus. The only thing that seemed to rattle Him was that he would be separated from His Father. Jesus experienced a peace in His life that I believe we all desire. Jesus was not exempt from suffering, by any means, but He successfully overcame any situation of suffering that came His way. Jesus probably suffered the loss of His earthly father as a teenager. He experienced poor relationships with His half-brothers and half-sisters, as they refused to believe in Him before His resurrection. He experienced the storms of temptation and the storms of betrayal. He understood what it meant to not have a place to lay His head at night. He knew what it felt like to be hungry to the point of starvation. He experienced suffering as people wanted to kill Him, as people mocked Him, as they beat Him, and as they finally crucified Him in a shameful death.

In this section, I want us to see the calmness of Jesus in the storms and unlock the secret to what gave Him this peace in the storms.

First of all, Jesus never seemed to be scared in the actual storms. Remember the story where Jesus was asleep in the boat and the disciples, who were experienced fishermen, were afraid that the boat was going down and would sink? They were calling out (or should we say, screaming) for Jesus to wake up and help. I can see Jesus calmly getting up and taking care of the situation. Do you remember what Jesus said to His apostles after He calmed the storm? His words are in Mark 4:40: "Why are you so timid? How is it that you have no faith?" Jesus acted as if there was no need for them to fear or be afraid. Why was Jesus not fearful?

The story of Jesus walking on water shows a trust and confidence amid the storms. This great, miraculous story is taken from Matthew 14:25-31:

> During the fourth watch of the night Jesus went out to them, walking on the lake. When the disciples saw Him walking on the lake, they were terrified. "It's a ghost," they said, and cried out in fear. But Jesus immediately said to them: "Take courage! It is I. Don't be afraid." "Lord, if it's you," Peter replied, "tell me to come to you on the water." "Come," he said. Then Peter got down out of the boat, walked on the water and came toward Jesus. But when he saw the wind, he was afraid and, beginning to sink, cried out, "Lord, save me!" Immediately Jesus reached out his hand and caught him. "You of little faith," he said, "why did you doubt?"

This shows us so much about the faith and calmness of Jesus compared to Peter. Jesus did not sink because He did not doubt. Peter was afraid as he looked at the wind and waves. Jesus was walking calmly in the midst of the wind and waves, yet He was not afraid. One of the gospels says that Jesus was intending to pass them by as He was walking on the water. Jesus was taking an early morning stroll on the water without any fear, because He had just been in the presence of God.

One of the most graphic stories of demon possession is Mark 5:5-10:

> And constantly night and day, among the tombs and in the mountains, he was crying out and gashing himself with stones. And seeing Jesus from a distance, he ran up and bowed down before Him; and crying out with a loud voice, he said, "What do I have to do with You, Jesus, Son of the Most High God? I implore You by God, do not torment me!" For He had been saying to him, "Come out of the man, you unclean spirit!" And He was asking him, "What is your name?" And he said to Him, "My name is Legion; for we are many." And he began to entreat Him earnestly not to send them out of the country.

This man was full of so many demons he would beat himself to try and stop the torment. The gospels refer to the man as being naked, cuts on his body from the rocks, and extremely strong. He comes running at Jesus. What would be your first impulse or reaction if a crazy man came running at you naked and screaming? Jesus was not afraid as He spoke to this man and released him from the captivity of Satan. Jesus did not fear Satan but always had trust in God. Over and over Jesus appears to not fear but, rather, to love and trust. Fear proves we lack complete trust in God.

What was the secret for Jesus, time and time again? I believe the secret was Jesus's prayer life and complete trust in the Father. I have mentioned this earlier in the book, that Jesus put prayer time with His Father over food and sleep. As seen in the walking on water story, Jesus had just come from a long night prayer session with His Father. Jesus did not doubt because He knew His Father could and would do anything for Him. Peter had this same Father, but Peter just didn't know Him the way Jesus did. Jesus had invested His entire life in knowing the Father. Did regular prayer keep Him trusting? Did this time set apart with God continually remind Him of who was really in control? I believe it did. Jesus walked on water because of His trust and His relationship to the Father. When Peter had this same faith and trust, he walked on water also, until he began to doubt.

If you want peace in the storms, you are going to have to walk as Jesus walked. You are going to have to make talking to God and listening to God a regular pattern in your life. This should not be timed or hurried, just as Jesus did not see prayer as an action that simply needed to get done that day, but as a lifestyle and something He lived and relished. You are going to have to see time with God as more filling than food and more restful than sleep. You are going to have to discipline yourself to be dependent on God as you are dependent on air to breathe. I believe Jesus confirms to us by His example that prayer is the secret to peace.

Living many years in Florida, we have experienced a number of hurricanes. There is what's called the eye of the storm or the eye of the hurricane. This eye can be miles long, and as a fierce hurricane is going directly over you, you can find yourself in the eye of the storm—no clouds above you and no wind or rain, yet the storms are all around you. The storm is all around you, and still you experience calmness. I see prayer as experiencing the calm in eye of the storm. The bigger we see our problems, the smaller God appears; but the bigger we see God, the smaller our problems appear. If you want calm in your life, you need to get close to the One who has the power to calm. Peace is not the absence of trouble but the presence of God. Where there is "no prayer," there will be "no peace."

CHAPTER 8 WORKSHEET

What did you learn about suffering?

_____

_____

_____

Was there ever a time you questioned God in suffering?

_____

_____

_____

How did God bring you through those times of suffering?

_____

_____

_____

How can God use you to serve those who are suffering?

_____

_____

_____

What does God's peace look like for one in suffering?

_____

_____

_____

CHAPTER 9

The Shadow of the True Church

Salvation is found in no one else, for there is no other name under heaven given to men by which we must be saved.
—Acts 4:12

The question always comes to my mind whether or not I have ever personally encountered Satan. We always say Satan is tempting us, when it could really be his angels or evil spirits. I believe Satan is working extremely hard on the things which will affect the majority of people. I would think presidential elections, terrorism, false religions, and "church leadership" are places where Satan works the most. I would like to be such a threat to Satan because then I would know God is truly using me. Remember in Acts 19:15, where the spirits say we recognize Jesus and we know Paul, but who are you? If I am wanting to live a peaceful life without Satan really bugging me, then I should just go through the motions. If I want God to use me to the fullest, then Satan is going to know and the evil spirits will also.

I would love the body of Christ, through unity, evangelism, and love, to become such a threat to Satan that he would not know what to do with us. Could this be why the church in America as a whole has such peace and lack of persecution? Could Satan have learned from the first century that the church becomes strong and unstoppable during persecution? If

Satan can deceive people into believing their purpose is tied to this world and that it is ok if Christians are lukewarm and stagnate in their faith, is he not successful? Some scholars believe the letters to the seven churches in Revelation address time periods from the first century until the time in which Christ returns. The final church discussed in Revelation 3 is the church in Laodicea which is lukewarm because of materialism. If this represents the final days before Christ returns, we just may be getting close. A few Scriptures which have got me thinking about the last days are these:

- Matthew 24:12—"Because of the increase of wickedness, the love of most will grow cold."

- 2 Timothy 3:1-5—"But mark this: There will be terrible times in the last days. People will be lovers of themselves, lovers of money, boastful, proud, abusive, disobedient to their parents, ungrateful, unholy, without love, unforgiving, slanderous, without self-control, brutal, not lovers of the good, treacherous, rash, conceited, lovers of pleasure rather than lovers of God—having a form of godliness but denying its power. Have nothing to do with them."

The popular question today is, who really is a part of the true church? Are Catholics, Mormons, Baptists, non-denominational, or Pentecostals part of the true church? Satan has confused the world, and we have helped. I grew up in a non-denominational church, and we were told that we were the church that followed the first-century pattern. I was fine with that. It sounded right to me, and I was glad I was a part of the group going to heaven. It was all about what I did that pleased God and what I didn't do that displeased God. When I debated others, I knew I was right because I had been told I was right. I had more pride in my heart than I ever had love. I was more of a Pharisee than a disciple or follower. I was more about "being right" than I ever was about the body and unity of Christ. I was more about condemning than saving, and judging rather than mercy.

Because of my own study, this all has changed. Now, I am very clear about where I stand. I believe in God's grace, justice, unity, and even God's one church while also believing there are false teachers. All of these things you will find in the Scriptures.

I later realized I did not want to be what the first-century church became. It started out giving, sharing, and unity, but quickly turned to legalism, works of the Law to save, and "We are more holy than you." It quickly became messed up. There was chaos in the assemblies, and divisions in their relationships with other churches. The clergy looked a lot different than the apostles, and yet they were still considered saints according to 1 Corinthians 1:2: "To the church of God which is at Corinth, to those who have been sanctified in Christ Jesus, saints by calling, with all who in every place call upon the name of our Lord Jesus Christ, their Lord and ours." I want to be at the heart of why God gave us the church. I want to be a part of the people who are "the called out." It does not matter what sign or name they have on their building, where they meet, their race or nationality, or what style of worship they enjoy. I want to be the twenty-first century church God desires in today's day and age, which in spite of our imperfections we bring to a spiritual body of Christ. I do believe faith in God the Father, His Son, Jesus, and the Holy Spirit are the ingredients for salvation throughout all of the Scriptures. I do believe what it says in 1 Corinthians 12:13: "For we were all baptized by one Spirit into one body—whether Jews or Greeks, slave or free—and we were all given the one Spirit to drink." The entrance into the true body of Christ is when we were baptized into it. Why would we even say otherwise? To think differently would go against what this Scripture clearly states. I do not believe the Bible teaches us to accept everything within the church. We are given instructions about things we are not to accept within the church. According to 1 Corinthians 5:9-11:

> "I have written you in my letter not to associate with sexually immoral people—not at all meaning the people of this world who are immoral, or the greedy and swindlers, or idolaters. In that case you would have to leave this world. But now I am writing you that you must not associate with anyone who calls himself a brother but is sexually immoral or greedy, an idolater or a slanderer, a drunkard or a swindler. With such a man do not even eat."

These Christians were not to associate with "Christians" who were living in these sins. A person who has chosen to rebel against the will of God and become a slave to sin should be disciplined for the sake of saving their soul.

Also in 2 Timothy 4:2-5, the Bible clearly says there will be a time when people will find themselves teachers who will teach what they want to hear, not what God really says.

> Preach the Word; be prepared in season and out of season; correct, rebuke and encourage—with great patience and careful instruction. For the time will come when men will not put up with sound doctrine. Instead, to suit their own desires, they will gather around them a great number of teachers to say what their itching ears want to hear. They will turn their ears away from the truth and turn aside to myths. But you, keep your head in all situations, endure hardship, do the work of an evangelist, and discharge all the duties of your ministry.

Maybe this is why we have homosexual churches with homosexual ministers? This is people finding teachers who will teach what they desire. The Scriptures teach that homosexuality is against the will of God just like other sins. This is an issue discussed in Romans 1:26-27. "Because of this, God gave them over to shameful lusts. Even their women exchanged natural relations for unnatural ones. In the same way the men also abandoned natural relations with women and were inflamed with lust for one another. Men committed indecent acts with other men, and received in themselves the due penalty for their perversion."

I do not trust my flesh because it would be just like me to look for someone to agree with me and find the easy way out. What good will that do for me in the end? I have maybe seventy to eighty years to live deceived, and then all of eternity to live separate from God. There are deceptions even within the church, and these are seen when we try to teach what we think instead of what the Bible says. We are going to learn more about interpreting Scripture in a later chapter, but at some point we have got to quit trying to figure out what the Bible means and take it for what it says, whether it is something we have believed or not.

The true church cares more about the name of Christ than the name on their church building; its members care more for reaching the lost than selfishly getting all they want; they have a vision for maturing the saints and strengthening the Kingdom, not just their own church; and preserve unity with those who follow and love Jesus Christ as the Messiah, and His Holy Word.

For the Sake of the Name

We are all given names when we are born. Sometimes names are given which mean something. For example, the name of Moses means to be drawn out of the water. At times, much thinking goes into a name for your newborn child. As my wife, Teresa, and I found out we were having twin boys during her first ultrasound, the wheels were in motion as we began to contemplate names for our boys. We wanted Bible names, so we thought about Joshua and Caleb, but they seemed too common. I will say some names were not even an option. I could see the name Jacob, but not the name Esau. Needless to say, names like Judas were not considered. I always liked the Bible name of Justus. Justus was with Matthias and was qualified to be an apostle in Acts 1:23. He must have been an eyewitness of Jesus as well as a faithful follower of Him. After discussing the name of Justus with my wife, we agreed our firstborn's name would be Justus. As a dad, I also liked the fact the name Justus sounded like a gladiator's name.

After numerous days of wracking our brains, my wife and I could not agree on any other boy names in the Bible for our second son. Deciding on one name had been hard enough, but deciding on two names was downright impossible. So, I went to a reinforcement I knew would never let me down—my mom. At this point, Teresa and I just needed to agree. My mom's idea for a name was brilliant.

She said, "What about the name Jordan?"

As we thought a few minutes, it just sounded right, Justus and Jordan. It is not a name of a male in the Bible, but it is the name of the river in which Jesus was baptized. I figured close enough, right? With much relief, we finally decided to name our twin boys Justus and Jordan. I had prayed from the time we found out we were having sons that they would grow up to be the best of friends, so I was going to incorporate this somehow in their names. Jonathan and David in the Bible were the best of friends, even though Jonathan was probably much older. So our firstborn would have the middle name of Jonathan, and our second born would have the middle name of David. It was settled! Their names would be Justus Jonathan Verge and Jordan David Verge.

Sometimes a name can represent who you are or who you will become. Many names of people throughout the Bible described them well. For example Amos, a prophet of God, means burden-bearer, and Obadiah, another Old Testament prophet, means servant of God. When you study their lives, you realize the name fits them.

Jesus saw the need to change people's names to better represent how God saw them, such as He did with His apostle Peter. Jesus changed his name from Simon to Peter, which means stone or rock. This represented what Peter would become. I wonder that as Jesus changed Peter's name and also called James and John the "Sons of Thunder," whether the others just laughed at the idea of these two younger sons of Zebedee being Sons of Thunder. I'll bet to others, they never would have seen this possibility in them, but Jesus saw something deeper. He saw the potential of what God could do in and through them. I am glad God sees more in me than what is revealed right now. I wonder what name God would give me to best describe my life and what I will become. I'll bet the name would probably make everyone laugh, but that would not matter because it would come to pass.

Sometimes names were changed by God to give new identity, as with Saul, whose name was changed to Paul. I believe names were changed at times to represent the difference, or should I say the conversion, which happened when a person surrendered to Christ. The Bible defines this conversion as a death, burial, and resurrection which would take place, thus symbolizing a new birth with a new life. Names can serve more of a purpose than what your mom yells out when you are in trouble.

The name "Christian" is a term which has lost meaning. Many have also succeeded to take the name of Christ out of the term Christian. In many ways, the term Christian does not describe a Christ-follower, but a churchgoer. I learned this as a teenager who was appalled at the leaders of our Fellowship of Christian Athletes (FCA) club in high school. Many threw around the name Christian in our school as they described themselves. If you went to church, you were a Christian. Doesn't Christian mean follower of Christ? This was the last thing these FCA leaders were. I did not see people reading their Bibles in school or praying before their meals. I do not even remember a prayer said before our Christian club meetings. The club was a joke, as our leaders were sexually active and partiers every weekend; yet they bore the name Christian, and they represented this "Christian" club. I don't have to tell you I was not a part of that club for long. Sadly, I grew up realizing this was not only the way it was in high school, but that same thinking would continue in the adult world and in the church. I ought to see Christ in a person who calls themselves a Christian.

Names do have significant meanings, but no name has changed the world the way the name Jesus Christ has. Many would argue that they stand for Jesus, but they deny the unity in His blood that makes us family. How many different ways can we say we are a church who follows Christ? How many more names are we going to come up with to place on the front of churches, or on the side of our church buses? Have we become a church which is more focused on the name of Christ for salvation or the name of the denomination or church of which we are a part?

We hear over and over it is all about Christ, and actions usually show it is more about church names and the practices they have. It becomes about why you should choose to worship here and not there. The name of a church or denomination seems to supersede the name of Christ for some. Have you ever gone to a church that has said, "This is what our church has always done." We seem to divide over church names when we are supposed to be unifying under Christ. In today's religious world, it has little to do with following Christ and more to do with your church affiliation.

God forgive us if we have taken Christ out of the church. If you have Christ, you are connected to all the believers around the world, even those who do things a little differently than you.

The church in the first century was called "The Way" from the book of Acts. There were not different denominations segregated within the true church. The Way was the name known for those who followed the message of Christ, believing Jesus was the Messiah who died, was resurrected, and who is coming back. You were either a part of the church, "The Way," believing and following the true message of Jesus, or you weren't. What you did was important, but if it was not rooted in love, it was pointless.

This is seen in 1 Corinthians 13:2-3: "If I have the gift of prophecy and can fathom all mysteries and all knowledge, and if I have a faith that can move mountains, but have not love, I am nothing. If I give all I possess to the poor and surrender my body to the flames, but have not love, I gain nothing." There were things which pleased God as well as things which displeased God. God can teach you what pleases Him through His Spirit, but you still have to make the choice to love God and please Him every day.

There were people during the life of Christ and before the destruction of Jerusalem in AD 70 who were false christs according to Matthew 24:24: "For false christs and false prophets will appear and perform great signs and miracles to deceive even the elect—if that were possible." There were also people called Gnostics who lived during the first century and denied Jesus coming in the flesh. However, according to 1 John 4:2-3: "This is how you can recognize the Spirit of God: Every spirit that acknowledges that Jesus Christ has come in the flesh is from God, but every spirit that does not acknowledge Jesus is not from God. This is the spirit of the Antichrist, which you have heard is coming and even now is already in the world."

Needless to say, there were false teachers during that time who rejected the truth of Jesus and the truth of His message. When you reject Jesus as the Christ, you are rejecting God and His saving message. This is the reason many religions today, including Muslims, are lost, because they have rejected Jesus as the Messiah, Savior of the world. The fact remains, people knew of "The Way" in the first century, and you were either a part of it or you were not. To the church back then, it was quite clear. The story in history says one day John went to a pool in the city and saw one of the false teachers there. As John saw him in the pool, John walked out and left, saying something like, "I refuse to be in here with this man in fear that the roof will fall in."

What defined "The Way" of the first century? Was it the church's views on women's roles or was it their views on spiritual gifts? Could it have been the Christians's views on the true day of worship, also referred to as "the Lord's day?" Maybe "The Way" was defined by the particular worship style used in the congregational assemblies. Could it be that none of these possible explanations defined "The Way" or the true church, even though today we have used these very issues to define and divide the church?

I believe none of those issues defined the true church. Is there a role for men and women in the church? Absolutely, there is a role in the letters...but is a misinterpretation of this of eternal significance? We have already heard of the issues the church in Corinth had, and yet they were still members of the Lord's church. Let's take a look at some key issues Corinth had that did not separate them from Christ. I will warn you that this is pretty ugly. Paul addresses this messed-up church in Corinth, which had major issues in following God's plan when it came to:

- Unity—1 Corinthians 1:12

- Disfellowship—1 Corinthians 5:9-13

- Communion—1 Corinthians 11:27-30

- Spiritual gifts—1 Corinthians 14:16-17

- Women's role—1 Corinthians 14:33-35

- Resurrection of the dead –1 Corinthians 15:50-53

Those are some of the issues just one church had during the first century, and I haven't even gotten to the second letter to the Corinthians or the other letters in the New Testament. Let's face it, in our legalism, we have cut people off from the church for far less than the things listed in 1 Corinthians. It has always been about the name of Jesus, and it still is today.

Now, two thousand years later, we have "churches" which teach about Christ but are divided on so many other things. Today, we have cut off our brothers and sisters in Christ over the same issues which actually were part of the churches in the first century, declaring they are not part of the true church if they practice these things. We have reached a place where we are confusing the world about Christ and His church. We live in a time when people would rather just stay away from the battle of churches. We are fighting the wrong battle if we are fighting the battle of denominational names and church affiliations. When are we going to realize we are members of Christ and are on the same team, and that our enemy has deceived us to turn against each other instead of the spiritual battle against the evil forces?

It is disturbing to me that we have fights under the same denominational name over different styles and different methods. We are even divided under the same church name. In the Baptist church, you have the First Baptist, the Southern Baptist, and the Missionary Baptist, to just name a few. We can't even agree under the same church denomination.

Let me validate this point by telling you a disappointing personal story where I learned churches will even disassociate with people under their same church name.

Our youth group had gone to Jamaica for eleven years. One of the main reasons our youth went to Jamaica every summer is because the people there speak English and we can study the Bible with them individually. I am not against mission trips where groups are led to work on service projects in other places where the people speak different languages, but why not also go to where we can speak to them about Christ?

For years, our group had stayed in a house owned by a church that was affiliated with our church. Each year we would rent this house and pay good money to stay for seven to ten days during the summer. During the year, we would raise money while training intensely to go to this receptive culture and teach. We would start out with so many youth who showed interest, and work our way down to the committed twenty or so who would allow the Holy Spirit to lead them. To say these youth were not scared or intimidated at first would be an understatement. The youth were young people who were going to talk to those of all ages about Jesus Christ. They were ready to answer questions, even though some had never done this before.

Every year we would go and be absolutely blown away by all the amazing things God would do with our team. It is a glorious sight to see people come together for the purpose of Christ, become selfless, devote themselves to prayer, and just watch God through His Spirit work. The relationships we built, the friends we made, and the people who found Jesus Christ not only benefited the Jamaicans but was a benefit to us, as well. We saw firsthand what God can do, and we also saw how Satan would try to stop it.

One year as we were going to show the *Passion of the Christ* movie to the entire adult community, the power went off in the entire city for hours. That was okay, because God brought a larger crowd the next night. It was obvious Satan was against us. In the midst of opposition, we would prepare and learn to be selfless instruments of God for the Jamaicans

Relationships and love were abounding as we continued to go year after year. We built such a rapport with the people; they got to know our love for the Lord and our love for them. They knew we did not teach religion but relationship. They knew we did not teach a name on the building but the name of Christ on the heart, and they also came to know that we taught God's Word, not our opinions. This was different for them, because many of the churches started by legalistic Christian Americans were trying to start legalistic Christian American churches in Jamaica. We battled legalism there, but we knew God was using us and our example to teach them about freedom in Christ.

Every year, God confirmed He was leading us and that He was with us.

We realized how much of a blessing this rental house was when I received a letter stating we were no longer invited to stay at that house or work with those churches. These were my brothers and sisters in Christ who disassociated themselves with us because we had an instrumental music service at our local congregation. My thoughts were, *You have got to be kidding, right? You are more concerned with the method in which our church worships God over the salvation of people you claim to love.*

My own church affiliation had gone against us. What was I to say to our youth? Should I say, "By the way, the body of Christ, the church Jesus died for, our source of encouragement in a predominantly corrupt world, has turned her back on us, treating us as if we are heathens. Oh by the way, this is the church, your family, who loves you with the love of God."

I am trying to teach our youth that the church was given to us by God and we need to be a part of Christ's church, but are they hearing the words or experiencing the reality of the times? I do not know how God is going to look upon this church and their leaders who made this decision, but God forgive them and teach them. This is an example of what can happen every day in the "church" world, but now it is personal to me.

I was told growing up that the church of Christ is the Lord's church. I was told if I wanted to be sure of heaven when I die, I needed to be a member of this church. Believe it or not, they even had a Scripture reference from Romans 16:16, where it says, "Greet one another with a holy kiss. All the churches of Christ send greetings." I was also told we must be a church of Christ from this verse, but we were not to greet with a holy kiss. Go figure, one part of the verse is very important, even of eternal significance; however, the other part we would not dare to practice. They also never showed us the numerous Scriptures referring to the church of God, because I was taught the church down the street was not right with God if they don't have our name.

Once I studied the whole name thing, I realized the name for our church was used fewer times than the other names of churches. The names mentioned in the Bible were not names of denominations like we have made them today. They were not mentioned in Scripture for us to fight about and separate over, yet you could never tell that based on what we have done since then. I want to be very clear. This is not a church of Christ problem only, but a problem in the church as we know it today.

I thought it was so clear from Scripture that the name we ought to be concerned about is the name of Christ, not the "church name." Even though this was a no-brainer to me, I did not think it would be as hard as it was to convince others. Just the thought of changing our church name where I once ministered from Metro Church of Christ to Metro Church stirred controversy and questions by even our own members. We were "messing" with their traditions. What would their families say? And, to be honest, testing the beliefs and convictions that many had been taught. Had we become more attached to our church name than the name of Christ? Our elders stepped up to the plate and moved forward by the Spirit of God with the change, teaching, and discussing with some who had issues.

Many of us have fallen into the same Satan's trap the Pharisees fell into during Jesus's time. Because of pride and self-righteousness, we have turned to our works and accomplishments to inherit salvation, disregarding grace, mercy, and forgiveness which God pours forth freely and is found only in Jesus. When we make salvation only about how we worship on Sundays, the day of the week we are to worship, miraculous gifts of the Spirit, meeting in luxurious church buildings, and so many other issues, we have turned to our works to inherit salvation. Even though there is God's will in Christian living and Christian worship, salvation is given based on God's grace and Jesus's performance, not God's grace based on our performance. This is tough for a legalist to believe and understand. Just as King David needed God's grace for going against the will of God in committing adultery and murder, we also need God's grace when we sin going against the will of God. We all need God's grace in our lives and in our churches, no matter who you are and where you go. All Christ-focused churches are filled with imperfect people and imperfect ministers, including myself, but we are covered with the blood of Jesus and made to be the family of God.

So, do all the churches need to change their names? Changing names is not always the answer, but changing our focus is. It is not about the name of a church but the name of Christ. We will never unify if we keep grasping the name on our signs. There is one body, according to Ephesians 4:4, and it is those who hold to Christ instead of holding to a church name. This may shock some of you, but your church affiliation will not save you in the end; it will be your love for Jesus and the relationship you have with Him.

Today, because so many churches are venturing out of a "church affiliation," my fear is we will become another smokestack church trying to use our limited resources to make a difference in a lost and dying world. Metro Church's leaders were not out to start another church name or denomination but were willing to stand strong in the belief that we are not Christians under a name, but under *the* name, Jesus Christ. Haven't we tried and failed to reach the world for Christ individually and separate from each other? It is a big assignment and can be accomplished, but only if we work together. We must join together and teach everything in the Bible while teaching that our traditions are just traditions and our preferences are simply our preferences. We must be all right if someone practices things a little differently than we do, as long as they are under the name of Jesus Christ, having been clothed with Christ and covered by His blood. We have got to trust God's grace to cover where they are wrong and trust His grace to also fill in for where we are wrong, because none of us are right about everything. Division happens because of pride; unity is experienced because of humility.

Legalistic "churches" have had a hard time interpreting the Scripture in Mark 9:39-40, where Jesus says: "No one who does a miracle in my name can in the next moment say anything bad about me, for whoever is not against us is for us." Even the disciples were ready to take action against those who were acting in the name of Jesus, just because they were from another group. Jesus was merciful because they were doing things in His name and for His glory. There may be a lot of things people are doing in Jesus's name which we do not do and do not understand, but as Jesus said, "Whoever is not against us is for us."

A church finally made good headlines when Metro Church merged with the South Seminole Christian Church less than a mile away. This merger shocked the community because Christians were actually getting along and joining together instead of dividing. It is actually sad this made headlines, because the truth of how the church is viewed became visible to all. Christians getting along should not be major headlines in the papers but rather a way of life in demonstrating God's love.

This merger was not because every belief and method were exactly the same, but because whether we meet in the same building or a mile down the street, we are under the name of Christ and are a part of God's family. This can only happen with those who are led by the Holy Spirit to preserve the unity given by the Spirit.

Whether you are the Church of God, the Church of Christ, Disciples of Christ, The Way, or any other name you claim, it is not about whether your name is in the Bible or not, but whether you are teaching and living the Name from His Word. The true church is under the name and authority of Jesus Christ. You are either a part of the Name (Jesus Christ), or you are not. That is a line in which we should draw for fellowship.

For the Sake of Unity

Do Christians even want to unite? I am convinced many are ready to quit the fighting that has been led by pride, and work together. I also understand the power of our enemy, who will do anything to destroy unity. I think we are witnesses of this today. In the first century, Satan used intense persecution to challenge unity. Acts 8:1-2 says, "And Saul was there, giving approval to his death. On that day a great persecution broke out against the church at Jerusalem, and all except the apostles were scattered throughout Judea and Samaria."

How badly do you want unity within the church? Would you die for it? Many in the first century did, and Jesus most definitely did, but would you? Well, right now you may not have to die for unity, but you must live for it. Living for a cause is sometimes harder than dying for one.

In striving for unity, we are faced with the discouraging thought that we are only a few people. Can we ever really obtain unity in Christ's church today? I have asked myself this question time and time again. We are slow to unite with other Christians in fear that some may leave our churches and go to their churches. It is us and them. We are worried about paying the bills and affording our multi-million dollar buildings and properties; we cannot afford to have people go elsewhere. God forgive us, and may You bless our leaders in the church with vision for the kingdom of God throughout the entire earth. We also struggle with experiencing unity in the individual churches where we meet. Why is this? Is unity as Christians a concept we will never experience? I, for one, am tired of us versus them, and I desire to learn how to live in unity and promote unity, one person at a time.

Unity was a struggle even in the first-century church. The church was divided over issues as crazy as who you were baptized by. We see this in 1 Corinthians 1:10-17:

> I appeal to you, brothers, in the name of our Lord Jesus Christ, that all of you agree with one another so that there may be no divisions among you and that you may be perfectly united in mind and thought. My brothers, some from Chloe's household have informed me that there are quarrels among you. What I mean is this: One of you says, "I follow Paul;" another, "I follow Apollos;" another, "I follow Cephas;" still another, "I follow Christ." Is Christ divided? Was Paul crucified for you? Were you baptized into the name of Paul? I am thankful that I did not baptize any of you except Crispus and Gaius, so no one can say that you were baptized into my name. Yes, I also baptized the household of Stephanas; beyond that, I don't remember if I baptized anyone else.

Jesus knew Satan would be out to destroy the unity of the church. This was why Jesus prayed for unity for His followers in John 17:14-19, saying:

> I have given them Your word and the world has hated them, for they are not of the world any more than I am of the world. My prayer is not that You take them out of the

world but that You protect them from the evil one. They are not of the world, even as I am not of it. Sanctify them by the truth; Your word is truth. As You sent me into the world, I have sent them into the world. For them I sanctify myself, that they too may be truly sanctified.

Why is Jesus praying for protection for His followers from the evil one in this passage? The evil one is out to separate them. He tried with the persecution of the church in the beginning of Acts, and he has continued in various ways ever since. Some of the ways he has continued is in false teaching, unresolved conflict, gossip and slander, materialism and greed, and an arrogant, unloving heart.

Sadly, Satan is succeeding as the church continues to divide and separate to this day. Without even realizing it, we are falling into his trap so our teaching is less about Jesus and more about why we do what is right, and why everyone else does what is wrong. May we learn that unity is possible because of Jesus and unity is distributed by the Spirit, and not by people.

I believe we can experience perfect unity, the unity Christ has with God, because Jesus prayed for it. I believe obtaining perfect unity is as easy as one thing. Are you ready? Are you on the edge of your seat? Have you been waiting a long time to hear this? Can it really be so simple? The ingredient is selfless, self-sacrificing, agape love, according to Colossians 3:14, where it says, "And over all these virtues put on love, which binds them all together in perfect unity." This is the love for God and the love for others. It is not an overwhelming love for ourselves, but a selfless love. It is our love for ourselves that stands in the way of perfect unity. It is that simple. Love results in unity, and selfishness destroys it. Change yourself and align yourself with the will of God, and you will experience the joy of unity with those fellow believers of Christ all over the world.

It is hard to give up yourself in church for the sake of unity. We most likely have chosen a church based on our very preferences. I charge us all to be the Christians God has called us to be as members of His church. May we know and follow the truth from His Word and be people who are not deceived by religious dogma, traditions, or feelings.

CHAPTER 9 WORKSHEET

What name do you think Jesus would give you?

_____

_____

_____

How do you feel about the church in general?

_____

_____

_____

What would you like to see change in the church?

_____

_____

_____

How can God use you to make those changes?

_____

_____

_____

What can you do to help preserve the unity in the church?

_____

_____

_____

The Shadows Unexpected

The coming of the lawless one will be in accordance with the work of Satan displayed in all kinds of counterfeit miracles, signs and wonders, and in every sort of evil that deceives those who are perishing. They perish because they refused to love the truth and so be saved.
—2 Thessalonians 2:9-10

In the killing of the terrorist Osama bin Laden, I saw how easy it is for people to disregard the truth. I learned in that story how people do not want to believe the truth, even when the evidence is extensive. So much controversy was stirred over something so obvious. After the killing of this notorious terrorist, many said they would not believe it unless they saw the pictures of Osama bin Laden's dead body themselves.

Let's look at the proof after his death. The U.S. president came before the world and announced the great news of justice. The Navy SEALs who executed the mission with excellence, witnessed his dead body. The Navy SEALs confiscated all of bin Laden's information on computers and videos, which proved it was bin Laden's compound. Al-Qaida itself also confirmed that bin Laden had, in fact, been killed. They even had DNA evidence to prove Osama's death, yet some still refused to believe.

Do I really believe this is the scam of the century and that Osama bin Laden will be seen again on this earth? That is absurd. Bin Laden will never walk the earth again, yet people want proof in pictures...even though they would no doubt deny the authenticity of the photos. Satan uses our own stubbornness to deceive us from seeing the clear truth of things.

The rejection of all the evidences as well as the eyewitness reports were also rejected in the time of Christ. Jesus was raised from the dead, which had over five hundred personal eyewitnesses, yet many others refused their testimony because they did not see Him with their own eyes. The lives of the apostles were great proof the resurrection took place. These men went from scared and timid to fearless and confident. How has Satan deceived the world about the resurrection when there was so much proof? Do we really believe that the apostles and other witnesses would die for a lie or a hallucination? Many said Jesus was never raised, yet no one ever came forth with Jesus's dead body.

The controversy over Osama bin Laden's death teaches us how deception and blindness hold people back from knowing and believing the truth. There are so many ways we can be deceived if we do not use the minds God gave us. Satan is out to trick us from seeing the obvious truth, and not just concerning Jesus, even though that is where he starts. Satan is at work in deceiving Christians in places we least expect it.

Deception of Christianity

This topic does not even seem right. Christianity is about being a follower of Christ and having a close relationship with Him. How can there be deception in that?

Believe it or not, many come to Christ for selfish reasons. I believe Satan wants us to be a Christian for all we can get, instead of who we get. Have you ever found yourself following Christ because of what He does for you, and getting mad at Him when he does not do what you want?

Have you ever found yourself trying to bring someone to Christ with the motivation of what you might get in recognition and praise? Following Christ in that way is not of God, but it is from Satan. Living in America can easily bring this out in us because we do not suffer much persecution, at least for now.

How can a person follow Christ selfishly? Here are a few ways. Many follow Christ because of the blessings they can obtain through Him. Those blessings include financial blessings, protection, guidance, self-worth, and so on. None of them are bad, but being a Christian has never been about those things. The problem is that when we are following God because of these things and we suffer setbacks, we fall apart because we believed God was always going to protect us. That is how we get confused, and you hear many say, "Why did God not heal my child? Where was God when this was happening to me? If God is the God of love, why did He let this all happen when He could have stopped it? I thought God would protect my family." Because we have not been taught accurately about God and His sovereignty, many refuse to follow God because God did not do for them what they believed He would always do.

I was getting ready to do a teenage class on how to have a relationship with Christ, and I was praying intensely about how I could help the young people understand and enjoy this relationship. I was sitting in the Orlando International Airport, waiting to go on a survey trip to Jamaica for our youth mission trip that summer, and God answered my prayers. I am not the most creative person, but God laid a story into my heart to help us understand the way God intended this relationship with Christ to be.

The story begins when judgment day arrives, and shows how it will be different than we had ever expected. I am standing before the Almighty God, and I hear the best news I could ever hear. The Father looks into my eyes and with a soft, gentle smile says, "You get to choose if you want to go to heaven or hell."

I cannot believe what I just heard. I knew that in my life I was a Christian and I was going to be in heaven one day, but this was great. This is the easiest decision of my life. Or is it? The Father looks at me as I am smiling from ear to ear, and says, "There is only one thing I must tell you. Open up each of the doors so you can make the best choice. Whatever door you walk through, your choice will have been made, and you will spend all eternity there. So choose wisely."

I go to the first door and I open it, making sure I do not get close to the threshold. As I look in, it is worse than I ever could have imagined. Just the smell from the room is like death. It must be hell. I am so glad I am a Christian. I would not have ever wanted anyone, for all eternity, to experience what I have just seen. Then it happens—and I cannot believe what I see. It appears to be Jesus on His throne within this terrible place. I look at the Father and I ask, "Is that really Jesus sitting there?"

He looks at me and nods and, in a whisper, says, "Yes, my son."

I am so confused because everything I had ever thought was so different from this. I did not know I would have a choice, and I had believed Jesus would be reigning in heaven.

I walk over to the second room and open the door. It is absolutely amazing. What seems to be heaven is far better than I could ever have imagined. It is all I had dreamed and more. I am ready for my eternal rest. Life was hard, and I was looking forward to rest. I had been waiting for this all my life and now it is mine; but as I look into the room, I am shocked once again. Standing in the midst of heaven is what appears to be Satan. What am I to do? I look to the Father, confused once again, and ask, "Is that really Satan?"

Once again, the Father nods his head and answers, "Yes." Immediately He asks, "What door do you choose, for you must enter immediately."

Let us stop the story right here and answer the question honestly. Which door would you choose? Do you choose the room with Jesus in misery or the room with Satan in bliss?

After you honestly answer that question, I must tell you the story is not over. What you do not realize is if you walk through the threshold of what appears to be hell, it actually becomes heaven; and if you go through the threshold of what appears to be heaven, it actually becomes hell. What the Father wanted to know was whether you really loved the Son enough to be anywhere with Him, even if it seemed you would be in hell for all eternity. Do you sincerely want to be with Christ so much that even if you would have to be in hell for all eternity, you would still choose that? Is Christianity about your love for Christ, or about going to heaven and having eternal rest, no pain, and no sorrow?

Would it be crazy to think something like this could happen? Is not Christianity all about my relationship and love for Christ? Answering the question before knowing the ending exposes your heart.

The point of the story is: do we love Christ? Are we in a personal relationship with Him? If Christianity is about what you will gain in this world, you may be greatly disappointed. If you are a Christian because of what you will get in eternity, you may be disappointed, as well. Not that eternity in heaven will not be amazing, but because eternity is about being with God, my best friend and the love of my life, forever. I will live in a shack, sleep on rocks, and even have nothing, if I but get to be in God's presence for all eternity. The mansions talked about in heaven do not entice me, but the heavenly relationship with God is what I desire.

Is it not scary to believe that Satan might even have deceived people when it comes to Christianity? He may deceive some, but do not let Him deceive you. Pursue a genuine love for Christ that will escort you into eternity.

Deception of Our Closeness to Christ

I have to admit, there are times I do not feel real close to God. That relationship has suffered because at times God seemed so far away. We may have all experienced this same thing in our lives. Sometimes it can be caused by tragedy, or loneliness, or it can be because of our sin. My closeness to God seems to be dependent on how I feel at the moment.

I grew up in a church that taught me when I sin I am not close to Christ until I make it right. As a teenager, I felt guilty because of making poor decisions. I had high standards for myself, so I was always coming up short. My relationship with God really suffered because of this teaching and deception. Growing up, I did not hear much about God's grace but more about God's anger and condemnation. I guess they thought if I knew too much of God's grace, I would abuse it. I wish I had known Romans 6:11-14, where it says:

> In the same way, count yourselves dead to sin but alive to God in Christ Jesus. Therefore do not let sin reign in your mortal body so that you obey its evil desires. Do not offer the parts of your body to sin, as instruments of wickedness, but rather offer yourselves to God, as those who have been brought from death to life; and offer the parts of your body to Him as instruments of righteousness. For sin shall not be your master, because you are not under law, but under grace.

I lived with so much guilt because I was still battling the sin Christ had already forgiven. Can Satan deceive us in our closeness to the Son? Of course he can, and he does. Getting Christians to feel unforgiven and distant from God will cause us to go into a cycle of sin, guilt, and distance from God and His church, to a hardened heart.

Later on, I began to study and learn of God's grace and the truth of Christ's closeness to His people. I have seen people who claim closeness with God but seem so far removed; and I have seen Christians who feel so far away, yet seem extremely close to God. It seems Satan is deceiving people on both sides. The people who talk too much of judgment and condemnation need to hear more about God's grace; and the people who can only talk of God's grace, need to be challenged by God's judgment and condemnation.

Some believe in God, but to them He is a distant God. Adam and Eve experienced a closeness with God who was not distant. Since Adam and Eve ruined this closeness by sin, the Old Testament seemed to reveal a distant God who was appeased by sacrifice, laws, and rituals. God's desire has always been to be close to His creation. Being a holy and righteous God, He appeared to be far off, even though He sought closeness. Satan has tried to convince the world that God is far off. Instead, God did not become like us but came to be with us and within us.

We make statements about getting closer to Christ. How many times have you heard a prayer, asking God to help us get closer to Him? I believe, from the Scriptures, we are as close to God as we ever will be on this earth. According to 1 Corinthians 6:19-20: "Do you not know that your body is a temple of the Holy Spirit, who is in you, whom you have received from God? You are not your own; you were bought at a price. Therefore honor God with your body." We are the temple of the Holy Spirit, and He lives within us. We have God living inside of us. It does not get any closer than that. According to the Scriptures, this closeness will never change unless we get rid of the Spirit in our life.

In 1 Thessalonians 5:19, we can quench the Spirit in our life. In Galatians 5:4, we can fall away from God. We can fall away not because of sin but because our hearts have become hardened by sin. This happens because we feel so guilty and worthless that we run away from God instead of running to Him. I believe we need to quit listening to the deceiving spirits and begin to listen to the Holy Spirit inside of us. The Holy Spirit says we are not to practice sin and live in sin; but if we do sin, we have an advocate who defends us. In 1 John 2:1-2 it says, "My dear children, I write this to you so that you will not sin. But if anybody does sin, we have one who speaks to the Father in our defense—Jesus Christ, the Righteous One. He is the atoning sacrifice for our sins, and not only for ours but also for the sins of the whole world." Jesus deals with our sins. Keep loving God and doing what He says, and when we make mistakes, do not get bogged down with what Jesus died for two thousand years ago.

People say, if we are as close to God as we will ever be, then why do we feel closer to God at times and not at others? That is just a feeling we have based on whether or not we have been experiencing God. This is the reason why, on a mission trip, I can feel so close to God. My closeness has not changed. On a mission trip, I have given up all of myself and my personal comfort to be completely led by God. I may be more in prayer and service, so I am seeing and experiencing God in a powerful way. Because of so much of my time and energy being saturated in service and prayer, I experience something so great that it is a feeling I always want to have. We call these the mountaintop experiences in our life.

We long for a mountaintop experience, and that could be why we go to seminars and retreats or have days of fasting—to help us get back to the top of the mountain in our relationship with God. The closeness to God has not changed, whether we are on the mountain or not. I am here to tell you that we can experience God all the time in our lives if we can get past this deception of needing to get closer to God. We can be selfless right here and now. We can be bold and unconcerned about our comfort here and now. We can saturate every day in service and prayer to experience God in His fullest. We can live by the Spirit and see the amazing power of God each day and not just at conferences, mission trips, or even Sunday mornings. We always say we are strapped for time but, for the most part, we do what we want to do in this life. Once, I heard a minister say that the busier his day was going to be, the longer he would spend with God in prayer that morning. It was because the more he had to do, the more he needed Christ to be with him and lead him.

We envy what others have in their relationship with God, and we wonder why their sins are not holding them back. They are still making mistakes at times, but they are not weighed down by them. We are actually deceived into thinking that they do not have struggles. We need to realize they are living in the truth that their sin was taken away 2,000 years ago. They are not deceived to stay in sin and call it forgiven. They are actually living lives where they do not practice sin. When they do sin, they repent and trust the forgiveness of Jesus.

What we need to be praying for is the possibility we will experience God the way He designed for us to experience Him on this earth. If we truly surrender to God and no longer are deceived into believing that God is not close to us or is close only at certain times, it is then we can start making steps toward having a true relationship with God.

Even though you want to read the rest of this chapter, please take a few minutes to stop and pray. Ask God to allow you to surrender everything to experience this relationship with Him—this relationship that cost the very life of Christ. Also ask God to guard your mind from all the lies that are said to be truth. Thank Him for the closeness you have because of the amazing gift of His Holy Spirit. May God lead you to true devotion and abundant life, having God with you always.

Deception of the Pursuit of Feelings

Did you ever think that Satan or his angels go to church more regularly than you do? Satan and/or his followers are at church buildings, Bible studies, accountability groups, fellowship dinners, and even Bible classes with consistency and purpose. Satan is out to deceive and turn as many as possible away from God. Satan knows he has only a little time left, according to Revelation 12:12: "Therefore rejoice, you heavens and you who dwell in them! But woe to the earth and the sea, because the Devil has gone down to you! He is filled with fury, because he knows that his time is short." Today, could the deception with believers be also in how they are touched by Christ as well as how they experience Christ? Many people are now seeking churches and ministers who will give them some religious experience. They are looking for an hour a week to give them an emotion that will get them through the following week. Emotions come and go, but God's Word planted in your heart will always be there.

I see people looking for this religious experience all the time because they are flying from emotion to emotion and church to church. They are attending churches, seminars, and even reading Christian books, searching for what will give them the next religious high. The deception of Satan could be in the pursuit of that next high or the next emotion, rather than seeking Christ. Satan or his followers may be at these church services in order to distract believers from seeing Christ while giving them every opportunity to pursue the next best experience.

Today's churches in America have to accommodate this trend by spending so much money to give their members the best experience. If they don't, the people have proven they will leave and find it elsewhere. Now churches are in competition. They are spending millions of dollars each year to have the best Sunday experience and facilities when Christ would prefer the millions of dollars be spent on meeting the needs of people and spreading truth around the world. When Christ envisioned His church, did He see it this way, or is this another thing Satan has perverted?

Our worship has often been backward. Churches are putting on high dollar services so we can leave feeling full of the Spirit. The Bible actually teaches that our worship is not to help us be full of the Spirit but it is a result of being full of the Spirit. According to Ephesians 5:18-21: "And do not get drunk with wine, for that is dissipation, but be filled with the Spirit, speaking to one another in psalms and hymns and spiritual songs, singing and making melody with your heart to the Lord; always giving thanks for all things in the name of our Lord Jesus Christ to God, even the Father; and be subject to one another in the fear of Christ."

A problem in churches today may be with bringing in true Spirit-filled Christians. Many people today are tired of all the politics in church, so they try to do it on their own or with a few other people. That is not what Jesus intended the church to be.

My relationship with God is not based on what happens every Sunday, but on what happens daily and even hourly with Him. My worship is not what happens on Sunday but in how I live my life every single day. My knowledge is not primarily what I learn on Sundays but on what God teaches me every day from His Word. My convictions as well as my emotions come through His Word and His Spirit. It is not eloquent ministers with good illustrations and funny jokes who convince, but it is the Word of God. Hebrews 4:12 says, "For the word of God is living and active. Sharper than any double-edged sword, it penetrates even to dividing soul and spirit, joints and marrow; it judges the thoughts and attitudes of the heart."

Have we been deceived into looking for the wrong things? Are we looking to fill our churches with people who only want a Sunday experience? If not, then we need to work harder at teaching a religiously ignorant society how to be taught by God and His Word. We need to quit spending God's money on bringing about emotions in people through a one to two-hour religious experience, and realize that experiencing Christ is when His true worshippers come together and worship in spirit and in truth according to John 4:21-24:

> Jesus declared, "Believe me, woman, a time is coming
> when you will worship the Father neither on this moun-
> tain nor in Jerusalem. You Samaritans worship what you
> do not know; we worship what we do know, for salva-
> tion is from the Jews. Yet a time is coming and has now
> come when the true worshipers will worship the Father
> in spirit and truth, for they are the kind of worshipers the
> Father seeks. God is spirit, and his worshipers must wor-
> ship in spirit and in truth."

Because God is spirit, He is not impressed with physical things like hearing our music, raising hands, bowing down, and even singing if it is not
from every ounce of our heart, mind, and soul. If you do not believe this
to be true, consider someone who is tone deaf and cannot sing in tune for
the life of them. Their singing is beautiful to God if it is from the heart,
regardless of the physical sound. If it is from our heart, God would expect to see some emotion and expressions of worship.

Also, those in the church need to quit jumping around from church
to church looking for the best experience. Finding a group of Christians
who teach the Word of God and live daily for the purpose of Christ is a
good thing. Once you have found that group, commit to serve the body
of Christ there, get involved, get along in love, and use the gifts God
has given to glorify Him and encourage each other. As Christians, we
already have Jesus. The search should be over. We need to quit looking
for Him on Sundays and start experiencing Him every day. If you want a
powerful worship experience, then put Christ on the throne in your life
to stay, submit to God and His will daily, and allow His Holy Spirit to be
free in your worship. Then, brothers and sisters, you will have meaning-
ful worship every day of your life.

There are so many churches that believe emotions are evil because
other believers have pursued emotions rather than Christ. God created

emotions, but He does not want us to pursue them and be driven by them, just as He does not want us to fight them and disregard them. Many have chosen to follow Christ because of being fearful of hell. Fear is the emotion which drives them to that decision. Fearing God is not wrong, but would God not rather you be motivated by love rather than by fear? Just as pursuing emotions is a distraction from Christ, allowing no emotion is just as much as a distraction as it is a deception. What we do not realize is that emotions will naturally be stirred up in our lives when we, through un-blinded eyes, see Christ. When was the last time you were moved to tears by meditating on the beautiful words of a song about Christ?

There have been times in my life where I literally could not control my emotions. One of those times was at my baptism. As I was getting changed in the back room in the church before I was to be baptized, I could not stop shivering, even though I was not cold. I could not talk because I understood the enormity of this decision. I was dying to myself and fully surrendering my life to Jesus.

Another time when I could not control my emotions was when I was at a big youth rally in Gatlinburg, Tennessee, a few years ago. They took a clip from the movie *The Passion of the Christ* and set it to the song by Phillips Craig and Dean entitled, "Your Grace Still Amazes Me."

Many of you might have had a similar experience if you saw this movie. These are not religious experiences we are pursuing, but the emotions are natural and unrehearsed. It is a shame for those of us who grew up in a church where no emotion could be shown. If emotion was shown, it was believed to be for attention, or too much like the other church down the street. Today I struggle with free worship because of my upbringing, and shame on me when I hold back emotions or feelings stirred by the Holy Spirit. It is not always about holding back emotions in congregational worship, but it can even be while hearing a song, serving in the hospital, or when I am recommitted at home in my study.

The deception is not in the feelings or in the emotions, but the deception is in our sole pursuit of these feelings and emotions to experience Christ. Do you remember the passage of Scripture where God was not seen where all expected Him, but in the whisper? 1 Kings 19:11-13 says:

> The LORD said, "Go out and stand on the mountain in the presence of the LORD, for the LORD is about to pass by." Then a great and powerful wind tore the mountains apart and shattered the rocks before the LORD, but the LORD was not in the wind. After the wind there was an earthquake, but the LORD was not in the earthquake. After the earthquake came a fire, but the LORD was not in the fire. And after the fire came a gentle whisper. When Elijah heard it, he pulled his cloak over his face and went out and stood at the mouth of the cave.

May our pursuit be to experience a true relationship with Christ, and may we exalt Him in all we do. May we allow the Holy Spirit to be free to express Himself by challenging us, motivating us, and committing us to worship the King of kings and the Lord of lords in the way He deserves.

Deception in Seeing Christ

In my Bible study, I have also learned the desire to see Christ is not the end of the matter, either. Some have said. "If I could just see Christ, it would change everything." How many people in the Bible have seen Christ, and it did not change their lives one bit? The deception is going from seminar, to retreat, and to conference, having a desire to see Christ when the whole time we are simply looking to see something great or hear the next best thought.

Take the rich man, as an example, in Matthew 19:16-22:

> Now a man came up to Jesus and asked, "Teacher, what good thing must I do to get eternal life?" "Why do you ask me about what is good?" Jesus replied. "There is only One who is good. If you want to enter life, obey the commandments." "Which ones?" the man inquired. Jesus replied, "'Do not murder, do not commit adultery, do not steal, do not give false testimony, honor your father and mother, and love your neighbor as yourself.' "All these I have kept," the young man said. "What do I still lack?" Jesus answered, "If you want to be perfect, go, sell your possessions and give to the poor, and you will have treasure in heaven. Then come, follow me." When the young man heard this, he went away sad, because he had great wealth.

He saw Jesus face-to-face and went home sad.

What about King Herod? He was glad to see Christ, and the Scriptures say he had wanted to see Him for a long time. Well, the time came in which his encounter with the I AM, Jesus Christ, happened. Luke 23:8-10 says, "When Herod saw Jesus, he was greatly pleased, because for a long time he had been wanting to see Him. From what he had heard about Him, he hoped to see Him perform some miracle. He plied Him with many questions, but Jesus gave him no answer."

Herod saw Jesus but then mocked Him.

So many times I hear people say if they could just be before Christ, their lives would change. If they could only go to good churches with good preachers, they would be different. There are going to be many people who experience Christ through me or through Christ's church collectively, and turn away saddened. There will be some who will mock and openly reject Christ by their own words. I am sad to say, many are like Herod in our churches. They say they want to see Christ or they have this desire to see Him, but their motives are not right. It may just be about how it makes them look to their family or friends. It may be because it makes them feel good about themselves to show up to church every now and then. It might help them make acquaintances for growing their businesses. Whatever the reasons may be, they are seeing Christ and choosing to walk away from Him unchanged.

This is the same response for the one who reads God's words and does not apply them. Jesus always says it best, and this time in Matthew 7:24-27:

> Therefore everyone who hears these words of mine and puts them into practice is like a wise man who built his house on the rock. The rain came down, the streams rose, and the winds blew and beat against that house; yet it did not fall, because it had its foundation on the rock. But everyone who hears these words of mine and does not put them into practice is like a foolish man who built his house on sand. The rain came down, the streams rose, and the winds blew and beat against that house, and it fell with a great crash.

How many people hear the Word of God every week on Sunday and then do not put it into practice? Many wonder why the storms of life hit and their lives crash down. According to Jesus's words, it is because they heard but did not apply what they heard. I like to ask the question, "What is going to be different in your life this week based on what you have studied and learned today?" I agree there were those like Zacchaeus, who saw Jesus and his life truly was changed. We need to be like Zacchaeus, who see Jesus and then let Him change their lives.

Let us hear the words of Jesus with a soft heart and choose to follow what our Lord says.

Deception of the Fear of God

Here is another section where we want to first ask the question, "What is the deception in fearing God?" I am glad you asked, because this topic has been watered down for many years. Many have gone to the other extreme and, because of the reaction from the belief that God is a lightning-throwing God, some have taken on the mentality that God is more like our spiritual Santa Claus whom we are simply supposed to admire and respect.

Is that true? Many have tried to get people to be afraid of God in order to lead them to God. As I mentioned earlier in the book, God would rather we be motivated by love, even though we should fear, as well. The deception today is that I do not need to fear God but rather only respect Him. This is a great thought if God were our companion, but He is not. Some use the verse in 1 John 4:18, where it says, "There is no fear in love. Perfect love casts out fear because fear involves punishment." Is this contradicting the entire Bible where God desires to be feared?

I believe this is fear of judgment when we will all stand before the Lord. John writes before the previous verse, in 1 John 4:17, "Love is perfected in us so we may have confidence in the Day of Judgment. Learning to fear God the way He desires us to fear Him will result in a deep respect and submission to Him."

I want to give a full picture of God as the Bible teaches. God is light, and in Him there is no darkness at all, according to 1 John 1:5. God will not ever tolerate sin. Sin is evil and darkness, and causes separation and hardships. Sin and evil are in opposition to the very character of God. He knows what is best for us in this life, if we will only listen to Him.

Ask the young man in my office who was in so much pain because his girlfriend got pregnant and they made a terrible decision. Instead of making the right choice, he did not fear God but rather feared his parents, so they aborted the child. After the fact, when he came to my office with much pain, there was nothing he could do. He now held the guilt of his sinful decision. God's way of a sexual union in marriage would have made his life a whole lot easier with a whole lot less pain. Keeping the marriage bed undefiled is not to hurt us or keep us from fun; it is for the best life possible.

Ask the woman whose marriage went under major stress because she aborted her firstborn in high school with a high school boyfriend. She had never told her future husband. Her husband found out as they were having complications with their first son after his birth where the doctor stated, "This situation could have been caused from the abortion you had years ago." Lies and deception do not lead to a healthy and satisfying life.

How has Satan deceived us to believe God's way is some kind of punishment to control us? This was the very lie He told Eve, and she believed him. God's instructions are there because He loves us. I love my sons enough to not allow them to play in the road. I am not punishing them, even though at times they think I am, but I love them so much that I do not want life to be harder for them or to end abruptly.

Let me reference some stories in the Bible about the vastness and holiness of God. If you have studied these stories and are not afraid of God, you need to restudy them.

Throughout the Bible, God has shown His holiness and justice, starting with the punishment of Cain. After that, He destroyed all but eight people in the world through a worldwide flood. He has burned wicked cities; struck Miriam (Moses's sister) with leprosy because she did not like that Moses married a black woman; had Achan and his family stoned to death because of stealing; killed the baby born by Bathsheba because of her and King David's adultery; killed Uzzah as he touched the holy ark of the covenant while he was trying to save it; brought nations to kill and exile His rebelling people; struck down Ananias and Saphira because they lied. Should I keep going?

The Bible even goes on to say many are sick and some have died because they ate and drank judgment on themselves as they took the Lord's Supper (communion) without recognizing the Lord, as it says in 1 Corinthians 11:29-30.

Can you believe that our God will kill or destroy a person in judgment? He has, He does, and He will. I do not believe in "natural" disasters because nothing happens outside the knowledge of God. Do you believe it is a coincidence that more disasters are occurring around the world as the world continues to become more corrupt? Corrupt cities are being judged right before our eyes. I understand no one wants to say these things aloud, but God has given me a message to proclaim, "God judges wickedness and rebellion, even now in our country."

There are so many Bible examples where God judges even His own people. What about Moses, who was a man who had such a relationship with God to be envied? God spared his life as a child and raised him up to be a vital instrument in the release of His people in Egypt, yet God would not allow him to enter the promise land. The Scriptures would actually allude to the point that God killed and buried Moses even before His body gave way to death. This is seen in Deuteronomy 34:1-7, where it says:

> Then Moses climbed Mount Nebo from the plains of Moab to the top of Pisgah, across from Jericho. There the Lord showed him the whole land—from Gilead to Dan, all of Naphtali, the territory of Ephraim and Manasseh, all the land of Judah as far as the western sea, the Negev and the whole region from the Valley of Jericho, the City of Palms, as far as Zoar. Then the Lord said to him, "This

is the land I promised on oath to Abraham, Isaac and Jacob when I said, 'I will give it to your descendants.' I have let you see it with your eyes, but you will not cross over into it." And Moses the servant of the Lord died there in Moab, as the Lord had said. He buried him in Moab, in the valley opposite Beth Peor, but to this day no one knows where his grave is. Moses was one hundred and twenty years old when he died, yet his eyes were not weak nor his strength gone.

Because Satan saw Moses not get to enter the promise land, Satan must have believed Moses was his, so he made claims to the body of Moses when he died according to Jude 9: "But even the archangel Michael, when he was disputing with the Devil about the body of Moses, did not dare to bring a slanderous accusation against him, but said, 'The Lord rebuke you!'" If Satan believed he had rights to Moses, who was a great man of God, doesn't it get you to wondering about yourself and what Satan will think about you after you die?

God is a just God and would not even make an exception for Moses to enter the promise land. This tells me something in and of itself. On one occasion, Moses tries to convince God to allow him to enter the promise land. These verses will give some insight about our relationship with a Holy and Almighty God. From Moses's conversation with God, I see a parent/child relationship. The story is taken from Deuteronomy 3:23-26.

At that time I pleaded with the Lord: "O Sovereign Lord, you have begun to show to your servant your greatness and your strong hand. For what god is there in heaven or on earth that can do the deeds and mighty works you do? Let me go over and see the good land beyond the

Jordan—that fine hill country and Lebanon." But the Lord was angry with me on your account and would not listen to me. "That is enough," the Lord said. "Do not speak to me anymore about this matter."

It seems as if Moses starts out by trying to butter up God and then convince Him to let him enter the promise land. God tells Moses that it is enough and not to ask again. Boy, have I heard those words a lot growing up. It may not have been wrong to ask God, but that better be the last time. Moses feared God so much that the Scriptures never record Moses asking again. I believe Moses knew better. God had made His decision, and that was it. The word of God had been spoken into existence that Joshua would be the next leader. God is not to be treated as a best friend where we can say whatever we want to say. Let me put it this way. My boys need to have a loving relationship with me as their daddy, but they also need to be afraid of me at times.

This may be the problem today in society. Children need their dads, and dads can reflect and teach the principles of God to a child in such impacting ways. The same hand that loves on them, scratches their backs, holds them, and provides for them is the same hand that disciplines and punishes them out of love, for their own good. The same hand that gives to them the things they want is also the same hand that out of love withholds and takes away dangerous things which can bring them harm. The Bible talks about the hand of God to heal and to destroy. If children do not have a fear and a respect for both their parents, the teenage years will be extremely difficult. When mom or dad says, "Enough, and do not ask us again," it should mean exactly that. What are we teaching our kids when we count to three when we want them to do something? One is enough! We must learn to move immediately when God says something to us and not wait until He counts to three.

I heard a lady in a store count to three to get her child to stop taking things off the shelf. She counted slowly, and the boy still was not stopping. She got to two and then she said, "You better quit…two and a half, almost at three." I wanted to shout out, "Three already! He is not listening to you!" God did not look at Moses and say, "You better stop. I am counting to three." As a parent, when I say, "Stop!" I mean stop right this instant. The counting-to-three technique does not work very well when your child is running toward a busy highway.

Do we fear God and respect what He says? We should, because He is the all-powerful, perfect, and excellent God. I will be transparent with you about my personal fear of God. You might criticize me for this, but fearing God has kept me from sin. Many years ago I was dabbling in some things I should not have been doing. After a deep study on the fear of God through the Scriptures, I knew that if I did not deal with this in my life, then God would do whatever He needed to do to teach me. As my wife was pregnant with twins, I could not help but know God was in control of the health and survival of my boys. I knew from the story of David and Bathsheba that God could punish unrepentant and continual sin. Because of this fear of God's discipline, God gave me the strength to overcome this struggle immediately.

When you hold your child for the first time, you do not want God ever to take them away because of your hardness of heart or rebellion toward God. I would rather get my life together than have God wake me up through hardships to save my soul. I truly believed that out of God's love, He will do whatever it takes to open our eyes. Many may scrutinize me for this belief, but I believe the Scriptures teach that fearing the Lord will keep us from sin. Take a look at Exodus 20:20, where it says, "Moses said to the people, 'Do not be afraid. God has come to test you, so that the fear of God will be with you to keep you from sinning.'"

Why would Abraham be willing to offer his son Isaac as a sacrifice? What would lead a father to do this to a son whom he loved? The

Bible says that after Abraham was really going to obey God by sacrificing his son, then God says in Genesis 22:12, "'Do not lay a hand on the boy,' he said. 'Do not do anything to him. Now I know that you fear God, because you have not withheld from me your son, your only son.'" Abraham feared God more than anything, and he proved it here. This was not just a healthy respect. This was fear in not obeying all God has asked him to do.

How does God define fear in the Bible? Let's take a look at a few Scriptures to see what God says.

- Daniel 6:26—"I issue a decree that in every part of my kingdom people must fear and tremble before the God of Daniel. For he is the living God and he endures forever; his kingdom will not be destroyed, his dominion will never end."

- Isaiah 8:11-13—"The Lord spoke to me with His strong hand upon me, warning me not to follow the way of this people. He said: 'Do not call conspiracy everything that these people call conspiracy; do not fear what they fear, and do not dread it. The Lord Almighty is the one you are to regard as holy, He is the one you are to fear, He is the one you are to dread.'"

- Matthew 10:28—"Do not be afraid of those who kill the body but cannot kill the soul. Rather, be afraid of the One who can destroy both soul and body in hell."

- Luke 23:40-41—"But the other criminal rebuked him. 'Don't you fear God,' he said, 'since you are under the same sentence? We are punished justly, for we are getting what our deeds deserve. But this man has done nothing wrong.'"

- 1 Peter 1:17-19—"And if you address as Father the One who impartially judges according to each man's work, conduct yourselves in fear during the time of your stay upon earth; knowing that you were not redeemed with perishable things like silver or gold from your futile way of life inherited from your forefathers, but with precious blood, as of a lamb unblemished and spotless, the blood of Christ."

It seems quite clear with many stories and Scriptures that God wants to be feared. This fear includes respect and reverence but seems to surpass that meaning alone. God wants us to tremble before Him. Men and women in the Bible trembled before angels. How much greater is God above the angels? Isaiah trembled before God in Isaiah 6 and saw himself very clearly as he was in the presence of God. It was not until his sins were forgiven that Isaiah had any confidence in God's presence. We are also to draw near the throne of grace in confidence because we are forgiven in Jesus Christ according to Hebrew 10:19-22:

> Therefore, brothers, since we have confidence to enter the Most Holy Place by the blood of Jesus, by a new and living way opened for us through the curtain, that is, his body, and since we have a great priest over the house of God, let us draw near to God with a sincere heart in full assurance of faith, having our hearts sprinkled to cleanse us from a guilty conscience and having our bodies washed with pure water.

This confidence does not give us a right to forget whose presence we are in and who is the magnificent God.

How does a true, godly fear of God impact our lives today? Let us also look at what the Scriptures say about this.

- Deuteronomy 5:29—"Oh, that their hearts would be inclined to fear me and keep all my commands always, so that it might go well with them and their children forever!"

- Proverbs 8:13—"To fear the Lord is to hate evil; I hate pride and arrogance, evil behavior and perverse speech."

- Proverbs 15:16—"Better a little with the fear of the Lord than great wealth with turmoil."

- 2 Corinthians 5:11—"Since, then, we know what it is to fear the Lord, we try to persuade men. What we are is plain to God, and I hope it is also plain to your conscience."

- 2 Corinthians 7:1—"Therefore, having these promises, beloved, let us cleanse ourselves from all defilement of flesh and spirit, perfecting holiness in the fear of God."

These few verses teach me so much about the importance of fearing God and the impact it will have on my relationship with God. Since this understanding, my posture in prayer is less upright and more bowed low in humility. My prayers are now more of seeking God's will and less telling of my will. My heart desires holiness, and it is less about what I can do and still be a Christian. My pursuit is more about fearing the Lord and less of a pursuit toward wealth and pleasures in this life. I am learning to understand that I do not have any rights before God but, rather, a greater appreciation for the sacrifice of Christ, which humbles me to know I can come into His presence and He wants me there.

Do not let our hearts be deceived. How could we ever fear Satan when we should fear God? Satan wants to keep us from fearing God because when we do, we become just like he was when he lost his fear of

God in heaven. It is when we water down our fear of God or lose our fear of God that we find ourselves in a bad place. We get caught up in sin and find ourselves thinking that for whatever reason, God does not see us or He just always forgives. The message of this section of the book is clear from Proverbs 23:17, where it says, "Do not let your heart envy sinners, but always be zealous for the fear of the Lord."

Deception in Loving our Neighbors

How can we be deceived in loving our neighbors? Would it shock you if I told you that everyone is not your neighbor? Would you be surprised if I told you the Bible does not expect you to love everyone? Yes, you read this correctly. We hear all the time, "Love God and Love others!" This slogan is used in many churches as their Vision statement, and is seen on billboards without any explanation. This deception and misinterpretation has confused many as they see a contradiction with God. If you misinterpret this, then there is a contradiction, but we know there are not any contradictions with God. This section is going to cause some of you to be very angry with me. I hope this frustration leads you to study out what I am writing. Please, give me a chance to explain before you make your judgment. I know these are very deep concepts, and it will take an open mind to hear me out.

This commandment of loving your neighbor as you love yourself is found in Leviticus 19:18. How could God say this commandment and then tell the Israelite to go in war and kill and destroy these perverse and evil people. How can you go and kill in war while loving them? I don't believe you can. How can God send those He loves to hell? I don't believe He will. Does God love everyone? There are Scriptures which say God hates. We have always heard people say that God hates the sin and not the sinner. Can God hate the ungodly? Psalm 11:5 says, "The LORD tests the righteous and the wicked, and the one who loves violence His soul hates." Also in Psalm 5:5 it says, "The boastful shall not stand before Your eyes; You hate all who do iniquity." There are a handful of other verses which say God hates. How can God truly love His people and not hate the evil doer? God's justice is because of His love. God's vengeance and punishment for the wicked is because of His justice as He demonstrates His love for the righteous. What God will do in the future to the wicked, rebellious, and ungodly in Revelation is not out of His love for them, but because of His love for His church.

I do not believe the Israelites saw loving their neighbors as including everyone, even when it came to defending themselves in warfare. They must not have seen the invading armies or wicked groups as their neighbors, or God would have been telling them to break His commandment. We know God would not ask such a thing. Could it be that the Hebrew knew God's commandment was not to love everyone but only their neighbors? God used a specific word to describe a neighbor, which did not include everyone. In verses such as Exodus 22:21 and Deuteronomy 10:17-19, God gives requirements to His people in how to treat strangers and aliens in their land, especially as they became their neighbors. There was a difference in Scripture between a neighbor and sojourner in the land. Even if these people were from other places, they were to be treated as neighbors while they lived in the land. Leviticus 19:34 makes this quite clear when it says, "The stranger who resides with you shall be to you as the native among you, and you shall love him as yourself, for you were aliens in the land of Egypt; I am the Lord your God." God used the same terminology of loving you neighbor as you love yourself in how to treat these new residents who lived now in their midst.

Now we have to define neighbor, or should we just let Jesus define "who is our neighbor?" People in Jesus's time must have understood that the term "neighbor" did not include everyone. This is why a lawyer approached Jesus and asked Him to define this for him. The story is told by Jesus in Luke 10:29 where He is asked, "Who is my neighbor?" The motive behind the man's question was "to justify himself." This lawyer seems to have had a very narrow view of a neighbor. Jesus told him a story to answer his question and to broaden his view of this word neighbor. This is the story we refer to as *The Good Samaritan*.

We need to first start with a little background between the relationship of Jews and Samaritans. During the time of Jesus, Samaritans were considered "half-breeds." Jews would go miles out of their way to avoid traveling through the region of Samaria. On numerous occasions, Jesus would travel through Samaria and was never prejudiced in dealing with them. Jesus told this story about two Jewish leaders who did not love their neighbor as they loved themselves. To this lawyer, loving one's neighbor might have only meant Jew to Jew. Jesus was illustrating that one's neighbor was more than your race. The Samaritan in the story somehow knew that his neighbor included his Jewish neighbors, as well. At the end of Jesus's parable, Jesus told the lawyer to follow the example of one he originally did not think he needed to love. Jesus did not contradict the Old Testament command, or even add to it. Jesus simply explained the heart of God who told His people from the beginning to love their neighbors, and also defeat wicked armies.

Goliath was not a neighbor whom David was expected to love. David was given the power to defeat Goliath by the hand of God. Some people say David killed under the old law and now things have changed. So, let's discuss this. The law of loving our neighbors and loving our enemies has never changed. God always taught his people to love their neighbor while also teaching them to love their enemies. Once again, how can you love your enemy and then kill them? I don't believe you can. When Jesus said to love your enemies in Matthew 5:43-44, he was not correcting or changing something in the Law of Moses. In fact, you will not find it anywhere in the law to love your neighbors and hate your enemies. Hating your enemy was not from the Law of Moses but from those who try to make the Bible say what they want. The Pharisees and scribes were good at twisting the Scriptures to fit their lifestyles and wickedness. In the Sermon on the Mount in Matthew 5-7, Jesus did not introduce a new concept of loving your enemies. God always expected His people to love their enemies. The listeners to Jesus's teachings of the Sermon on the Mount were not warriors getting ready for battle. These were ordinary people from small towns such as Galilee and Capernaum. Jesus reminded them how to deal with each other in minor, personal offenses which can occur in everyday life.

It has always been about loving your enemies, but we must define the word enemy from the context of the Bible. Just like the word neighbor does not encompass everyone as we have been told, the word enemy did not encompass every person, either. Let me explain. The Law of Moses in Exodus 23:4-5 says, "If you meet your enemy's ox or his donkey wandering away, you shall surely return it to him. If you see the donkey of one who hates you lying helpless under its load, you shall refrain from leaving it to him, you shall surely release it with him." The Israelites would have known that this law was more than dealing with an ox or donkey. It was a way an Israelite could show love to his enemies.

The passage is not dealing with how the Israelites were to treat those who would invade their land. It would be absurd to think the Israelite was to treat a soldier of an invading army, a thief, or a murderer this way. The enemy God is referring to in these verses is also considered a neighbor. This enemy lived close enough to discover his ox in trouble. Just as the passage in Matthew 5:39 which says, "If someone strikes you on the right cheek, turn to him the other also," refers to an enemy who is a neighbor, not an evil invading soldier or murderer whom you allow to hurt you worse. Jesus is not telling us not to defend against an evil person who breaks into our house and rapes our wife. By the way, take our daughter since we need to go the extra mile. God commanded His people to show undeserved kindness to their enemies, and He also instructed them to go to war against certain cities and countries. The Israelites did not ever seem to see this as a contradiction, and we shouldn't either. When we read Scriptures such as Proverbs 25:21-22, "If your enemy is hungry, give him food to eat; And if he is thirsty, give him water to drink; For you will heap burning coals on his head, And the Lord will reward you," we must use the same logic we used earlier in seeing that this has no application to the battlefield or defending against evil. This refers to a neighbor who has made himself an enemy. Nowhere in the New Testament does Jesus ever forbid his people from serving in the military. John the Baptist challenged the soldiers to repent and bear fruit in repentance by not taking money by force from anyone. Jesus dealt with a Roman centurion, where Jesus never said he needed to give up his position. Instead, Jesus commends him for having extraordinary faith.

Some use Jesus as the example because He never engaged in warfare and never carried a sword. This argument would not hold up because Jesus also didn't marry. Using the same logic, we should also not marry, and that would not coincide with the rest of Scripture. Many of our veterans come home from war with guilt for some of the orders they had to follow. The commandment has not changed, and war exists to fight evil and defend the innocent. Imagine where America would be today if we practiced loving our neighbors and loving our enemies as encompassing everyone. When evil nations would invade, we would just let them take over the country and we would serve them by going the extra mile. As they are killing and beheading, we would not run or fight, but if anything, we would stand still so the killing would be a little easier for them. The fact is, God has used godly nations to expel the wicked, defend the helpless, protect God's people and promote peace. Not all countries do this, so it may not always be a good thing to fight in a nation's military. As of now in the United States military, America seems to fight against evil while defending the helpless.

To conclude this challenging section and chapter, there are numerous reasons people are confused about the teaching in Christianity. Many do not know how to interpret Scripture correctly and thus they contradict themselves, causing an unbelieving world to see what appears to be cracks in God's Word. The problem is the cracks are in man's interpretation, not in God's Word itself. We must all be students of God's Word instead of only being students of fallible pastors and teachers who teach a lot of what they were taught by those they respected. Satan is out to distort God's Word at every turn to confuse Christians and the unbelieving world. The next chapter will give us some more tools to interpret God's Word correctly so we are not walking in the shadows.

CHAPTER 10 WORKSHEET

What have you learned in this chapter?

_____

_____

_____

If you are a Christian, what was your motivation in coming to Him?

_____

_____

_____

What is the real motivation of why you want to go to heaven?

_____

_____

_____

What hinders you from being free in worship to God?

_____

_____

_____

Have you had a healthy fear of God? Why or why not?

_____

_____

_____

CHAPTER 11

The Shadow of Interpretation

We have not received the spirit of the world but the Spirit who is from God, that we may understand what God has freely given us. This is what we speak, not in words taught us by human wisdom but in words taught by the Spirit, expressing spiritual truths in spiritual words. The man without the Spirit does not accept the things that come from the Spirit of God, for they are foolishness to him, and he cannot understand them, because they are spiritually discerned.
—1 Corinthians 2:12-14

As we are humbly learning from this book, we may be asking, how did I miss it, or can these things be right? This chapter will teach us how Satan has twisted the Scripture for so many. It is amazing how others's views take us away from the simplicity of God's Word. We all have the ability to know God's Word regardless of our education level or ministry experience.

In order to interpret the Scriptures correctly, we must understand the uniqueness of the Bible. The Bible was written over a 1,500-year span by more than forty authors in different places and times, during different moods, and on three continents. It was written in three languages, and it deals with hundreds of controversial subjects in a harmonious manner.

So how can a person without any Bible education understand God's Word? Over the centuries, many believed they needed an interpreter or teacher in order to understand the Bible. Many have gone to pastors, religious leaders, and priests, but were misguided by them. Did God really write the Bible through these forty authors for only religious leaders to understand? If this were the case, then the fate of all who were not educated in the Scriptures would be in the hands of these religious leaders. I do not believe this was the design of God, even though it is practiced today. God has preserved His Word over the centuries, and now some of the world has the Bible translated in their own language. I believe it is God's plan to get a copy of His inspired Word in the hands of each person on the earth. It is the Word of God that changes hearts and leads people to repentance.

I mentioned earlier that our faith is not a one-day occurrence; it is a process in which God continues to teach and develop us through His truth. We grow in our knowledge and understanding of God through His Word, and we have ministers and pastors learning side by side with us because none of us have all the answers. The people who stand up before us on Saturday or Sunday to teach may have some insights in what they have learned, but if they are honest, they will admit they continue to learn all the time. This is the reason I mentioned earlier about why we need to examine the things we have been taught from the Scriptures. We search from church to church for the greatest teacher and preacher. We look for the next pastor or minister who will excite and motivate us to live a life with Christ. But what we may have forgotten is that Jesus Christ is the greatest teacher who has ever lived, and there is authority in His Words. Even ancient philosophers and teachers marveled at His teachings and authority. Allow this chapter to teach us about how we can clearly interpret God's Word for ourselves.

The entire message of the Bible is not clear to those who have not read the entire book. I believe the message about Christ's plan can be clearly seen if the Bible is read cover to cover, even though there are verses throughout which may be difficult to understand. Remember the

Ethiopian eunuch on the road who was studying Isaiah in his chariot. God sent to this eunuch Philip, a treasurer to the Queen in Ethiopia, to teach Christ to him. To say we do not have a need for teachers would be absurd, and would contradict the Scriptures which talk about how God gave some gifts to be teachers. There are also verses where the Word of God does not tell us everything there is to know, but we do have what we need in the Scriptures to believe that Jesus is the Christ, the Son of God. Some examples are:

- Deuteronomy 29:29—"The secret things belong to the LORD our God, but the things revealed belong to us and to our children forever, that we may follow all the words of this law."

- John 20:30-31—"Jesus did many other miraculous signs in the presence of his disciples, which are not recorded in this book. But these are written that you may believe that Jesus is the Christ, the Son of God, and that by believing you may have life in his name."

- 1 Corinthians 13:9-12—"For we know in part and we prophesy in part, but when perfection comes, the imperfect disappears. When I was a child, I talked like a child; I thought like a child, I reasoned like a child. When I became a man, I put childish ways behind me. Now we see but a poor reflection as in a mirror; then we shall see face to face. Now I know in part; then I shall know fully, even as I am fully known."

- 2 Peter 3:16—"He writes the same way in all his letters, speaking in them of these matters. His letters contain some things that are hard to understand, which ignorant and unstable people distort, as they do the other Scriptures, to their own destruction."

God did give us some things in the Bible that people will find difficult to understand, while there are other things we will find out after we are in our resurrected spiritual bodies. The Bible remains clear, though, that we need the Spirit's guidance to teach us and help us understand the things we read and learn.

Some of these difficult passages may include the man of lawlessness in 2 Thessalonians 2, or the entire book of Revelation, but God made His plan of salvation through faith in Jesus Christ evident in all of the Scriptures. Parts of Revelation may be more difficult if they are referring to future times that have yet to be accomplished. Revelation may make great sense to those living in its fulfillment, just as it is easy for us to understand the prophecies of Jesus Christ from the Old Testament Scriptures after they have been accomplished.

Satan is out to deceive us on the important things, especially those things that affect our eternity. But Satan is out to divide us over things that don't matter. For example, Jesus being the only way to the Father cannot be challenged or changed, according to John 14:6, where it says, "Jesus answered, 'I am the way and the truth and the life. No one comes to the Father except through me.'" God will not change this or make exceptions for those who try any other way. Salvation is not through Mohammed, Buddha, or even as some say today, through us. Even though many on earth try to distort this truth, the fact remains that Jesus is the cornerstone of Christianity and salvation, as well as the rock of eternity with the Father.

How can a simple person who has very little education in the Scriptures interpret God's Word correctly? First, God has promised that if we seek, we will find. It does not mean if we seek for the answers we want that we will find them. This is a promise given by Jesus Himself that will never be broken. We can camp out on God's promises, depend on them, and even die for them, illustrating the degree of security that these promises hold.

I believe that many of us today have not asked for God's truth in the Scriptures, or even want to hear God's truth. Maybe it is because we are deceived into thinking we already have it. Or it might be that if we learned the truth, it would cause problems in our families or it would call us to live to a higher standard than what we are currently living. Maybe God's truth would challenge our upbringing and traditions in which we seek comfort. Questioning the salvation of loved ones is not a comfortable thing to do. Let God determine salvation for others while you are faithful to what you know. I have been to many funerals and the person is always said to be in heaven and rest. I know that is a comforting thing to hear, but it is just not true. Most people on the streets say they are going to heaven when they die. They are comforted by this thought, but according to the Scriptures, it just isn't true. Where there is knowledge, there is responsibility. You are receiving the knowledge. Now comes the responsibility of living out knowledge and wisdom. If your heart is open and sincere in following Jesus Christ, do not fear truth, but embrace it.

How many of us pray for the Holy Spirit to help show truth every time we study the Scriptures or listen to a teacher? I have to admit that I sometimes get too comfortable with what I know and what is being taught, so I do not pray for the Holy Spirit's involvement. Stop right now and humbly ask God to teach you through the truth of His Word, and make this a common practice as you continue to learn.

These few pointers will give you some direction in how to interpret the Scriptures correctly. It may seem cliché and simple, but start and end every learning time with prayer, asking the Holy Spirit to teach you. Do not do this as habit, but lay yourself before God, showing Him that you want to clearly understand everything He desires you to know. Prove to God that you will be obedient to what you learn because you love Him.

Ask God for wisdom, understanding, and humility. Even though this seems simple, how often do we do this? How frequently do we pray for the Spirit's involvement in our study during class time at church, or for His wisdom during the lessons or sermons we hear? Maybe we are not receiving wisdom because we are not asking for it. God reminds us that He will give wisdom in abundance if we would just ask Him, according to James 1:5: "If any of you lacks wisdom, he should ask God, who gives generously to all without finding fault, and it will be given to him."

One way many get confused in their understanding is over the interpretations of what some say the Bible is saying. If I read a verse and say it means this, and someone else reads that same Scripture and says it means that, how will we know which interpretation is correct?

Listen closely to this way of interpretation, because this is the key to knowing truth. I believe we are to read and understand the Bible as a whole. We get things messed up when we try to pick and choose the Scriptures we like or ones easy to follow, and then disregard or teach away the ones we have difficulty with. If the literal sense makes sense, then do not seek an alternative interpretation. Who are we to interpret whether God meant this or that? How do we know what God meant? If He said this but meant that, how will we ever understand? He expects us to read it and understand it exactly as it says.

In all languages there are allegories, metaphors, and similes. Of course, these are in the Scriptures, as well. For example, the Bible refers to Jesus in heaven as a Lamb on His throne. In the Bible, it also refers to Jesus as a rock. When you get to heaven, you are not going to see a big rock, and you are not going to see a lamb. These are metaphors which pertain to Christ. The Bible also speaks of us being a tower of strength. God is not asking us to be a tower or a building. We may be laughing at this point because we understand this and know it is quite obvious. Exactly! The metaphors or similes in the Bible are obvious. If God said something to us that He wanted us to interpret differently than what it says, then I believe He will tell us. An example of this is in the parables throughout the gospels.

Let us test these interpretations from the Bible as a whole. Let's first go to 1 Peter 5:8: "Be self-controlled and alert. Your enemy the Devil prowls around like a roaring lion looking for someone to devour." We know that if we see the words "like" or "as" it is a simile. So, Peter says Satan is not a lion but is like a lion in how he is on the attack. The Bible shows that Satan is on the earth bringing havoc, tempting, hurting, and is not omnipresent (2 places at once). That is easy enough, right?

Let's try a harder one. Let's take a look at Matthew 5:40-42, where it says, "And if someone wants to sue you and take your tunic, let him have your cloak, as well. If someone forces you to go one mile, go with him two miles. Give to the one who asks you, and do not turn away from the one who wants to borrow from you." What does Jesus want you to do? He gave the temple tax that was asked of Him in Matthew 17:24-27, and it was made clear that your money and your things should mean very little to you. It is taught in the Bible that people are more important than things. We also learn in God's Word not to let someone continue to take advantage of us, or to be foolish in our stewardship.

The next thing to understand in interpretation is the importance of reading and studying the Scriptures within their immediate context. Read them in the context of the chapter in the Bible and within the context of the book of the Bible. A person can make the Bible say whatever they want by taking Scriptures out of their context and putting them together. For example, a verse says, "Judas went out and hanged himself," and another verse taken somewhere else from the Scriptures says, "Go and do likewise." This one is not too difficult to figure out. These verses have been taken out of context, and you should not put them together.

Let me give you a more complex example. Church leaders tend to use a Scripture quite often to bring encouragement and comfort to the congregation. The Scripture I am referring to is Matthew 18:20, where it says, "For where two or three come together in my name, there am I with them." Apparently, some ministers have forgotten to read the context correctly. In Matthew 18:15-19, the context is about confronting a brother who is in sin. The entire section of the chapter reads this way:

> If your brother sins against you go and show him his fault, just between the two of you. If he listens to you, you have won your brother over. But if he will not listen, take one or two others along, so that every matter may be established by the testimony of two or three witnesses. If he refuses to listen to them, tell it to the church; and if he refuses to listen even to the church, treat him as you would a pagan or a tax collector. I tell you the truth, whatever you bind on earth will be bound in heaven, and whatever you loose on earth will be loosed in heaven. Again, I tell you that if two of you on earth agree about anything you ask for, it will be done for you by my Father in heaven.

Ministers have used this Scripture to prove that God is amongst us in the church, when two or more are gathered. Don't we also learn from the Bible that God is with us even when we are not with the church or members of the church? Well, from the Scriptures, the church is wherever you are as a Christian, regardless of how many people are with you. We should be encouraged by that. We don't even need two gathered to have God with us. We each have the Holy Spirit in us all the time. The context in Matthew 18 is really about the confidence in God's support as we confront followers of Christ who are in sin. He is with us, and He is in approval of calling His people in sin to repent. This is just another way the Scriptures are not interpreted correctly within their immediate context and the context of the Bible. I could write another book about all the Scriptures taken out of context by ministers and teachers. It is actually really sad many believe those things without ever studying and questioning the interpretations.

Another thing to remember when interpreting the Scriptures is that, in most cases, the books of the Bible were not written directly to you. Therefore, you must learn about whoever the initial recipients were and why the book was written for them. A lot of the things in the Scriptures can be taken literally, like the verses I mentioned earlier. Do not make it harder or more difficult than it has to be. Take most things at face value, and use the simplest interpretation.

Another example of this is Galatians 5:19-21: "The acts of the sinful nature are obvious: sexual immorality, impurity and debauchery; idolatry and witchcraft; hatred, discord, jealousy, fits of rage, selfish ambition, dissension, factions and envy; drunkenness, orgies, and the like. I warn you, as I did before, that those who live like this will not inherit the kingdom of God." You can take it to the bank that a person who practices and has given themselves over to sexual immorality will not inherit the kingdom of God. We can try to rationalize this based on our lifestyle or the culture, but the fact remains, and God will hold true to His Word. Sexual immorality was wrong four thousand years ago and is still displeasing to God today. Acceptance of that behavior by those who call themselves Christians should not be tolerated.

I was raised believing that the correct way to interpret the Scriptures was through what were called command, example, and necessary inference. First of all, I did not even understand what this meant until years later. I was taught that if something was a command in the New Testament—a good example of someone in the Scriptures or if it was implied by the Scriptures—then God has given us the authority to do it. If what I was going to do was not a command, example, or implied in the Scriptures, then I did not have any authority from God and I would, therefore, be displeasing to God. I was told to speak where God speaks in the Scriptures and to keep quiet where God does not speak.

As I grew older, I began to realize that our church did not practice all the imperatives or commands in the New Testament even though they said to interpret Scriptures this way. For example, we did not greet one another with a holy kiss as stated five times in five different books of the New Testament. I noticed we also did not make women put on coverings during prayer, according to 1 Corinthians 11. I was told it was a matter of culture, even though Paul uses the creation and order of things to be his proof in 1 Corinthians 11:3-10:

> Now I want you to realize that the head of every man is Christ, and the head of the woman is man, and the head of Christ is God. Every man who prays or prophesies with his head covered dishonors his head. And every woman who prays or prophesies with her head uncovered dishonors her head—it is just as though her head were shaved. If a woman does not cover her head, she should have her hair cut off; and if it is a disgrace for a woman to have her hair cut or shaved off, she should cover her head. A man ought not to cover his head, since he is the image and glory of God; but the woman is the glory of man. For man did not come from woman, but woman from man; neither was man created for woman, but woman for man. For this reason, and because of the angels, the woman ought to have a sign of authority on her head.

If we really want to get technical, the reasons in this passage that women were to wear head coverings were: men are the head of women, men were created first, women are the glory of men, women were created for men, and because of the angels. Some say that hair is the covering but read the text again where it says that if a woman does not cover her head, than she should have her hair cut off. This means she had hair, but it was not her covering.

I am not debating whether we should practice these things today in American churches, but what I am attempting to get across is that every time someone did not have an answer as to why we did not do something the Bible spoke of, the answer was always related to cultural reasons.

I also knew that we did not follow all the commands in the gospels. For example, in Luke 3:11, where it says, "John answered, 'The man with two tunics should share with him who has none, and the one who has food should do the same.'"

We were not even consistent in our method of interpretation. Who came up with this method?

I did a study recently on all the commands in the four gospels. The Bible says we are to practice all the things Jesus commanded. This is seen in some of the last words Jesus said to His apostles in Matthew 28:19-20: "Therefore go and make disciples of all nations, baptizing them in the name of the Father and of the Son and of the Holy Spirit, and teaching them to obey everything I have commanded you. And surely I am with you always, to the very end of the age."

The apostles were to teach everything Jesus commanded. So, I wanted to know everything He commanded. After I wrote pages of commands as I read the four gospels, God spoke to me. It was obvious I needed to check myself to see if I had been doing what Jesus commanded, but I learned that all of Jesus's commands are summed up in loving God with all of our being and loving our neighbor. The reality is we do not do either of these if we are caught up in our money, our success, our food, our sleep, and so on. Jesus proved that God was more important than sleep and food. Love leads us to all the commands, and following all the commands without love is just loud, annoying noise to God, according to 1 Corinthians 13:1-3. Learning to love as Jesus commands and having a heart of love as Jesus had will lead us to go beyond our own capabilities in following Jesus and being a light in a dark world.

Remember, we are under grace and a law of liberty, but that does not mean liberty to go against what God has clearly said. If the Bible speaks consistently about a topic, then it is important, and we need to pay attention. If it is not mentioned much, then it cannot be the most important thing we need to know. Of course, simply being in God's Word makes it important, but legalism will destroy the church.

I see the root of Christian living is choosing to love God and to love our neighbor. Jesus says if you love Him, then you will obey His commands. John 14:15 says, "If you love me, you will obey what I command." I do not know how God is going to deal with those who say they love Him but who are not obedient to His Words. That is where the merciful judge is going to act fairly, and some are going to appreciate God's mercy while others will be crying, "Lord, Lord." According to Matthew 7:22-23, "Many will say to me on that day, 'Lord, Lord did we not prophesy in your name, and in your name drive out demons and perform many miracles?' Then I will tell them plainly, 'I never knew you. Away from me, you evildoers!'"

Do not get caught up in the difficult passages of the Scriptures, but live true to what you have learned while allowing the Holy Spirit to open your eyes even more as you grow in Christ. Allow this book to be a tool for God to help open your eyes to things you need to re-examine and re-study in order to be faithful and obedient to what God has given you today.

As I close this chapter, let me pause here and just say we live in a world where the Bible is translated into many languages. In America, we can get Bibles for free, such as at a Chinese restaurant I visited where they had complimentary Bibles near the cash register. Many hotels still have a copy of God's Word in the night stand next to the bed. I do not know of a church that will not give a Bible to someone who wants one. Or you can go to any dollar store and buy an entire Old and New Testament Bible for one dollar. I believe we live in a time where ignorance will not be tolerated. Ignorance cannot be an excuse, yet many believers rely on ministers instead of examining God's Word for themselves. We live in a time where we can search libraries, history, and subjects just by a few clicks on a computer or, for some of us, on our phones or tablets. As a Christian, I will not be biblically illiterate in this day and age. I will not allow Satan to deceive me into believing people rather than God. This will take commitment on my part to pray and to study and search the Scriptures daily to know and follow God's truth.

CHAPTER 11 WORKSHEET

Have you learned more from God in your personal study or from pastors and teachers?

_____

_____

_____

What are hard things in Scripture for you to understand? Pray God will give you revelation.

_____

_____

_____

Have you read the Bible through? If not, will you create a plan to do this in the next year?

_____

_____

_____

Do you pray before your study? If not, how can you remember to do this each time?

_____

_____

_____

What is a study you would like to do in Scripture? When do you plan to start? How do you plan to start?

_____

_____

_____

CHAPTER 12

Shadow of Salvation

Enter through the narrow gate. For wide is the gate and broad is the road that leads to destruction, and many enter through it. But small is the gate and narrow the road that leads to life and only a few find it.
—Matthew 7:13-14

If Satan is the great deceiver, it only makes sense that one of his biggest strategies would be to pervert the salvation process, confusing people who are seeking salvation in Christ. Salvation is the defining point where he loses in the lives of people. Do we think Satan is just going to sit back and allow people to choose to follow Jesus? Absolutely not! He will distract, distort, deceive, and do anything else that will keep people from deciding to follow Jesus. I have seen this first hand with people who are getting so close to surrendering their life to Jesus. I have seen people need to move away suddenly, or go to the hospital or emergency room because of a sudden illness, lose a love one, and so many other terrible things, just because Satan is fighting for them. In the first few centuries after Christ, history shows people would actually fast for those who were contemplating this major decision of choosing Christ. Maybe they knew something more on the topic of spiritual warfare.

Satan tries to distort every good thing and use it to his advantage. Look at the good things Satan ruins. Take the Internet and the benefit of using it to reach the world for Christ by touching a few buttons. Yet we see pornography is destroying the minds of many adults and children because of Satan's influence through a good thing like the Internet. The last statistic I heard was that there are fourteen pornographic websites for every one non-pornographic website. The use of social media to hurt others and elevate oneself is just another example of how Satan has used the Internet and technology to destroy lives.

Another example of distortion is the way the United States of America was established as one nation under God with the freedom of religion. This freedom has turned into an opportunity for Satan to get Americans to accept every religion. Because of this law, we have a post-modernist belief that says, "Do not judge me, and I will not judge you. Let me serve my God and you serve yours." According to our nation's Founding Fathers, freedom of religion was freedom to worship Jehovah God. We, as a nation, are afraid to say Jesus is the only way to eternal life for fear of criticism and resentment from our own countrymen as well as from the rest of the world. Our government just might be afraid for the same reasons. I have seen an official sworn into a United States government position by placing his hand on the Koran instead of the Bible because of his Muslim faith. I am not writing a political book, but the reality is we are not one nation under Jehovah God anymore, no matter what is claimed. We do not hold to the principles and teachings of the Bible or to what our Founding Fathers desired in terms of freedom. Because of this, America will have to suffer the consequences for its decisions, and our leaders will be held accountable by Jehovah God and His Son, the Messiah. Maybe earthquakes, 9/11, tsunamis, and Hurricane Katrina are things that God has used to try to wake up this nation and our world. What many call natural disasters such as forest fires, famines, and droughts may not be from "mother nature," after all. Our responsibility is to make sure we are living simple lives and are always ready to meet our God. Satan sure likes to twist anything good, and by being deceived, we all pay the penalty.

I mentioned earlier in this book that some things will challenge our thinking and our traditions. These things will challenge the way we were raised as well as the church in which we worship. Remember, I do not believe I have all the answers for this life, but I do believe God's Word has the answers we need. I believe we are all capable of reading God's Word for ourselves and of following Christ and His Word instead of following religion. Satan perverted God's Word in his dealings with the Son of God in the wilderness in order to try and deceive the incarnate God (God in the flesh). How much more will he try to pervert God's Word for those who read occasionally? Just consider the things from the Word of God, because is it not obvious Satan would pervert the way of salvation?

There are doctrines of demons, according to the Scriptures. So, what are they? Anyone who does not believe that Jesus, as the Son of God, came in the flesh, lived a perfect life, died for the sins of the world, was resurrected on the third day, ascended to the Father, and is one day returning, has given in to false teaching. First John 4:2, says, "Every spirit that confesses Jesus has come in the flesh is from God; and every spirit that does not confess Jesus is not from God." Also, everyone who does not believe the Bible is completely infallible and inspired by God, is also led astray. First Peter 1:25, says, "The Word of the Lord abides forever." In Galatians 1:9, it says, "But even if we or an angel from heaven should preach a gospel other than the one we preached to you, let him be eternally condemned." This statement alone rules out some "churches" because they are founded on the belief that an angel from God gave someone a new revelation. I do not deny the fact that an angel appeared to someone to give them a "new revelation" but, according to the Scriptures, that angel will pay the penalty as well as those who follow what it said. Even 2 Corinthians 11:14-15, says, "And no wonder, for Satan himself masquerades as an angel of light. It is not surprising, then, that his servants masquerade as servants of righteousness. Their end will be what their actions deserve."

Could it be we have believed a lie? How will we ever know unless we recondition or allow God to transform our minds to see the Scriptures the way He wants us to see the Bible instead of the way we have always been told?

Some things may be very clear from the Scriptures, but because of family, traditions, feelings, or pride, we fail to see the truth. Jesus says it perfectly in Mark 8:34-38:

> "If anyone wishes to come after Me, let him deny himself, and take up his cross, and follow Me. For whoever wishes to save his life shall lose it; but whoever loses his life for My sake and the gospel's shall save it. For what does it profit a man to gain the whole world, and forfeit his soul? For what shall a man give in exchange for his soul? For whoever is ashamed of Me and My Words in this adulterous and sinful generation, the Son of Man will also be ashamed of him when He comes in the glory of His Father with the holy angels."

What will you give in exchange for your soul? Is it your devotion to your parents's beliefs? Are they your traditions because you will not read God's Word for yourself? Or is it your pride in that you cannot be wrong? Are any of those worth losing your soul over?

In my life, I have seen where I have been completely wrong due to believing only what I have heard from people I respected. Reading God's Word for me, with the power of the Holy Spirit to help, changed my heart. I realized the people I respected so much are still good people and are following Christ the best way they know how. I also realized God has been a part of my life every step of the way, even if I was taught some incorrect interpretations of some things in the Bible. It did not make me less of a "believer" because I found out through my study there was more to salvation than what I had been taught. The truth is, God has always been faithful to me, taking me through every experience to bring me to where I am today. I would be a liar if I said I have arrived in complete knowledge. Those will be the words I say as Jesus, the love of my life, escorts me into heaven. Regardless of your past, do not question God's faithfulness to you. He has brought you through everything in your life to where you are now, even to this moment when you are reading this book.

What are some ways that Satan might have distorted salvation? I mentioned earlier that salvation through any name other than Jesus Christ would be distorted. The process for becoming a Christian is debated by denominations and church leaders everywhere. Is it really supposed to be that difficult? Or can we safely say Satan has something to do with that? It is difficult for us, who have always been told what to think and believe without being encouraged to examine the Scriptures ourselves, to do so. We must be like the church in Berea mentioned in Acts 17:11: "Now the Bereans were of more noble character than the Thessalonians, for they received the message with great eagerness and examined the Scriptures every day to see if what Paul said was true."

If the church was doing this back when an apostle was teaching, then we should be doing the same and even more today. Instead, many want to debate about what their pastor has said or what their tradition has been. May we see the light and not fall into Satan's hold any longer. My pastor is not infallible, my traditions are not infallible, and even the pope is not infallible. In 1 John 1:8-10, John is speaking to Christians:

> If we claim to be without sin, we deceive ourselves and the truth is not in us. If we confess our sins, He is faithful and just and will forgive us our sins and purify us from

all unrighteousness. If we claim we have not sinned, we make Him out to be a liar and His Word has no place in our lives.

According to these verses, there should never be any man or woman who claims to be without sin, and if someone does, he is an obvious false teacher where God's truth is not in him. Also, in Romans 3:10-12, 23, it says,

> As it is written: "There is no one righteous, not even one; there is no one who understands, no one who seeks God. All have turned away; they have together become worthless; there is no one who does well, not even one. For all have sinned and fall short of the glory of God."

There are plenty of educated, scholarly men who are wrong. Just read the commentaries from great men of faith over the centuries, and you can see this. Let us get back to the simplicity of God's Word, studying and living out what it says.

Here are some things we are told when it comes to salvation. Which one is correct, or are they all correct? Some say in order to be a Christian, you must be sprinkled as an infant because children carry sin from Adam. Some of them say you need to be sprinkled at an age where you understand your need for a Savior. Some say you need to be baptized whatever way you desire—whether it be sprinkled upon, poured upon, or immersed with water—because it really does not matter to God. Some say baptism should be through immersion alone because it symbolizes the death, burial, and resurrection of Jesus, according to Romans 6:3-4. Some say salvation is in a spiritual baptism, which does not include water. Some say you simply need to confess your belief in God to be saved. Others say you need to say a certain prayer, inviting Jesus into your heart and asking for forgiveness to be saved. Some say just to have faith, and you will be saved.

Is it not amazing how many different things believers have said to be truth? This is not even the complete list. These are just the more popular ones taught in many churches.

Are all of these ways true? Are any of them true? We know Satan has perverted the truth and has tried to hide the way of salvation. That is why Matthew 7:13-14 says only a few will find it: "Enter through the narrow gate. For wide is the gate and broad is the road that leads to destruction, and many enter through it. But small is the gate and narrow the road that leads to life and only a few find it." With only Jesus speaking truth, then all of those ways are not true. Some of them are traditions passed down from generation to generation while others are mankind's interpretations of a Scripture pulled out of its context or pulled from no context at all. A great example of this is in Revelation 3:20 where Jesus says, "Behold I stand at the door and knock. If anyone hears my voice and opens the door, I will come in to him..." This verse is in so many Bible tracks to bring people to the Lord when the context is that the message is to Christians in the church of Laodicea. There are so many verses on salvation in Christ, but this verse used in the majority of the church world is taken out of context.

We know some of these views of salvation have definitely been twisted and distorted by Satan. The only way we will find salvation is through humility and the involvement of the Holy Spirit through the Bible. It is the poor in spirit who will enter the kingdom of heaven. The first thing Jesus said to the people in the "Sermon on the Mount" was that they needed humility to accept the things He would say. Likewise, today, we will need humility to accept the things He has said.

The only way we are going to truly know salvation is to read through God's Word and understand salvation through the context of the entire Bible. If we pull a few verses out and make claims of salvation, it will easy to be deceived. In order to interpret correctly, we must read them in the context of the chapter in the Bible, within the context of the book of the Bible, and within the context of the entire Bible based on your knowledge so far. A person can make the Bible say whatever they want by taking Scriptures out of context and putting them together.

Some believe salvation is something an individual decides for oneself. Many seem to understand from the Scriptures that you need to believe in God, confess Jesus as Lord or Master, and repent of your sins by asking God to forgive you. The difference is, at what point is a person forgiven, and at what point does a person actually receive salvation and the gift of Holy Spirit as their seal for salvation? Is it when you pray, when you call on His name, when you realize you need a Savior, or while in the water of baptism?

Does it even matter at what point we are saved? It is our faith in Christ that saves us, and our sincere faith is validated in immediate responses to true faith. According to the examples in the book of Acts, people came to Christ by faith, repentance, confession, and then they were immediately baptized. There is definitely importance in each part, so let us follow each part as soon as we come to faith as the Bible says, and quit debating on the exact point in which salvation took place. Salvation is by grace through faith!

There are Scriptures like Acts 10:43 that say if you believe in Him, you will be saved. Other Scriptures say if you repent, then God will wipe away your sins, as seen from Acts 3:19, where it says, "Repent, then, and turn to God, so that your sins may be wiped out, that times of refreshing may come from the Lord."

There are other Scriptures that say God will forgive you and wash away your sins when you are baptized (immersed) into Christ, such as Acts 2:38: "Repent and be baptized, every one of you, in the name of Jesus Christ for the forgiveness of your sins. And you will receive the gift of the Holy Spirit." Another example is Acts 22:16, where it says,

"And now what are you waiting for? Get up, be baptized and wash your sins away, calling on his name." Does forgiveness happen when all these things are completed, or is salvation initially given when there is true faith in Christ? Could baptism be a completion of the salvation process of doing all that God has asked us to do to be saved? If so, salvation would be based on works and not God, right? Receiving salvation may begin with faith in the working of Christ, but salvation is not completed with faith alone.

Let us see the importance in each of these things and follow the examples of those before us who have come to faith without questioning and dividing. If we see each of these as important when it comes to faith and obedience, then as long as we believe with all our heart that Jesus Christ is the Messiah, let us hold on to our love and faith as we obey and follow all that God has asked us to do. The point where we need to question our salvation is if God is teaching us, and we are rejecting what He says to be true.

In the next few sections, we will address some specific issues that could have been perverted and twisted from the Scriptures.

Shadow of Sprinkling Instead of Immersion

Since we are attacking deception, let us not be deceived into thinking that baptism into Christ is anything other than immersion based on the Word. The very word baptize in the Greek means to immerse or submerge. The reason the Greek word is so important is because the New Testament was written in Greek. There are different Greek words for *sprinkle* and *pour* which are also found in the New Testament, but every time the New Testament deals with baptism, it uses baptize, meaning immersion.

From the Greek word baptize, these are the definitions from *Thayer's Greek Lexicon* (Biblesoft, Inc. Copyright © 2000, 2003).

Baptizo:

1. properly, to dip repeatedly, to immerge, submerge (of vessels sunk, Polybius 1, 51, 6; 8, 8, 4; of animals, Diodorus 1, 36).

2. to cleanse by dipping or submerging, to wash, to make clean with water; in the middle voice and the 1 aorist passive to wash oneself, bathe; so Mark 7:4 (where WH text rantisoontai); Luke 11:38 (2 Kings 5:14 ebaptisato en too Iordanee, for Taabal; Sir. 31:30 (Sir. 34:30; Judith 12:7).

3. metaphorically, to overwhelm, as idiootas tais eisforais, Diodorus 1, 73; ofleemasi, Plutarch, Galba 21; tee sumfora bebaptismenos, Heliodorus Aeth. 2, 3

The symbolism used in Romans 6:3-4 reminds the Christians in Rome about their conversion and their freedom from the Law. The symbolism in these verses relates to death, burial, and the resurrection of Jesus. Instead of a physical grave in the ground, water symbolizes the grave we enter and come out of, representing death and a new life.

Have you ever been to a beach with beautiful, white, powdery sand that looks almost like snow? Imagine if I took you to the beaches in Florida and said I was going to bury you in the sand. As I say that, imagine I grab a handful of sand and throw it on you. You would look at me as if I was crazy. It would be obvious if I was going to bury you in the sand at the beach, I would first dig a hole (a grave), have you get in the hole, and then cover you with sand all the way to your head. Even that is not a complete burial in the sand. Burial in baptism, using the Greek word meaning "to immerse," would also be just as absurd if it involved sprin-kling water on someone, calling that a baptism, and completely misrep-resenting what the Bible said and meant. I believe part of the problem is that we do not use proper terminology, and many lack understanding in what baptism is really about. This confuses so many people. Baptism means immersion. Therefore, sprinkling and pouring are not baptism because neither of these are immersion. When you ask someone if they were baptized, you are asking if they were immersed or fully submerged, based on the meaning of the word.

In the first century, they clearly understood the difference in the terms because initially baptism was not a Bible term. Because baptism was connected to the idea of a ship being sunk or a cloth being dyed a certain color, there was not any question around defining water baptism. If we would start using the correct term, then it might be pretty simple to understand whether or not we were baptized in the way the Bible says. Today in our culture, baptism is a religious word that has come to mean sprinkling, pouring on, or immersing a person with water. There are also meanings in our culture of a spiritual baptism that does not include physical water. This is why many are confused.

If we would just take the actual word in the Bible and what it means, not what our culture says but what the Bible says, and practice it, we will be obedient to the words of Christ. Do we have the liberty today to take a Bible word, change its meaning and practice how it is defined by our culture? I would think not.

On the other hand, God is the judge, and He knows each man's heart. How arrogant it would be for me to say a person poured upon because of their faith is condemned? I have seen ministers baptize over and over the same person because the entire body did not go under the water. If we honestly believe because a hand was out of the water that this person was disobedient, we really have other problems, and we will be judged with the same measure in which we judged. God knows each person's heart, and I'll trust in Him in all things.

Shadow of Infant Sprinkling

Let us address infant baptism for a moment from the truth of God's Word. This is a common practice in some churches today, but is this really what God intended? I deal with so many confused people who are not sure if the pouring or sprinkling they experienced as an infant is legitimate with God for their salvation. The main reason for infant sprinkling or pouring originates with the scriptural interpretation that because everyone is born into this sinful world, then we are all sinful. Many get that thought from a misinterpretation of Romans 5:12-13, where it says, "Therefore, just as sin entered the world through one man, and death through sin, and in this way death came to all men, because all sinned—for before the law was given, sin was in the world. But sin is not taken into account when there is no law." It is obvious how a person can misinterpret this passage by way of simply reading through it quickly and not looking carefully at what it really says. Notice Paul does not say that sin spread to all men but, rather, death spread to all men.

In Genesis 3, after the temptation and fall of Adam and Eve, God makes it very clear to them that not only had sin brought them physical death, but they also were sentenced to a spiritual death. According to Paul in Romans 5, sin came into the world through Adam and, because of sin, death spread to all men, and they will all die a physical death. The wages of sin are death, according to Romans 6:23, so all of us who have come after Adam deserve death. Romans 5 says all have sinned. This is what made Jesus's sacrifice so important; He did not deserve death because He never sinned. Since He did not have to die for His own sins, He could die for our sins.

The Bible says Jesus was born into a sinful world, without any special wisdom or privileges. Jesus grew in wisdom, according to Luke 2:52: "And Jesus grew in wisdom and stature, and in favor with God and men." He was just as we are, except without sin. Jesus, having been born into this sinful world, proves that infants have not inherited Adam's sin. If this were the case, then Jesus would also have inherited Adam's sin and, therefore, would have deserved death. This would not align with God's entire plan.

I appreciate parents who want their children to be saved, so they do what they know best. I see infant sprinkling, infant pouring, or infant immersion as a pledge by the parent or parents to raise the child in the Lord. By no means is it commanded. It should be obvious that this is a decision made by the parent or parents of that infant and not the infant. Therefore, it cannot be a decision of personal faith on the part of the infant. The Bible teaches each accountable person must make a decision for Christ and stand before God with their own faith. On judgment day, parents, friends, ministers, or even spouses will not be there to stand with you or for you. Jesus Christ is the only one who can and will stand with you, but only if you have personally chosen Him. Even if you had godly parents who dedicated you to God as an infant through sprinkling, you must still make a personal decision of faith to surrender to Christ and be obedient to His Word.

Also related to this belief about baptizing infants, Jesus seemed to have a special relationship with children. In the Scriptures, children seemed extremely comfortable with Him. And Jesus expects us to be like little children for the reason stated in Matthew 18:1-4 (NASB):

> At that time the disciples came to Jesus, saying, "Who then is greatest in the kingdom of heaven?" And He called a child to Himself and set him before them, and said, "Truly I say to you, unless you are converted and

become like children, you shall not enter the kingdom of heaven. Whoever then humbles himself as this child, he is the greatest in the kingdom of heaven."

Children are innocent and pure. They are almost too trustworthy. I realized this first hand when my sons, Justus and Jordan, would just jump off the bed toward me whether I was ready or not. They believed their daddy would always catch them. Was it not awesome as children when you did not have to be concerned about bills, jobs, cooking, and so many other adult things? You just had a childlike faith, and would trust everything to be fine. This is the way God wants us to be, even as adults. We must become as pure, innocent, and trusting as little children in order to enter the kingdom of heaven. We must have full reliance on Him and Him only, as a new babe. We do not need to be converted as children, but we must be converted to become like children.

Shadow of "The Sinner's Prayer"

I had a friend who was in a church basketball league where they played in a local church gym. On the wall of the gym in big letters they had several admonitions about how to be saved, complete with scriptural references. The first saying was "Hear the Word of God," with the Scripture reference, Romans 10:14—which says, "How, then, can they call on the One they have not believed in? And how can they believe in the One of whom they have not heard? And how can they hear without someone preaching to them?" The second admonition was "Believe," and the scriptural reference was John 3:16—which says, "For God so loved the world that he gave His one and only Son, that whoever believes in Him shall not perish but have eternal life." Underneath "Believe" was "Confess," with the scriptural reference Romans 10:9—which says, "That if you confess with your mouth, 'Jesus is Lord,' and believe in your heart that God raised him from the dead, you will be saved." The fourth word was "Repent," and the Scripture was Luke 13:3—which says, "I tell you, no! But unless you repent, you too will all perish." The final saying was "The Sinner's Prayer," but there was not any scriptural reference associated with it. During the break, my friend, trying to be funny, went up to the wall and read them aloud. After each one, he pointed out the Scripture. When he got to "The Sinner's Prayer," he got a laugh out of all of us when he said, "Now, what is wrong with this picture?"

No matter how we try to get around it, the Bible does not speak of a special prayer a person must say in order to be saved. This may be tough for many of you, and I might have hit a nerve with this one. The idea of a "Sinner's Prayer" did not come about until just a few hundred years ago.

Billy Graham through his revivals would teach and practice it during the last century. Indeed, every Christian concert you go to, every pamphlet you receive, and with most of the preachers on TV, there is some special prayer without any scriptural base, other than Romans 10:13, where it says, "Everyone who calls on the name of the Lord will be saved." Even then, it does not say "Pray a certain prayer," or "Repeat a prayer after me" in order to receive forgiveness and be saved. Saying a prayer and having a heart of repentance are not wrong, but by no means does the Bible say it must be done this way.

I believe the focus on the sinner's prayer was to get people to repent and call out to God. I believe we shouldn't be telling people what they need to say, or telling people to repeat after us. I believe prayer needs to come from the person's heart in their own words to God. Some people know they need God but do not truly believe or are not ready to fully surrender to Jesus Christ. I do not see people in the Bible repeating a prayer after someone in order to receive salvation.

I understand there are times when people realize they need God, but God must be leading them to repentance, confessing, and even a full surrender of life and will to the Almighty God. Because of this Sinner's Prayer, more than ever we are seeing people who have said a prayer to receive salvation, but with no conversion or true surrender in their lives. We see many so-called "Christians" who were never changed but just wanted to go to heaven instead of hell. This seems to have hurt the message of true Christ followers because so many say today that they do not want to be Christian because Christians are hypocrites.

True Christ followers are sincere and surrendered, but "Christians" may have just said a prayer to go to heaven. Satan has deceived so many who believe they have salvation only to hurt the witness of those who are true Christians. For example, how many of you have encountered people who claim Christianity but live worldly and ungodly lives? They claim Christianity because they said a prayer, but Satan uses them to confuse the unbelieving world of true New Testament Christianity. Satan also uses them to bring selfishness and worldliness to the churches, though they never surrendered to Jesus in the first place. This prayer without discipleship and teaching has brought much damage and confusion to what the unbelieving world believes about Christianity, as well as damage to churches when they must battle with those who never surrendered to follow the ways of the Lord but simply prayed and asked God to forgive them and come into their heart.

Being the Christian owner of a country store in Montana, I have seen so many "Christians" who come in drunk and cursing, holding onto their addictions, upset that the church will not help them more, and are generally terrible examples of Christianity, but all the while talking about their choice to follow the Lord. If this is what Satan causes the world to see, no wonder the witness of Christians is not taken seriously.

I was at a Christian concert in the old Amway Arena in Orlando, Florida, in January, 2007. A group of popular Christian bands were there for Winter Jam. Some of the youth from our church went, and we were blown away by the performances as well as the worship. There must have been around five thousand people there that night. They had a guest speaker during the middle of the show who was personal and honest in what he was speaking. But as usual at these things, they did the whole "Sinner's Prayer" thing where a couple hundred people did what they were told and recited a prayer because they knew they needed God.

I am always moved in my spirit because I want to speak up and congratulate all these people who want to make things right with God. I want to take them and teach them about repentance, about confessing Jesus as the Messiah, and about fully surrendering their life to God because of their faith in Christ. If this was during the time of the apostles, once they understood and were willing to put their faith and trust in Jesus, they were taken that very hour to be baptized for a new identity in Christ, as Paul did with the jailer and his household after he said he believed in Acts 16:29-33. This Scripture shows us the immediate response of faith. It shows us the teaching of coming to faith in Christ, and the appropriate response. They did not argue the point of salvation. They saw the importance in each response to faith. Repentance, confession, and obedience are all responses to true faith.

I am not trying to be legalistic but, rather, obedient. No one has ever been able to show me where calling on the name of the Lord means a special prayer, or to prove that God desires a certain prayer to bestow salvation upon someone. Grace is not given on the basis of works, but is a gift of God when we humbly submit by faith to the Lordship of Jesus Christ. Could this prayer be part of the journey we are on to find faith in Christ? Of course! However, there are clear examples from the Scriptures as to why one should not stop at a prayer when calling out to God. The demons also made confessions of Jesus being the Son of God when Jesus approached them, as in Mark 5:7-8: "He shouted at the top of his voice, 'What do you want with me, Jesus, Son of the Most High God? Swear to God that you won't torture me!' For Jesus had said to him, 'Come out of this man, you evil spirit!'" This example shows me that a confession of faith is good but not the end-all when it comes to obedience and change.

Are we following traditions instead of the Scriptures? Some churches only baptize certain times a year. Where do we find that in the Bible? Our churches should exist for the purpose of teaching examples of faith to a lost and dying world. Each week, the goal should be seeing people saved and obedient to the plan of God. We need to be celebrating the death of the old life as well as the beginning of the new life. I do not believe we should make baptism more than what the Bible makes of it, but let us at least give it the same importance as the Bible does.

We have many experiences where we try and minister to people through the country store. We have a lot of regular customers whom we see all the time. Sometimes we see them three times a day. As time goes by and we share our lives with them, they come in and share their lives with us. Recently a young woman came in very upset. She had started going back to church and was reading her Bible regularly. This woman was battling her demons and addictions, and God was bringing her to a desire to change. She came in and told us that as she had been reading the New Testament, she was convinced she needed this new start and wanted to be baptized. You might ask why she was so upset. She went on to tell us that she had gone to her minister only to find out that she cannot be baptized in the church until the summer. She said, "Why can't these churches and preachers just follow the Bible?"

I have to agree!

If you have said this Sinner's Prayer, then praise God that your heart was calling out to God and wanting change, but do not stop there. The Bible says those who believe (John 3:16); confess Jesus as Lord (Romans 10:9); repent (Luke 13:3); call on the name of the Lord (Romans 10:13) will be saved. God says all these things for a purpose. Confession, repentance, and baptism are obedient responses to faith in Christ. They are all works or actions which validate our faith.

Could it be that many have emphasized the importance of one of these acts over the other, when they are all important in the heart and life of a person finding God? Once again, I believe Satan has confused the world about the simplicity in God's Word of salvation of Christ by faith. Do not find yourself in the web of deception, unable to see the truth right in front of us in the Scriptures; and do not find yourself wasting your entire life debating with those who are saved when people are dying every day without salvation in Christ.

Shadow of Faith Only and Salvation by Works

There are not enough good things you could ever do to earn your way to heaven. If that were possible, then Jesus would never have left heaven to come to earth. Jesus left heaven because, no matter how hard we try, we can never earn our way to heaven. We are one-hundred percent indebted to Jesus to receive salvation. But to say it falls only on Jesus for us to receive salvation is not true, according to the Scriptures. Jesus did the initial work for our salvation, but fulfillment takes our acceptance and response. If this were not the case, then Jesus dying for the sins of the world would save everyone, no questions asked, and no matter what they did. We know the belief that "all people will be saved" is contrary to the Word of God, so it is accurate to say we must play a part in our salvation.

Our part is a decision of faith that leads to obedient responses of faith. We see that people were set free from sin when they obeyed the form of teaching they were entrusted with, according to Rom 6:17-18. Believing includes action, according to Hebrews 3:18-19: "And to whom did God swear that they would never enter his rest if not to those who disobeyed? So we see that they were not able to enter, because of their unbelief." In Hebrews 3, disbelief and disobedience go hand in hand. Therefore, belief and obedience go hand in hand, as well.

Why do people say baptism is a work? It is a work just like saying a prayer is a work, but it is not a work that earns your salvation. It is an immediate response of faith that leads to transformation and a new identity in Christ. Whether we want to call it a work or action, it does not matter. It means the same thing. A better way to state it might be to say it is a result of faith or an example of active faith. The Bible says faith saves us, repentance saves us, confession saves us, calling on His Name saves us, and that baptism also saves us. So, are we saved by works or not? We discussed earlier that repentance, confession, and even saying a prayer are actions or works. Are all of these true, or are we saved by faith alone?

Even faith without works is dead.

Let us take a closer look at baptism saving us. In 1 Peter 3:21, it says, "and this water symbolizes baptism that now saves you also—not the removal of dirt from the body but the pledge of a good conscience toward God. It saves you by the resurrection of Jesus Christ." To deny this is to read something in the Bible and then say it is not true. I do not want to be the one to do that. The Bible says baptism saves you also. If the Bible says baptism saves you, then it does, even if we do not understand this statement fully.

How wrong would I be to say that baptism does not also save me when the Bible says it does? Just as how wrong would I be to say we are not saved by grace through faith? Do we choose to believe this or not? Why argue what the Bible says? I have heard people emphatically say baptism does not save us. Whether we understand this verse in its entirety or not, the fact remains that what God said is true. If the Bible says it, then I believe it.

Can we be saved without repentance? During the time of John the Baptist and the baptism of repentance, John expected people to bring forth fruits in keeping with repentance. He expected your faith to lead you to a transformed life. We would agree faith without works is useless. Would we then not also agree that faith without a response to faith would also be worthless? So, it is accurate to say faith in Jesus requires obedience, also known as works or actions, on our part. Remember, salvation comes through faith in Jesus Christ and Him alone. James 2:20 asks, "You foolish man, do you want evidence that faith without deeds is useless?" Colossians 2:9-14 says:

> For in Christ all the fullness of the Deity lives in bodily form and you have been given fullness in Christ, who is the head over every power and authority. In him you were also circumcised, in the putting off of sinful nature, not with a circumcision done by the hands of men but with the circumcision done by Christ, having been buried with him in baptism and raised with him through your faith in the power of God, who raised him from the dead. When you were dead in your sins and in the uncircumcision of your sinful nature, God made you alive with Christ. He forgave us all our sins, having canceled the written code, with its regulations, that was against us and that stood opposed to us; he took it away, nailing it to the cross.

Baptism is also a work of God because of our faith. Our faith is made complete by the things we do, according to James 2:21-24:

Was not our ancestor Abraham considered righteous for what he did when he offered his son Isaac on the altar? You see that his faith and his actions were working together, and his faith was made complete by what he did. And the Scripture was fulfilled that says, "Abraham believed God, and it was credited to him as righteousness, and he was called God's friend. You see that a person is justified by what he does and not by faith alone." A work completes our faith like with Abraham.

We see from verses like this that faith alone is worthless. The things we do matter. Salvation is so much more than faith only. According to these verses, faith by itself is not really faith, at all. The word faith in the Bible always seems to refer to action and obedience. Just as love in the Bible also seems to refer to action and obedience.

When God asked us to die, be buried, and be raised to walk a new life, why question that? We ought to be like the Ethiopian eunuch who could not wait to die with Christ, according to Acts 8:35-39:

> Then Philip opened his mouth, and beginning from this Scripture he preached Jesus to him. As they went along the road they came to some water; and the eunuch said, "Look! Water! What prevents me from being baptized?" And Philip said, "If you believe with all your heart, you may." And he answered and said, "I believe that Jesus Christ is the Son of God." And he ordered the chariot to stop; and they both went down into the water, Philip as well as the eunuch, and he baptized him.

The eunuch had somehow learned the significance and advantages that come through baptism.

The problem is, most people go to an extreme and say faith only means no works, including baptism. Repentance and confession, or a prayer of repentance and confession, is a response of faith; why can't we see baptism is clearly a response, as well? Repentance outside of faith in Christ does not save us. Confession outside of faith in Christ does not save us. Baptism outside of faith in Christ does not save us. It is our faith in Christ that saves us, causing us to respond sincerely in obedience. A person who has come to faith in Christ wants forgiveness, wants Jesus as their Master, and wants transformation and a change in identity and purpose. Our works do not earn us salvation but validate our faith in Jesus who gives us salvation. Salvation is not about our works but has always been about the works of Christ. Baptism serves the function of transformation. This transformation occurs as God's power is at work in us because of our death as we surrender to Him.

Are we so against following the Scriptures that we will continue to try to prove why we are right? There were certain demands, such as circumcision in the Old Testament, which God was serious about. Remember the story of Moses when God almost killed His faithful leader who was chosen to lead Israel out of Egyptian slavery? The Bible says it was because Moses's son, had not been circumcised. Genesis 17:9-14 says:

> Then God said to Abraham, "As for you, you must keep my covenant, you and your descendants after you for the generations to come. This is my covenant with you and your descendants after you, the covenant you are to keep: Every male among you shall be circumcised. You are to undergo circumcision, and it will be the sign of the covenant between me and you. For the generations to come every male among you who is eight days old must be circumcised, including those born in your household or bought with money from a foreigner—those who are not your offspring. Whether born in your household or bought with your money, they must be circumcised. My covenant in your flesh is to be an everlasting covenant. Any uncircumcised male, who has not been circumcised in the flesh, will be cut off from his people; he has broken my covenant."

It was a sign of the covenant. God demanded this not only from Abraham and his family, but it was necessary from all those who would follow, leading up to Christ. Sincere obedience has always validated a person's love and faith throughout the entire Bible.

Where Now?

Do not fall into the trap of asking hypothetical questions about whether or not you would have been saved or lost if you had not learned some of these things. As I mentioned earlier, our Christian life is a journey, and God has brought you to here and now. Be obedient to what you now know from the Bible. Work out your salvation with fear, knowing the demands and the truth that are in the Almighty God according to Philippians 2:12-13, where it says, "Therefore, my dear friends, as you have always obeyed—not only in my presence, but now much more in my absence—continue to work out your salvation with fear and trembling, for it is God who works in you to will and to act according to his good purpose."

Follow Jesus because you love Him far more than you love any other. The New Testament is clear, God wants every person who believes in Jesus to be water baptized (immersion), so follow His Word instead of people and their traditions. The Bible teaches there are some key reasons to be baptized. The reasons are:

- To follow the example of Christ—Mark 1:9-11

- Christ and the apostles commanded it—Matthew 28:19

- The early church believed it was important—Acts 8:35-39

- Baptism has a great deal of spiritual significance—Romans 6:4

The Bible also teaches the advantages that come when a person responds in faith in baptism:

- Baptism is where our sins are washed away—Acts 22:16

- Baptism is where we are guaranteed the gift of the Holy Spirit—Acts 2:38

- Baptism is where we are added to the church—the body of Christ—1 Corinthians 12:13

- Baptism is where we are clothed with Christ—Galatians 3:27

There is so much more listed in the Scriptures, but these are a few advantages.

There are a lot of deceptions and much confusion about baptism, so I wanted to spend some time clarifying, but do not get so caught up on baptism that we forget we are saved by God's grace through our faith.

If you are a minister of Jesus Christ, then teach truth and follow truth yourself. Do not be ashamed to say you have learned something new, because God's Word is constantly teaching us. As a minister, this is what happens when we read and study the Word of God. If, as a minister, you are afraid of admitting you learned something new or saw something different from the Bible, and you refuse to teach what the Bible teaches for whatever reason, then preaching may not be your calling.

Any of you can be obedient by finding water, just as the eunuch did on the desert road, and get baptized today. You do not need anyone there but the believer who is baptizing you according to the examples of Acts, and you can have a major celebration because God is celebrating your obedience. The number of people present at your baptism is not the point. It is about dying to yourself, desiring transformation by His Spirit, and receiving the advantages that comes to Christians. If God is changing your heart, do not run from the tugging on your heart, but rather embrace it and celebrate that God is speaking to you personally.

Putting off baptism seems to be a trend today because of what is taught in the churches. No one in Acts even put it off to the next day.

I was encouraged to talk with an important man after a syndicated radio show I was on for a book interview. This man got a copy of my book and through the Holy Spirit, it changed his life. For security purposes I cannot share his name, but he was a worker for the United Nations who was in Austria at the time. He called me and wanted to come to the United States to visit and learn more. To my surprise, he actually scheduled a flight, a hotel room and a rental car, and came to my hometown. He said he could do business while he was here, as well. When he got here, we set up a time and I got to meet him personally in an opportunity God could only orchestrate. I am proud to say, he came to faith in Christ and was baptized that very day. He was a man I will never forget. I have baptized numerous people over the years, but only this man asked if he could pray for me when he came up out of the water.

Baptism is so much more than declaring your faith publicly. We see this in the story of the eunuch in Acts 8. If baptism is just for showing others, the eunuch would have waited until he got back to the queen of Ethiopia and his hometown before he got baptized. In baptism, there is a death that occurs. Paul said he had been crucified with Christ, according to Galatians 2:20.

Do not reject the will of God because of stubbornness and pride. Be excited God has brought you to this place in your faith, and celebrate it with others. I knew a woman who had been sprinkled as a baby and, as she studied Scripture, she believed she needed to be baptized (immersed) in order to be completely obedient to what she knew about what God had stated. There is nothing like hearts that love God so much they are willing to do whatever God has asked. This reminds me of a story I heard about a slave girl. The story is entitled *Bought to be Freed* (copyright 2001, Youth Specialties Inc).

Back in the 1800s, a young Englishman traveled to California in search of gold. After several months of prospecting, he struck it rich. On his way home, he stopped in New Orleans. Not long into his visit, he came upon a crowd of people all looking in the same direction. Approaching the crowd, he recognized that they had gathered for a slave auction. Slavery had been outlawed in England for years, so this young man's curiosity drew him to watch as a person became someone else's property. He heard, "Sold!" just as he joined the crowd. A middle-aged black man was taken away.

Next, a beautiful young black girl was pushed up onto the platform and made to walk around so everyone could see her. The miner heard vile jokes and comments that spoke of evil intentions from those around him. Men were laughing as their eyes remained fixed on this new item for sale.

The bidding began.

Within a minute, the bids surpassed what most slave owners would pay for a black girl. As the bidding continued higher and higher, it was apparent that two men wanted her. In between their bids, they laughed about what they were going to do with her and how the other one would miss out. The miner stood silent as anger welled up inside of him. Finally, one man bid a price that was beyond the reach of the other. The girl looked down. The auctioneer called out, "Going once! Going twice!"

Just before the final call, the miner yelled out a price that was exactly twice the previous bid. This was an amount that exceeded the worth of any man. The crowd laughed, thinking that the miner was only joking, wishing that he could have the girl himself. The auctioneer motioned to the miner to come and show his money. The miner opened up the bag of gold he had brought for the trip. The auctioneer shook his head in disbelief as he waved the girl over to him.

The girl walked down the steps of the platform until she was eye-to-eye with the miner. She spat straight in his face and said through clenched teeth, "I hate you!" The miner, without a word, wiped his face, paid the auctioneer, took the girl by the hand, and walked away from the still-laughing crowd.

He seemed to be looking for something in particular as they walked up one street and down another. Finally, he stopped in front of some sort of store, though the slave girl did not know what type of store it was. She waited outside as the dirty-faced miner went inside and started talking to an elderly man. She couldn't make out what they were talking about. At one point the voices got louder, and she overheard the store clerk say, "But it's the law! It's the law!" Peering in, she saw the miner pull out his bag of gold and pour what was left of it on the table.

With what seemed like a look of disgust, the clerk picked up the gold and went in a back room. He came out with a piece of paper, and both he and the miner signed it.

The young girl looked away as the miner came out the door. Stretching out his hand, he said to the girl, "Here are your manumission papers. You are free." The girl did not look up.

He tried again. "Here. These are papers that say you are free. Take them."

"I hate you!" the girl said, refusing to look up. "Why do you make fun of me?"

"No, listen," he pleaded. "These are your freedom papers. You are a free person."

The girl looked at the papers, then looked at him, and looked at the papers once again.

"You just bought me…and now, you're setting me free?"

"That's why I bought you. I bought you to set you free."

The beautiful young girl fell to her knees in front of the miner, tears streaming down her face. "You bought me to set me free! You bought me to set me free!" she said over and over.

The miner said nothing.

Clutching his muddy boots, the girl looked up at the miner and said, "All I want to do is to serve you—because you bought me to set me free!"

This story is a great illustration of what our attitude will be if we truly understand what Christ has done for us. Following and serving Christ will be the only option. We will understand we have been given a whole new life with a whole new purpose. Once our death occurs and gives birth to new life, we can know we are freed from sin. Romans 6:6-7 says, "For we know that our old self was crucified with him so that the body of sin might be done away with, that we should no longer be slaves to sin—because anyone who has died has been freed from sin."

Just like the slave girl, we were bought to be set free. We do not serve God out of pressure or obligation, but out of love and thanksgiving.

Most Christian books end with a call to the reader to be saved. Satan does not want you to find salvation, but this book will not have a prayer you will recite or a Bible verse taken out of context from Revelation 3 that says Jesus is at the door knocking. God wants you to make a personal decision because of your love for Him. Are you going to surrender your life to Jesus by repenting of your sins, confessing Jesus as your Master and Lord, and be baptized into His name? Let that just be the beginning of a new life in Christ.

Conclusion

So, is now the time that you are ready to find my number or e-mail me your thoughts about what I have written in this book? I do have a website with contact information, and I would love to hear from you. It is TravisVerge.com. I would also love if now is the time you pray and ask God to help you understand as you study, and see if the things which are written in this book are true.

I want to say thank you for finishing this book regardless of the emotions that might have been stirred up by the things written. I hope my point throughout this entire book has been clear. Yes, I would like you to be stretched and challenged. And, yes, I would like you to see Jesus more clearly from the Scriptures. But the purpose of the book is to give you an appetite and a strong desire to study God's Word for yourself, and to devote yourself to Jesus and His church while realizing the only solid truth we know is of God and His Word.

I asked the young people in one of my Bible classes if the God and Bible they know is more from their own study or more from what they were taught by imperfect, fallible people. As I looked into the eyes of many of them, I received the answer. If things do not change for them, they will one day be just like many other believers, standing before God on the basis of what they had heard from people instead of what they learned from God through His Holy Spirit. That is a scary thought, since there are doctrines of demons out there. I do not want to be one of those people.

I told the youth that, in heaven, it will not hold any credibility if you say my minister, or Travis, said whatever. Just as it will hold no credibility if we say my parents said, my husband or wife said, my minister said, or, even, this author said this or that. My desire is for you to know Christ, and to have the boldness and strength to think for yourself. I love my minister, my heritage in the church, and my parents, but I understand they cannot save me. I am saved only on the basis of Jesus Christ and my obedience and relationship to Him.

This book is not your Bible by any means, but it is intended to point you back to the Bible. It is not meant to point you to your minister, to your priest, and especially not to me, because God knows we have sought other people long enough to confirm to us what we believe is right. Does it not seem as though so many in this world simply want to be told what to believe? Many also just want to have someone say they are right. Is it really about being right about everything, or is it about a relationship with and faith in Jesus Christ based on truth?

God gave us the Bible so we can accurately know what God wants us to know and follow what God wants us to follow. The Pharisees taught us that knowledge and "accuracy" are not enough. The Pharisees also taught us our standards can be high, but if you do not believe and love Jesus Christ, it is all in vain. Jesus taught us it is about knowing Him. And, in knowing Christ, we will know the Father. May we humble ourselves and go to none other except the all-knowing God.

Do not be misled into thinking I believe ministers are all wrong, so we should not listen to them. I was a minister, and I studied for hours each week concerning the things I taught. I take teaching very seriously, just as it says I should in James 3:1: "Not many of you should presume to be teachers, my brothers, because you know that we who teach will be judged more strictly." I believe I speak for most ministers when I say, "I want my listeners to study fervently what I teach." I would stay far away from any minister who did not want me to study from the Scriptures about what they had taught. I would stay away from anyone who did not encourage me to study God's Word daily. This would be a clear sign they believed themselves to be greater than they ought, and an authority when all authority should be given to Jesus.

As I stated in the introduction to this book, all Christians are ministers and priests, so they have access to the Father through Jesus Christ. As it says in 1 Peter 2:9-10, "But you are a chosen people, a royal priesthood, a holy nation, a people belonging to God, that you may declare the praises of him who called you out of darkness into his wonderful light. Once you were not a people, but now you are the people of God; once you had not received mercy, but now you have received mercy."

There is nothing wrong with wanting to be right so God is pleased with us; but accuracy without a relationship is empty. We must remember, knowledge without accuracy is also empty. Cornelius is a good example in Acts 10. The Scripture says he was a devout and God-fearing man. At Acts 10:1-2, it says, "At Caesarea there was a man named Cornelius, a centurion in what was known as the Italian Regiment. He and all his family were devout and God-fearing; he gave generously to those in need and prayed to God regularly." From these verses, this relationship was not enough. He also needed to be obedient. In Acts 10:47-48, it says, "Then Peter said, 'Can anyone keep these people from being baptized with water? They have received the Holy Spirit just as we have.' So he ordered that they be baptized in the name of Jesus Christ. Then they asked Peter to stay with them for a few days." In Romans 10:1-3, it says:

> Brothers, my heart's desire and prayer to God for the Israelites is that they may be saved. For I can testify about them that they are zealous for God, but their zeal is not based on knowledge. Since they did not know the righteousness that comes from God and sought to establish their own, they did not submit to God's righteousness.

We also learn that having the best intentions is not enough, either.

God has called me to this, and I realize many will criticize me. The prophet Jeremiah spoke things that people refused to hear, yet he continued to speak regardless of how much he suffered. I honestly believe Satan will try to stop this book as he did my first book. Being an author, I have learned Satan will try at all costs to destroy my credibility. That is fine because I do not have any credibility outside of the Word of God. But based on all that has happened with my first book, I know God is bigger than any plan or scheme of Satan.

I have never professed to be infallible and accurate about everything. I actually do not want you to take everything I have written to be truth unless you study it and find that it agrees with the Scriptures. I think you would agree as you read this book, I have tried to back everything with

Scriptures from the Word of God. Walking in the light and living by the Spirit is more rewarding than hiding in the shadows. If you allow God to expose the shadows in your life, you will never find yourself walking in shadows again.

CHAPTER 12 WORKSHEET

What has the journey of faith been like to bring you to today?

_____

_____

_____

Is there an area in your life where you have been lazy or rebellious to God's Word?

_____

_____

_____

Have you done all God has asked you to do in your responses to faith?

_____

_____

_____

What are you going to do about that now?

_____

_____

_____

How can God use you to help others not to be deceived by Satan?

_____

_____

_____

Appendix A

D. J.'s Journal Entry

Submit yourselves, then, to God. Resist the Devil, and he will flee from you.
　—James 4:7

On the night of her conversion, I asked D. J. to write in a journal that we gave her about what had happened that day as she remembered it, while it was fresh in her mind. I told her I was going to do the same thing. I copied her journal entry so you could see her perspective. It is quite mind-blowing if you have never been this close to a Satan follower who now believes in Jesus.

Tuesday, March 14, 2006

The spirits were getting increasingly controlling and angry. I woke up to a high-pitched screaming along with the low groaning that I fell asleep with. I had been waiting for two days for Travis to return to town from his youth trip. I was scared and alone. The spirits started tormenting me more than they usually did. They started throwing me against the walls, porcelain tub, and sink in the hotel bathroom. I was pulling my hair out in clumps and speaking things that I really did not want to say while they lead me to the major highway next to the hotel saying, "If we can't have you, no one will." As they kept trying to thrust me into the street, I tried everything to stop them. I wanted to be free of them, but I was afraid that if I reached out to any Christian or God, then I would surely die. So, for a long time I suffered in silence and attempted to detour Travis away from me. I started calling Travis with different excuses about why he could not come to the hotel. Each time, he insisted. By then, the spirits were screaming for me to go back home. Then Travis came to the hotel and the whole tone changed. Fear rose up in me as I saw Travis and Teresa come into the hotel room. I wanted to scream and run away, but I could not because of the kids. I tried my best to act normal so he would go away. The spirits had told me they would kill me if I reached out, so I tried to act normal, but the spirits were so angry. They began pulling out my hair and trying to control my body. My attempts to fight them made me look even more spastic I am sure. I talked as slowly and as quietly as I could. Secretly, I was glad to see both Travis and Teresa, but I was afraid to let them know that. That day, Travis seemed different, stronger, and more assertive.

As Teresa took all the kids out, I felt both relief and fear. I felt relief because I did not want the kids to see me that way and I felt fear because Travis and I were alone, face to face. Somehow, the spirits had merged their fear with mine. It was like I could feel what they felt and think what they thought. The spirits were so angry at him and the God in him. They were mad at me for being there. He started reading Bible verses while pain was echoing through my ears and head. Sharp squeezing was everywhere in my body. They tried to block my hearing. He would start reading, but every other word was interrupted by "Get out. Leave. He doesn't care about you. It's a trap. They will never believe you and they will turn against you." I continued to try to fight them while attempting to act in control. Travis then stepped it up. Now, he was asking to pray with me. I wanted so bad to yell, "Yes, please help me, I can't stand it anymore! They are hurting me! Help!" but I was afraid so I said nothing.

I let the spirits control my tongue. By this time, I was glad Travis was speaking with authority because I wanted to hear him through the spirits screams of "Ignore him! He is lying to you! Kill him!" I tried to reach out my hand to let him know that I was still in there somewhere, but they kept controlling my hand. I could see myself hitting him and kicking him but I could not stop, so I tried my best to hold back the strength of my blows. He started talking about baptizing me. I thought, "Are you mad?" Travis just would not quit. He kept on fighting.

He started pulling me out the door. The spirits were fighting and looking for an out. He turned to pick up his Bible and camera and the spirits darted me down the hall and outside telling me, "Run to the street! If we can't have you, then no one can!" I could hear him calling me from behind as I was scrambling, but the sounds were muffled. Travis yelled, "Do it for God and just stop!" That is all I could hear him say because the spirits were saying, "Ignore him! Do not listen to him! Listen to us!" I was so scared and realized that I did not want to die. I stopped and reached out my hand and allowed Travis to lead me to the pool to be baptized. The spirits fought and tried to hold on to anything along the way. My muscles were sore as I clutched on to metal fences and washing machines as it scraped my arms and added to the blood. I thought the pain would never end. With open gashes on my head and arms, I was about ready to die until we turned the corner and saw the hotel swimming pool.

The spirits had already been warring in me like rats running from fire. Travis had me repeat something with him and had me verbally say that this is what I wanted to do, but the spirits were holding my mouth. Travis prayed right there that God would let me speak and He did. Finally, I was able to say, "Jesus is Lord, and, yes, I do accept Him." No sooner had I got the words out of my mouth then I lost all control. The spirits spoke in a voice not like my own saying, "I hate you! You will never get her! We have a right to be here! We will kill you and kill her!" They said these things to Travis and he kept fighting every comment, punch, and kick while speaking back to them. He asked me one more time, "D. J.—not the spirits—are you sure this is what you want?" As I answered yes, we walked into the pool water. It was cold. The spirits fought some more and were yelling in my ear, "This is your last chance, don't get in." As I got in waist deep, the spirits jerked my head back and the pain was excruciating. They said, "This is our last chance. Don't go under. We will kill you!" Travis again asked if this were what I wanted to do and I yelled, "YES!" Then, the spirits let out an unearthly yell. It came from my inner depth. My head tilted back in pain as I literally felt like my rib cage was being ripped open from the inside out. My skin was burning like it was on fire. From the middle of the torment, I heard Travis say, "Good, then I baptize you in the name of the Father, the Son, and the Holy Spirit for the forgiveness of your sins and you will receive the Holy Spirit." Then, he placed his hand on my head and the pain was unbearable. I went under with his hand still on me. "Now we kill you" the spirits said in my head as I went under. I seemed to be pulled down and the water got bright and warm as if it were hit by lightning. I was propelled up into Travis's arms as I heard him say, "They are gone, D. J., they are gone." I looked at the water half expecting to see them in there, but there was nothing but silence. I was in shock. What was that sound? It was the water. I could hear the water as we walked out. Travis was talking to me excitedly, but I was half listening because I was distracted by the water, the birds, Travis's voice, the birds, the wind, Travis's voice, and my wet clothes. Everything was so different. The covering on Travis looked different and I knew I had one, too. Travis's voice was different. It was louder and uninterrupted by voices. We walked to the hotel room as I stumbled my way because I was unable to feel balanced after feeling and living life through the spirits for so long. When we got back to the hotel room, I towel-dried my hair and Travis stopped the video camera that had been recording. He began to read a verse (James 4:7: "Submit yourselves, then, to God. Resist the Devil, and he will flee from you.").

Before he could finish the verse, I began to cry. It was the first time I was able to hear the Scriptures uninterrupted by the spirits. Travis and I began to talk for a few minutes and, as we were talking, I saw myself in the mirror. There were no spirits! Then, I thought about my kids and I had to see them. We walked outside and, at first, could not find Teresa and the kids. We walked in circles around the hotel and I was still amazed at the birds, Travis talking, the lake, wind, and no spirits. Finally, from around the corner, there they were. I saw my children, uninterrupted, without spirits. I truly saw my children for the first time.

Made in the USA
Las Vegas, NV
19 July 2021

26701251R00164